This powerful new book, *The Supernatural Power of Prayer and Fasting* by my friend Ronnie Floyd, will challenge you to live life with a fresh new reliance on the supernatural power of God in your daily walk. Expect to grow more intimate with Christ as you read these pages and learn how to fast and pray.

—**Jentezen Franklin,** senior pastor, Free Chapel,
and *New York Times* best-selling author

I cannot imagine an emphasis more needed or longer overdue than Ronnie Floyd's book *The Supernatural Power of Prayer and Fasting*. This book has the potential to change not only your whole life but also the face of the church throughout the world.

—**R. T. Kendall,** minister of Westminster Chapel (1977–2002)

Never has the church, Christ's body, more needed the prophetic message Dr. Ronnie Floyd presents in *The Supernatural Power of Prayer and Fasting*. This is more than a book—it's an invitation to join the author in releasing God's supernatural power to change the very destiny of men, women, and nations in our generation.

—**Dr. Dick Eastman,** president emeritus, Every Home for Christ,
and president of America's National Prayer Committee

In every great revival throughout church history, prayer and fasting were the central components in God's display of his supernatural power on his people. That is why we could not be more excited about our friend Ronnie Floyd's new book *The Supernatural Power of Prayer and Fasting*! We believe this will be a necessary tool in every leader's library.

—**Shane Pruitt,** national next gen director, North American
Mission Board, and author of *Revival Generation*;
and **Paul Worcester,** national collegiate director, North American
Mission Board, and author of *The Fuel and the Flame*.

In this amazing book, *The Supernatural Power of Prayer and Fasting*, pastor Ronnie Floyd equips and engages us with praying and fasting as two biblically substantiated God-ordained activities that are legitimately supernatural! Read about them. Learn ways to practice them. And your life will no longer be the same!

—**Rev. Samuel Rodriguez,** president,
National Hispanic Christian Leadership Conference

Dr. Ronnie Floyd, in *The Supernatural Power of Prayer and Fasting*, has opened a kingdom door, and we have been afforded the opportunity to step through it to a new level of empowerment by the Holy Spirit. I encourage every pastor and Christian leader to obtain a box of books and sow them into your entire team!

—**Dr. James O. Davis,** founder and president,
Global Church Network (GCNW.tv)
and Global Church Divinity School (GCDS.tv)

The Supernatural Power of Prayer and Fasting is a transformative guide that reveals how these spiritual disciplines can profoundly impact your life and church. With practical insights and inspiring stories, this book will encourage you to deepen your faith as you experience the life-changing power of God's presence.

—**Dr. Grant Ethridge,** pastor, Liberty Live Church,
and author of *Parenting Your Parents* and *Goodbye Fear*

In a day when prayer seems more transactional than transformational, Dr. Ronnie Floyd clearly communicates the power of prayer and fasting in our lives. The wisdom with which he has written *The Supernatural Power of Prayer and Fasting* is the overflow of a life lived in the trenches of ministry, leading others to passionately pursue the Lord through prayer and fasting. This book is a must-read!

—**Dr. Nathan Lorick,** executive director,
Southern Baptist of Texas Convention

There has never been a revival in the history of the world that has not been given birth to, cradled by, or nurtured in prayer. Today is no exception. Mercy drops are falling, but the secret to the outpouring we long for is the kind of life we look for and will discover in the pages of Ronnie Floyd's new book, *The Supernatural Power of Prayer and Fasting*.

—**Byron Paulus,** founder and president, OneCry, and CEO emeritus, Life Action Ministries

Most Christians want to experience more of God in their life—more of his power, more of his presence, and more of the person and work of Christ. In his new book, *The Supernatural Power of Prayer and Fasting*, Dr. Floyd shows the way drawing from Scripture and his own personal experiences of prayer, fasting, brokenness, and sitting in the presence of God.

—**Robby Gallaty,** pastor, Long Hollow Church, and author of *Growing Up* and *The Forgotten Jesus*

Ronnie Floyd's book on *the supernatural power of prayer and fasting* is the best book ever on the subject. His profound understanding and practice of these spiritual disciplines are unparalleled, offering invaluable guidance to deepen your walk with God.

—**Julio Arriola,** Send Network Director for Texas of the Southern Baptists of Texas Convention

Ronnie Floyd has been a key catalyst for fasting and prayer in my life. He is one of the seminal voices on fasting in the church today. He lives what he preaches, and his life exhibits the fruit of walking closely with God. His influence and example are the main reasons Dr. Malachi O'Brien and I felt led to call on one million young people to fast and pray for the Roaring Twenties Fast.

—**Matt Brown,** evangelist, author of *Truth Plus Love*, and founder of Think Eternity

In his new book *The Supernatural Power of Prayer and Fasting*, Dr. Floyd illuminates the power of these vital practices as he shares decades of extensive wisdom and experience seeing God's heart and hands moved by the humility and dependency expressed in faith-filled prayer and fasting.

—**Kathy Branzell,** president, National Day of Prayer Task Force

Dr. Ronnie Floyd has not only done his homework, providing well-researched material, but he has personally experienced the challenges, trials, and triumphs accompanying fasting and prayer. Breakthroughs are available if we refuse to settle for where we are and move into the empowerment that awaits us as we experience *The Supernatural Power of Prayer and Fasting*.

—**Kay Horner,** executive director, Awakening America Alliance

Ronnie Floyd has produced a book that is both powerful and practical. The church needs a supernatural touch, and this volume, *The Supernatural Power of Prayer and Fasting*, gives the pathway to unlocking the transformative power of prayer and fasting.

—**Dr. Ted Traylor,** pastor, Olive Baptist Church, Pensacola, FL

The Supernatural Power of Prayer and Fasting will completely change your life. You'll be encouraged, uplifted, and convicted.

—**Shane Idleman,** pastor, Westside Christian Fellowship, southern CA

Especially for people caught in the busyness of life, Ronnie's *The Supernatural Power of Prayer and Fasting* offers a transformative guide—a beautiful book to help fill our still moments with God's presence, lifting our hearts to higher places and teaching us to listen to his gentle voice.

—**Dr. Drew Dickens,** host of the daily podcast Encountering Peace

Synonyms for prayer and fasting could easily be power and peace. Take a step on this wonderful journey closer to God's heart through Dr. Floyd's *The Supernatural Power of Prayer and Fasting*.

—**Gregg Matte,** pastor, Houston's First Baptist

This guidebook, *The Supernatural Power of Prayer and Fasting*, rings true because it is not mere head knowledge but experiential from one who has humbly pursued God for decades. This is the best book on fasting and prayer you will find, and I highly recommend it!

—**Bill Elliff,** founding and national engage pastor, The Summit Family of Churches, Little Rock, AR

The Supernatural Power of Prayer and Fasting

12 WAYS GOD WILL CHANGE YOUR LIFE

RONNIE W. FLOYD

BroadStreet
PUBLISHING

BroadStreet Publishing® Group, LLC
Savage, Minnesota, USA
BroadStreetPublishing.com

The Supernatural Power of Prayer and Fasting: 12 Ways God Will Change Your Life
Copyright © 2025 Ronnie W. Floyd

9781424567898 (faux)
9781424567904 (ebook)

This book details the author's personal experiences with fasting. The author is not a
healthcare provider. Prior to fasting, please consult your own physician or healthcare
specialist regarding the suggestions and recommendations made in this book.

Cover and interior by Garborg Design Works | garborgdesign.com

Printed in China

25 26 27 28 29 5 4 3 2 1

To Jesus Christ alone, who lived experiencing

the supernatural power of prayer and fasting,

I dedicate this book and my life. To you be all the glory!

"And Jesus returned to Galilee
in the power of the Spirit."

LUKE 4:14

CONTENTS

SECTION III
Experiencing the Supernatural Power of Prayer and Fasting Devotions

Introduction

God can do more in a moment than I could ever do in a lifetime. I believe in the supernatural power of God. God can do anything, anywhere, with anyone at any time. Yes, I believe in the supernatural power of God. Unfortunately, far too many Christians and far too many pastors and far too many churches are content with living life and doing ministry *without* the power of God.

If the apostles and the church of the New Testament could see into today's Christianity and present church world, they may ask us, "Why do you not believe in the supernatural power of God?"

God created the whole world, including the laws of nature. Scientifically, human beings live in this world and operate by these laws of nature. Yet God does not. He lives and operates above and beyond the natural.

God is the only God. He is supernatural and operates supernaturally. God is not bound by time or space or you or me. So who are we to try to qualify what God can do today versus what God did centuries ago? Who are we to try to rationalize God's acts and power using our finite human understanding?

If Jesus Christ has ever changed and transformed us personally, we should be the first ones to proclaim to everyone, everywhere, that Jesus forgives all sins, gives us purpose on this earth, walks with us through this life, and will take us to heaven after our last breath in this world. This happens solely because of the supernatural power of God.

Through spiritual conversion, Jesus changes us supernaturally; in sanctification, Jesus continually transforms us. He does this through the supernatural power of the Holy Spirit of God, who enters our lives the moment we decide to follow Jesus Christ. This is the only reason we can live by and experience the supernatural power of God.

God Continues to Change Me

I do believe God works in each of our lives in unique ways. He knows our past, present, and future; therefore, he doesn't work the same way in my life as he might in yours. He desires for us to know him intimately and to live in and by his supernatural power daily.

Through my personal experience and a transforming journey of mine, God used obedience to the biblical principle of fasting to change my life. I will never be the same again because of what God has done in my life, my family, and my ministry through prayer and fasting. Since I have tasted and seen God's goodness and favor and experienced his supernatural power, I cannot and will never again settle for spiritual powerlessness and lukewarmness.

God used prayer and fasting to change me. His movement was significant, dramatic, sudden, supernatural, permanent, and personal. It penetrated the deepest levels of spiritual warfare, providing breakthroughs to many obstacles in my life. Finally, one of my most profound personal strongholds was torn down. God uprooted and revealed the rottenness of my great pride that had previously stiff-armed God's power.

For me, prayer and fasting were God's gateway to supernatural power. Through these years, he repeatedly uses this biblical principle to restrain my flesh so that he can supernaturally unleash his power through me.

I was a college student when the Lord began to teach me about prayer and fasting. My zeal, passion, and curiosity led me to experiment with it. Yet it was not until a few years later that I began to understand, practice, and experience something powerful that occurred each time the Spirit led me to fast.

Then, in 1995, I had a life-changing experience through prayer and fasting. In my regular early morning quiet time with God, I felt God call me to go on a forty-day journey of prayer and fasting with him. I longed for God's power in my life, my church, and my nation.

After a few weeks of learning more about long-term fasting, I entered this journey.

Through these days, God moved in me profoundly and powerfully. God deepened my awareness of my personal spiritual brokenness. I knew my life, my family, and my ministry would never be the same. Following forty days of prayer and fasting, God permitted me to stand before the congregation I pastored to tell them what God had done in me. You see, I had entered that journey thinking God may use it to move in and change the people in our church, but God showed me through that experience that the biggest problem in the church was not them. It was me.

Therefore, on Sunday, June 4, 1995, I stood in the front of my church before thousands of people and expressed my deep repentance and brokenness over my pride and arrogance, telling them about this forty-day spiritual experience that had changed my life. God moved significantly on that day.

Even while I was preaching, people came to the altar weeping in deep repentance. What started at nine thirty that morning ended formally around noon. It blew up the entire morning schedule! Nevertheless, the moving of the Holy Spirit was so powerful that 70 percent of the morning attendees returned on Sunday night. Open confession and repentance of sin occurred, resulting in deep brokenness, powerful intercessory prayer, and a supernatural demonstration of freedom, worship, and praise. The evening service that began at six o'clock ended at ten. I will always remember it as the day when revival came.

Revival is the manifested presence of God in our lives. Since that day, I have never been the same, and our church has never been the same. The reality was this: on that day, the church got a new pastor, and the pastor got a new church, but neither ever went anywhere geographically.

What God did on and through that day and season of time launched our church into becoming something above and beyond what any of us had ever thought or imagined. Through these years, God has raised from us a mighty multi-campus church devoted to living out the Great Commandment and passionately committed to completing the Great Commission of Jesus Christ.

Over the course of my thirty-two years and seven-month tenure as pastor, through a successful succession in leadership, and to this day and beyond what God continues to do, I believe it all goes back to that moment, that experience, that season, and even to that day when revival came. The miracle began that day, and the miracle continues to this day.

While we do not live in the past, we have stones of remembrance that help us to never forget the supernatural demonstrations of the Holy Spirit like this one and many others. God is still writing the story in our hearts, personally and through our church collectively, even all these years later. I testify again to God's glory. The miracle continues!

I do not believe that my prayer and fasting made that day happen. It was not about me, but it was God alone. Spiritual revival is a sovereign move of God. God accelerates, ascends, and extends grace in action by the supernatural power of the Holy Spirit. Yet, unquestionably, for some reason, God used prayer and fasting to serve as the impetus in my life that positioned me to encounter the manifested presence of God like never before. When God so radically broke and moved in me, this supernatural spiritual breakthrough also moved those around me.

While God does not change, he changes us continually. Through the years and even to this very moment, again and again, God has used the supernatural power of prayer and fasting to change me and to keep on changing me.

God Wants to Change You

God does not call every person to an extended season of fasting. Yet in Jesus' mighty and well-known Sermon on the Mount, he instructs his followers about fasting. Jesus said:

- "When you give" (Matthew 6:2)
- "When you pray" (v. 5)
- "When you fast" (v. 17)

Therefore, in Matthew 6:1–18, Jesus presses upon us the need to practice giving, praying, and fasting. He clearly says there is a wrong way we can do these things and a proper way to practice these spiritual disciplines.

Furthermore, it is imperative to highlight and not diminish what Jesus did not say in this passage. He did not say, "If you give, if you pray, and if you fast." But he said, "When you give, when you pray, and when you fast."

Since the Bible mentions fasting numerous times throughout, and Jesus himself practiced fasting and taught about it, we know that fasting should play some role in our spiritual development and maturity.

So I encourage you to embrace prayer and fasting positively. This practice is about you and your walk with Christ. Since there will be moments when you pray and fast, we need to learn about it. Not only biblically and spiritually but practically and personally. I pray that God will use this book to help you in these ways.

For clarity, I have practiced various levels of prayer and fasting since my college days. At times, I have fasted from a meal a day to one full day, to three days, to seven days, to ten days, to twenty-one days, to twenty-eight days, to forty days. While I have undertaken all levels of fasts and have done it multiple times through the years, I only fast when I am convinced that God is calling me aside to be with him in a special way. Then, when I know this is happening, I find a way to do it.

Therefore, I am appealing to you to implement prayer and fasting into your life. Practice it only when you believe God is calling you to do it. It is not about the number of meals, days, or what kind of fast you will observe. In his time, God will make this clear to you; when he does, go and do it. With a pure heart and a clear focus, begin the journey and listen to what God may want to say to you.

You will discover that God will use prayer and fasting to change you. This spiritual transformation will occur from the inside out. God will never do any more *through* you than he does *in* you.

Opening Your Heart to God

Our fallen nature and broken lives skew our view of God and limit our ability to believe God wants to use us. Therefore, we need supernatural and God-sized intervention. The supernatural power of prayer and fasting will open your heart to God in ways you have never experienced. Why do I believe this?

Fasting is abstinence from food with a spiritual goal in mind. It is when you abstain from one of the most natural things your body desires, food, so you can pursue the God of heaven to do something supernatural in your life.

While prayer is a conversation with God, and fasting is abstinence from food with a spiritual goal in mind, prayer and fasting together lead to supernatural power within and through you. Therefore, be on the alert! Satan is your enemy, always trying to distort what God wants to do in your life. He knows how powerful prayer and fasting are. Satan will do all he can to distract you from practicing prayer and fasting. Then, when you still do it, he will try to appeal to your pride and twist the way you do it and even the reasons why you are doing it.

Prayer and fasting are not reduced to some formula you follow or a hoop you jump through to gain God's attention. Nor are they tests in mental and physical discipline. God's Word strongly rebukes those who fast with improper motives and selfish desires. God does not ever respond to prayer and fasting based on pretenses or impure motives. True prayer and fasting are attitudes of the heart and cries from your soul. This crucifying and purifying process will position you to experience the supernatural power of God like never before in your life.

This Book Is Different

This book is my third one on prayer and fasting. What I wrote originally in 1997 was revised and expanded in another edition released in 2010. But this book on prayer and fasting is different. After all these years, experiences, and journeys with God through prayer and fasting, I have learned things about this practice that I have never shared before. Now I want to share them with you.

Furthermore, I have also learned that the longer we live, the more battles and tests we will face. Nothing stays the same, including us. There are just some things in life you will not learn until God blesses you with years of living on this earth. I can testify today that through all the battles, all the tests, all the transitions, all the victories, all the defeats, all the blessings, and even through all the disappointments in life, God has been faithful to use prayer and fasting repeatedly to keep my eyes and my focus on Jesus Christ.

Yes, this book is not only different but very different. But the real reason it is different is that I am different. I have changed because God is changing me continually. Therefore, you are about to read a new book: *The Supernatural Power of Prayer and Fasting*. When you do, you will discover:

- How you know God is speaking to you and extending you an invitation you cannot decline.

- Twelve ways God will change your life when you practice prayer and fasting. These discoveries are real and life-changing, and I have never shared them in this personal and comprehensive manner. They will be profound and powerful, especially if you make them personal. As you open your heart to God, I believe he will change you, your family, your church, and your future. He may even raise you up to change your generation, your nation, and your world. God can do more in a moment than you can ever do in a lifetime.

- Forty days of devotions that you can use on your journey in prayer and fasting. Whether it is just you on the journey, a small group, or your ministry or church experiencing a spiritual movement of prayer and fasting, these devotions will inspire and elevate your faith to believe God, whether for a day, several days, or even forty days.

I am praying God will use this new book in a way that is above and beyond what you could ever pray or even imagine because of God's supernatural power now living in you that God wants to release through you like never before, all for the glory of God.

Are you ready? Let's go! Come on. Go with me now. You will experience the supernatural power of God through prayer and fasting. I believe in the supernatural power of God.

Section I

How to Know God Is Speaking to You

An Invitation from God
You Cannot Decline

God is extending to you an invitation you cannot decline. He is inviting you to experience his presence and power supernaturally. He desires to unveil and manifest his presence in and through your life.

Can you imagine with me what it would be like for the God of heaven, the King of kings and the Lord of lords, to extend to you an invitation to experience him personally? Furthermore, realizing who he is, can you imagine saying no to him?

Please do not say no!

He wants to infuse your spirit with a fullness beyond your most cherished dreams or imagination. It would be a moment when God seems more real to you than at any time in your life. He is not a God who, for even one moment, is interested in business as usual. Instead, he invites you to join him in the most exciting, appealing, creative adventure of your life, promising you that he is ready, willing, and able to carry you into an experience so lofty, so eternally memorable, that you will never be the same.

Will you accept the generous invitation he is extending to you right now? If so, I believe you will discover that he is not the God in a box you have in your mind or that your religious tradition has made him out to be. He is infinitely more than all these things.

Suddenly you sense God is watching you with his keen eyes, ready to engulf you with arms of love because he has been waiting for you to respond to him like this. Once you even hint at saying yes, you will begin to sense God pleading for you to enter his streams of blessing through the gateway that he has designated. Are you willing to say yes and enter this gateway to experience his supernatural power?

Prayer and fasting are God's gateway to supernatural power. Biblically, it is true. Historically, it is on record. Personally, I have experienced it. For each of these reasons and more, I have spoken and written about it for decades. I am convinced, now more than ever before, that God is calling each of us and his church across this world to practice prayer and fasting.

So why should you answer yes to God's invitation? First, consider the excitement of being moved by God himself because he has placed his touch and blessing upon you in an extraordinary way. The mundane and mediocre days will be gone. God will move you away from the dull and routine because you choose to experience his dynamic and robust presence flowing in and through your life supernaturally. God will take you and lift you higher than you have ever been raised. I am not talking about promotions and positions that may come to you, but I am talking about God lifting you into spiritual wisdom, understanding, and power. When you experience his powerful presence, your doubts, fears, and confusion will dissipate.

The good news is that what I have just described is not a dream. This fresh experience with your heavenly Father can be yours. God is still God. He is still on the throne. He has not changed, nor will God ever change. The God of the Bible is the same God who is waiting and willing to work in the lives of people like you and me today. Yes, the God of the universe who spoke the world into existence and knew the number of grains of sand on the seashore and the number of hair follicles on your head wants to unleash his power in and through you.

In This Urgent Moment

There has never been a more urgent moment for God to release his supernatural power upon us. The world has seen what we can do, but now is the time for the world to see what God can do. This is our last great hope.

Fear and uncertainty are gripping this world like nothing I have ever seen. The American and global economies are continually on edge. Inflation is absolute and out of control. Analysts are publicly discussing words like "recession" and "depression." Simultaneously, threats of war abound. Concerns about national security exist while many believe our security has been compromised. The world's powers are strengthening and testing the waters of their influence.

Furthermore, America is hanging by a thread because the sanctity and dignity of human life are in constant jeopardy. What is decided biblically is now debated politically. Even though the Bible is clear about human creation and human gender, the culture is proudly promoting abortion rights and even gender identity.

In these terrible times, lawlessness abounds while all these confusing things are also happening. While some groups disregard the laws of our land, others are weaponizing those laws for personal gain. Law enforcement officers from our nation's borders into our towns and cities are now mocked by many people and even some so-called leaders.

These troubled times are so dangerous now that mass shootings are commonplace in schools, workplaces, churches, public entertainment events, streets, and neighborhoods.

While our hearts are breaking over all these happenings, we must remember that Scripture warns us about these last days. Jesus said, "Because lawlessness is increased, most people's love will become cold" (Matthew 24:12).

It grieves me even to write these words, but they reveal that our nation is in dire need of God. We cannot fix ourselves. We need help. We need God.

We must understand these urgent times and ask God what he wants us to do. But then, we must be willing to do it.

Desperate times call for desperate actions.

While our needs appear to be national and global, I urge you to understand that our greatest needs are personal. Therefore, we must answer this moment and be willing to do whatever it takes to experience God and his supernatural power.

The Supernatural Power of Prayer and Fasting is more than a book title. Unquestionably, prayer and fasting are significant ways we can experience the supernatural power of God. When you join prayer with fasting, your prayer becomes extraordinary prayer. This kind of prayer is over and above the ordinary because one of the most natural things you do besides breathing is eating. Choosing a meal or a full day or several days to pray and fast about something is explicitly more than expected and appropriate at times by each of us individually, many of us as the church collectively, and then in rare moments, the country nationally.

Is God Inviting You to Pray and Fast?

In these terrible and dangerous times, God is speaking to us. Those of us who follow Jesus cannot act like God is aloof, unaware, or out taking a walk. God is speaking to you and me. God is speaking to his church. God is speaking to America. God is speaking to the entire world.

We need to hear God's voice and obey God's call. I believe God is inviting us to trust him. Not ourselves, our money, our job, our country, but only him. The followers of Jesus and the churches of Jesus cannot run scared from the evils of the world like our God is dead or is missing in action. This is when we need to stand out and stand up like never before, declaring through our lives and with our words that our God is real and alive. He is still on the throne and in complete charge of everything. Our God reigns, and we must live and lead as he does.

Therefore, how do you know when God is inviting you to pray and fast? How do you know this is an invitation from God you cannot decline? Any time you sense one of these seven things, or perhaps a combination of them, God may be inviting you to pray and fast.

Burden

One of the most significant biblical examples of someone having a burden that led to a season of prayer and fasting is in the book of Nehemiah. When this cupbearer to the king of Persia heard the news about how Jerusalem was in ruins and its gates were burned with fire, he became so overwhelmed with a burden that he prayed and fasted. This led Nehemiah to request that the king permit him to return to Jerusalem to rebuild the wall around the city.

What is a burden? When you have a burden, you get up with it in the morning, live with it through the day, and even go to bed with it in the evening. And no, I am not talking about your spouse! Nehemiah was wise enough to know that since God had placed the burden on his heart about rebuilding the wall around Jerusalem, Nehemiah needed to take the necessary actions to do it. Therefore, he accomplished it.

Throughout my journey of walking with Christ and practicing prayer with fasting, usually some burden motivates me to consider a season to draw aside with God. The greater the burden, the more it may impact the length of your fast. For example, when I entered my first forty-day journey in prayer and fasting, I was overwhelmed with a deep burden for our nation, church, and my life. Ever since those days with God to this day, I live with a deep burden about where America is as a nation. I did not ask for it nor understand it, but I have this burden about America. In various leadership roles, I have carried this burden with me everywhere. This burden was placed upon me in my thirties. Again, I did not ask for it but was overwhelmed by it.

You will discover that when God gives you a genuine burden, you will feel deeply compelled to carry it in prayer with fasting. The continual awareness that you are abstaining from food because of a specific burden on your heart will keep you focused on why you are walking with God in prayer with fasting.

Restlessness

There are times in your walk with Christ when you become restless. There is a passion that rises from within you that desires greater fulfillment. While God alone is our rest and only he calms the restless heart, I believe God uses our restlessness to speak to us. While God wants us to experience peace in life and about decisions we may be facing, there are times when we do not have peace. Does this make us wrong or ineffective? I do not believe it does. However, if we permit God to use restlessness in our lives, God will speak to us through it. For example, if we had the chance to speak with ten men and women who had just transitioned into new jobs and were living in new cities, I believe we would discover that restlessness played a part in opening their hearts to the next thing, which each is living out now professionally.

God wants us to be at ease and live with peace in our hearts daily. Therefore, if you are feeling restlessness, it may mean one of two things. First, it may mean God is speaking to you and wanting you to discover a new place to work and to live so you can experience greater peace. Second, it may mean that God wants to give you peace where you are because you are not trusting him with the details of daily life. Therefore, anxiety and worry consume you. This is not God's will, so somehow, God wants to give you a spirit of peace about who you are, what you are doing, and where you live while doing it.

So when you feel any sense of restlessness, God may be calling you into a season of prayer and fasting.

Desperation

In 2 Chronicles 20, King Jehoshaphat faced immense pressure when he discovered that Judah's enemies were upon them, and it appeared there was no way forward. The Bible tells us that he feared they had no chances for survival and victory. With great desperation, he turned his attention to the Lord and proclaimed a period of prayer and fasting throughout Judah. God answered their prayer and fasting, resulting in a great victory because their enemies destroyed one another.

Just as desperation moved Jehoshaphat to proclaim a season of prayer and fasting, desperation may move you into seeking God with 100 percent focus on him. So often, desperation precedes great movements of the Spirit of God. I have found this to be true personally, and I have found it to be true in leading a church or ministry through a season of prayer and fasting.

Before our Lord returns, we will walk through

difficult times in these last days. Yet I believe God is creating and will continue to create such desperation within us and in his church that we will pursue him fully. While events or experiences around us may raise concerns and contribute to our desperation, I believe the Holy Spirit is creating within us a holy desperation for God. We want God, and we desire to experience his mighty presence.

Parents are becoming more desperate about the times in which they are now raising their children. Pastors are becoming more desperate for God and his work to be accomplished in a mighty way through the church. Politicians who are followers of Jesus are pressed with desperation as they labor at the local, state, or national level. Powerful CEOs of corporations who are followers of Jesus are wrestling with desperation as they navigate their terrain of leadership with the Bible in one hand and the fierce challenges of the culture in the other.

The point is this: regardless of who you are and what you do vocationally, you know how difficult these times are becoming, and your desperation continues to increase. Therefore, how do you handle this, and what do you do?

Consider a day or a season of prayer and fasting. Or perhaps, eat only one meal a day for a week and use this time to shut the door and seek God sincerely for his holy power that will help you through this season of desperation. Desperate times call for desperate actions.

Be encouraged, friend, because I believe that each time God creates desperation within you or his people, he will do something mighty and powerful. This is why we must seek the Lord passionately.

Need

I am convinced that God creates a need, a problem, or a challenge to call us to seek him through prayer and fasting. This need, problem, or challenge is more significant than we are; therefore, we know we need God and his involvement to get through it.

I can testify that when my wife was diagnosed with cancer, God used her illness to call me to fast one day a week for one year, asking and trusting God to heal her. I can also share with you that when my two boys, Josh and Nick, were growing up, there was at least one year— and in seasons beyond that—when I would pray and fast one day a week for both of them to grow up loving Jesus and his church with a desire for God to use them powerfully. Then, when the church's needs were pressing upon me incredibly, I would seek the Lord through prayer and fasting for a season because I knew only God could bring about the change we needed.

Through great years of growth, building, and expansion of campuses, our church needed God's intervention financially. The generosity we witnessed then and even today is highly encouraging. But in many of those days, before we became debt-free, I cannot tell you how many seasons and days I poured out my heart to God in prayer and fasting, pleading with God for us to become debt-free. The need was great. The need was beyond me. It was beyond any of us ever meeting it. I knew that only God could do it. He began moving mightily, and our debt began to reduce greatly. I believe God had put it in my heart and leadership focus for us to see it occur. We saw the hand of God amaze us annually and continually.

Then, after praying and fasting again, it was in 2015 that we informed the church that one of our five major goals by the end of 2020 was to become debt-free. We continued to see the debt reduced at a greater rate repeatedly. Through God's great power and our people's continued generosity for years, the debt was eliminated on the afternoon of December 31, 2020.

Whatever the need, whatever the problem, and whatever the challenge, most often, seeds of prayer, faith, and at times fasting precede God's mighty and miraculous intervention. The intervention may be God giving you greater wisdom through the journey, or the intervention may be God meeting the need, resolving the problem, and eliminating the challenge.

Decision-making

When you walk with the Lord, one of the ways you want to please God is to make the decisions he desires you to make. Decision-making is a huge part of each of us. In many ways, our lives are the results of the decisions we make. Most things in life that come our way, we cannot control. What we can control is our response to them.

Simultaneously, we are entrusted with the responsibility of decision-making. Our decision-making is pivotal in how we respond to these things that occur that we most often cannot control. Yet there are decisions we are entrusted to make daily. We are the ones sitting in the chair of decision-making.

Followers of Jesus must be responsible people in their decision-making. The Bible must be our source for all decision-making, and the Holy Spirit's power must become the personal energy that leads us in all our decisions. We should be very committed to always want the Lord's will to be done. We want to make each decision with wisdom and prayerfulness.

When we stand on God's Word in our decision-making, we may not always receive praise from others. In fact, at times, it may result in ridicule and scorn. This is why we must pray and fast about many decisions that come before us. Even in Acts 13, the church at Antioch prayed and fasted about the leaders they selected and then sent out to God's glory. Who are we to think we do not need to do the same at times?

When I was a pastor, I prioritized the first twenty-one days of each new year as a time for prayer and perhaps even a time for fasting. If some of the members of our church believed that God was leading them to join their prayer with fasting, then they would do so. While only some of us observed fasting for all twenty-one days, many people chose a day to fast among those twenty-one days or perhaps would take only one meal a day during that time to focus their lives on the prayer initiatives we may have been praying for as a church or that they may have been praying for personally. We know that each of us, in new seasons like the beginning of the year, is faced with multiple decisions. Therefore, God can move in our lives and clarify the matters we are wrestling through.

So consider prayer with fasting when you are in the crucible of decision-making. Only God, through his Word, can give you a word about what you need to do, and only God, through his Spirit, can provide you with wisdom with peace about the decisions before you.

Preparation

One of the most significant values of prayer and fasting is the part it plays when we are preparing for something important. God uses prayer and fasting to prepare us spiritually. Prayer and fasting can reveal our sins and weaknesses, leading us to a time of confession, forgiveness, and restoration. They can purify us not only physically but also spiritually. When we are clean before the Lord and right with the people around us, we are on the track for God to use us. We get there with preparation; prayer and fasting can help us be prepared in the highest way.

I believe God is constantly humbling us, teaching us, using us, and preparing us for whatever may be ahead of us. Most significantly, this is true when we practice prayer and fasting. When I have had extraordinary preaching assignments given to me, I have drawn aside to prepare myself spiritually through seasons of prayer and fasting. I could give you multiple stories about these experiences and how God intervened in my life personally while I was in the fast, showing me what he wanted me to share. Then I could share with you what occurred while I preached the message and the results of it. My point is not about what I have done but that I believe in this. Preparation is vital to everyone's life, and many of these times, prayer with fasting is a powerful and effective way to prepare.

The bottom line is this: we need God. We need his power. Whatever occurs in life-change and leads to eternity is done by God and not by us. Therefore, we need to always be prepared for God to use us. Prepare yourself. Prepare your family. Prepare your organization. Prepare your ministry. Prepare your church. One of the most profound ways to prepare internally and spiritually, practically and publicly, is through prayer with fasting.

Fresh Power and Anointing

Jesus spent forty days in the wilderness praying and fasting before publicly entering the ministry. The Bible says in Luke 4 that he was led around by the Spirit in the wilderness, praying and fasting for forty days. Then, after forty days of prayer and fasting, he returned to Galilee in the power of the Spirit. He even proclaimed then that the Spirit of the Lord was upon him. Jesus experienced fresh power and anointing through prayer and fasting. Therefore, we need to know this can also happen when we pray and fast.

Whether you are a young mom at home with your children or working as a greeter at Walmart, a politician in Washington, a pastor of a church, a university student, the president and CEO of a major company, a provost of an esteemed university, or whatever you do in this world vocationally, you need fresh power and anointing from the Holy Spirit.

As a Christian minister, church staff member, or the church's lead pastor, do you ever pray and fast, asking God for fresh power and anointing upon your life and ministry? For the church you serve, do you ever draw aside in prayer and fasting, asking God for the church to have fresh power and anointing? If Jesus did this and the church of the New Testament did this, who are we to think there will not be days, times, and seasons when we need to humble ourselves before God, pray and fast, and plead with God to place upon us fresh power and anointing of the Holy Spirit of God?

Often, God gives us an invitation that we cannot decline. He invites us to join him for a day, a few days, or even an extended period of time to pray and fast. We may have viewed prayer and fasting as mystical and hard to understand. I do not believe it is. But we cannot ignore that there is something powerful about simply obeying what God says to do. This we may only sometimes understand.

Please understand that we can notice the obvious. The obvious is that we need God. God is the win, nothing else! The apostle Paul, under the Spirit's leadership, wrote: "That I may know Him and the power of His resurrection and the fellowship of His sufferings, being conformed to His death" (Philippians 3:10). We need to know Christ, the power of his resurrection, and the fellowship of his sufferings, being conformed to his death.

Through experiences of prayer and fasting, we get to know Christ. We experience his resurrection power leading, filling, and anointing us. Through profound experiences of suffering, prayer with fasting can sustain us and teach us. As we die to ourselves daily, the power of Christ lives through us.

This is the invitation from God that I pray you will not decline. When you enter this journey of prayer and fasting, you will discover, as I have and continue to discover through all these years, the many ways God changes you through the supernatural power of the Holy Spirit.

As we enter this next section of the book, I will share twelve ways God will change you. You will never be the same again.

Section II

Twelve Ways God Will Change Your Life

2

Experiencing God's Power

What is the most powerful invention in the history of the world? If you were to ask this question among a small group of people who knew one another, it would be fascinating to hear the various responses. Yet today's generation enjoys these inventions continually, rarely considering what it would be like to have lived before they existed.

Was the most powerful invention in the history of the world the automobile, the telephone, vaccines, the printing press, the computer, the airplane, the electric light, the radio, television, or perhaps something else?[1] One way to answer this question is to ask yourself which one of these inventions you could not live without. For example, can you imagine what it would be like to live without the power of electricity and the light bulb? This power source brings comfort and ease to life beyond what we can appreciate. Then what about the printing press? The invention of the printing press permitted literacy to expand worldwide. Now consider the power of transportation today. Without automobiles and airplanes, transportation would be minimal. Furthermore, the power of computer technology is beyond our comprehension. Yet we also realize that a failure in a computer system can result in hundreds of flights being delayed and canceled, inability to communicate, and loss of vital data, among other things.

It is startling to understand the power of any of these inventions, much less be able to comprehend their combined dynamic contribution to our lives today. But imagine for a moment: if all these inventions in the history of the world were gathered in one common place and one moment, their power all together could never compare to one moment in the presence of God. We must understand that every human being in this world, including every scientist or group of scientists and including science itself, only discovers what our God already knows. God is great and greater than everything. God is powerful and more powerful than everyone and everything.

When you practice prayer and fasting, you will experience God personally like never before and experience God's power in such a dynamic manner that it will change your life. Experiencing God's power day by day and night by night is God's will for you and me.

I pray for you to walk in obedience to God's Word and soon enter an experience of prayer and fasting.

The power of all power awaits you. Jesus spoke about the power of God the Father in remarkable ways. One expression of God's power that Jesus talked about was his power through signs and wonders. Remember when the laws of nature were temporarily put on hold as Jesus fed thousands of people with only five loaves of bread and two fish?

Jesus was willing to do what others never would have considered doing and could not do anyway. To the surprise of everyone, Jesus healed a leper and made him whole. When Jesus was teaching one day, some men of faith made a way and lowered their disabled friend through a roof so Jesus could touch and heal him.

How do we comprehend the mighty power of Jesus Christ? First, Jesus was so powerful that he defied death and raised his friend Lazarus from the dead. Then following Christ's death on the cross, God raised Jesus from the dead. These were awesome and convincing expressions and proofs of God's power.

The New Testament's core message is that God's power changes people, transforms worldviews, moves nations, and makes people new. Power is a recurring theme throughout the Scriptures, but we have only begun to understand and experience this power. There is so much more! When you are willing to enter a moment or a season of prayer with fasting, you will begin to experience God's great power that is still unknown and underused in many ways. God stands patiently waiting and holding a connection that will give us one of the greatest sources of power we will ever know. Pure and simple, it is the power of God that manifests itself through prayer and fasting.

Whatever wall you need to bring down or mountain you must climb, a breakthrough is possible. God's power is so great that regardless of the obstacle, it is not enough to overpower God. Whatever the depths of darkness you are in or the levels of spiritual warfare you are fighting, our God is greater.

When you discover the supernatural power of prayer and fasting and develop it in your life, you will experience God's power in such a way that spiritual breakthroughs that you thought were impossible can happen. Your place of entry into experiencing God's supernatural power is through prayer and fasting.

Realignment with God

Sometimes, the pressures and storms become so intense that we get out of alignment with God. Just as you can unintentionally drive your vehicle into a curb, which negatively affects your car's alignment, you can find yourself out of alignment with God. You never desired for this to occur, but it did. You may even go through a short season in your life and not realize you are out of alignment with God. You would never delay going to your eye doctor if your vision suddenly became blurred. However, our eyesight can become blurred over time, and we may not realize it until it becomes a problem that interferes with our ability to function. Then we address it.

Walking with Christ is much like this. We may go through something dramatic and know we must talk to God about it immediately. We take the necessary steps and ensure we align with God, his Word, and his will for us. However, usually, it does not happen like this. Our distance from God occurs over time, and things may be a little different for a season, but we attribute it to something else. But then, we realize our misalignment with God is unacceptable. We recognize that things have become a blur spiritually and that it is because we are not aligned correctly with God and his Word. Therefore, we must address this problem and realign ourselves with God.

Experiencing God's power is impossible when we are out of alignment with God. Practicing prayer with fasting draws us back into a correct alignment with God, his Word, and his will for us. The more aligned we are with God, the clearer our vision will be daily. These things will lead us to experience God's power.

Through the years, I have discovered that I can experience God's mighty power through prayer and fasting. When I fully align with God, the potential for God's power in my life and through me becomes unlimited. You can experience God's power through prayer and fasting.

What God Has Done

Throughout this book, I will share various stories of what God has done in my life through prayer and fasting. I do not do this to focus your attention on me but to open my heart to tell you what I have seen God do in me and through me because of prayer and fasting.

I want to help you understand that life, leadership, business, sports, politics, education, law, ministry, and your personal walk with Christ are not only about the level of your charisma or giftedness. Your charisma or giftedness may positively impact each area of life, but these things alone will not guarantee faithfulness, a life of integrity, and eternal fruitfulness. Your charisma and giftedness have a ceiling, but the supernatural power of God working in and through you is unlimited and eternal.

I was raised in a small town of five thousand people in Texas and grew up in a small Baptist church where thirty to forty people gathered weekly. Brief seasons or special days sometimes took us to an attendance of fifty or more, but these were rare. Yet through this small but strong family of God, I came to Jesus Christ in my teenage years. While I wanted to one day be the head football coach for the University of Texas Longhorns and then the Dallas Cowboys, God transformed my heart so dramatically within months following my experience with Jesus that I surrendered my life to a call from God into the ministry of the gospel.

When I entered college, I was on fire for Christ. This

fire continued to grow in me as I was on a major learning track, academically, biblically, and devotionally. As I met with God daily, I sensed he was working in me powerfully, transforming me. As a result, in my college years, I began to practice prayer and fasting.

Although the discipline of prayer is frequently taught and practiced among many followers of Jesus, prayer with fasting is rarely taught, and neither is the concept of experiencing the supernatural power of God in your life. This needs to change. I have been active in the church my entire life and have attended many religious meetings and conferences over the years. Still, until the mid-1990s, I cannot recall a single occasion when a teacher took center stage and called his or her listeners to fasting. Until then, I only remember one time when I listened to a recorded sermon about prayer and fasting in college. Beyond that, I do not recall receiving any teaching or instruction about prayer and fasting until the last three decades.

But God captured my heart through the recorded sermon by Manley Beasley Sr., and I began practicing this biblical principle a few times as a young college student. No, I did not know what I was doing, but my heart yearned for God's power so much that I was willing to do anything.

In those times, as I was raised to do and still do today, I accepted the Bible as God's authoritative and infallible Word. The Bible does not just contain the

Word of God, but the Bible *is* the Word of God. When the Bible speaks, God speaks. So I was determined to fully obey God's truth, including what God said in his Word about the supernatural power of praying and fasting. Through this commitment to biblical truth, I began to glimpse the power of God that could and would manifest in my life through prayer and fasting.

In my first year in college, I became fascinated with many biblical references to prayer and fasting. I did not learn about these in a formal classroom but through my own personal devotions. Through the next few years of ongoing learning and experiencing moments with God in prayer and fasting, I began to define it as I stated in the introduction of the book as the following: fasting is abstinence from food with a spiritual goal in mind.

Whenever you fast, you abstain from one of the most natural things your body desires: food. Why do you do this? You do it to focus entirely on pursuing the God of heaven to do something supernatural in your life. This is what I had interpreted fasting to be then, and after more years of study, I still believe and practice this. These times have been integral to my walk with God through my younger years and still today.

In the first chapter, I mentioned how prayer and fasting became a weekly practice when my wife, Jeana, was diagnosed with cancer. I remember it like it was yesterday, on a Monday, January 15, 1990, when our doctor informed us that Jeana had cancer.

How could this be? My young and beautiful wife—with cancer? Our son Josh was nine, and Nick was six. I was desperate and powerless to deal with the fear of not knowing the future. I knew I needed God's power at this challenging time in our family's life, so I began fasting one day a week that entire year, asking God to heal my wife. Soon after her diagnosis, God gave me a Scripture verse to stand upon, asking God daily to heal her. God gave me a word from Isaiah 43:1–3 about my wife.

Do not fear, for I have redeemed you;
I have called you by name; you are Mine!
When you pass through the waters,
    I will be with you;
And through the rivers, they will not overflow you.
When you walk through the fire,
    you will not be scorched,
Nor will the flame burn you.
For I am the Lord your God,
The Holy One of Israel, your Savior.

As I studied these words, I believed God was promising to heal her.

My wife is alive after all these years through God's anointing and blessing, the work of doctors and nurses who performed surgeries, conducted and monitored radiation and aggressive chemotherapy treatments, and God's healing power. I believe God placed within me great faith and wisdom from his Word through weekly encounters of prayer and fasting, all for the healing of my wife.

Still, one of the most humbling things we know is that God chose to heal Jeana and give us a long and fruitful life together. This is one of God's greatest blessings our family has ever received. I am not saying everyone should fast as I did through that entire experience, but God chose it to break me, shape me, and prepare me for life ahead. A day or season of fasting is a call from God, not one we think up and then decide to do. Fasting must have a spiritual goal or purpose so important to us that we are willing to abstain from food, using the time we would be eating to spend with God for him to speak to us.

I believe that when we become so desperate for God that we have nowhere else to turn, as I was then and have been so many times through the years, we should enter prayer and fasting. So consider this question: Could our desperation be God's calling to us to come to him through prayer and fasting? This level of desperation is precisely what I felt again in the winter of 1995. I shared some about this experience in the Introduction of this book. I was so desperate for God to revive my life, church, and nation that I answered God's call to pray and fast for forty days. While that was my first call to pray and fast for forty days, that calling has come to me several times.

Since January 1, 1990, I have written at least a one-page prayer to God daily. Yes, I have done it after all these years and to this very day. These journals chronicle my daily spiritual life since that first day in 1990. Shelves in my library are filled with these prayer journals. One day I would like to read through all of them because I know at least one thing will be evident: God has intervened in my life repeatedly. Many of these pages record a consistent and faithful prayer life while others have come during days, periods, or seasons of prayer and fasting.

It has been all for God. I have never desired in my flesh ever to fast. I love food and the fellowship around the table with others. Yet for some reason throughout the years, God has pressed upon me a calling to him through prayer and fasting. Whether it is just for a day, a few days, or an extended season, each time God has been faithful to meet me and see me through during that time. He continually provides me with his sustaining power.

I could spend paragraphs and hundreds of words testifying to you the miraculous works of God in me and many times through me, all because of God's work in the first seasons when I combined prayer with fasting. But I will tell you the hand of God has moved in my life sovereignly and providentially. What God placed in my heart in college, he continued to mature through decades of encounters with prayer and fasting. What God put in me then was all preparatory for the life God would call me to live. Through epic moments of God's miraculous moving in response to preaching to thousands in the Superdome in New Orleans in 1996, to 1.3 million men in Washington, DC, Promise Keepers Stand in the Gap Rally in 1997, to Awaken America rallies we led across this nation in the late 1990s, to teaching and preaching to thousands of people in major prayer gatherings in back-to-back national conventions in 2015 and 2016, and then to lead the National Day of Prayer in 2018 and 2019, including the National Gathering of the National Day of Prayer in Statuary Hall in the United States Capitol Building in each of those years, as well as many more blessed experiences across this nation and world, in person as well as through media and technology, I can tell you the ongoing practice of prayer and fasting influenced all these experiences and so many more I did not mention.

Please understand that while all of this has been so blessed by God and things far greater than I could have ever thought about have happened, the most incredible story, the greatest miracle of what God has done, is through the people called Cross Church. Through this church, God has touched and is still touching the world. This is where God taught me so much to launch all he has ever done through me elsewhere. Yes, it was through prayer and fasting not only by me but by many others there and, at times, the entire church family. Together we have seen God do things above and beyond everything we have ever thought or imagined. Therefore, the miracle continues at Cross Church because of God's amazing and astounding grace.

While this is just some of the story, another part of the story has been challenging, especially after God called me away from Cross Church in my thirty-third year of service as their pastor. Sensing God's leadership to this new calling upon our lives, Jeana and I left our beloved church. From the day I resigned through the seven weeks I spent with them preparing for the transition and then completing a succession plan on my final day of departure, I cried like a baby almost every day. But in obedience, we did what we believed God called us to do.

Quite honestly, this was a devastating experience for me. When we left Cross Church, we felt we would serve in this new leadership role for seven to fifteen years. But for some reason, the Lord called me for a specific season to provide leadership through a very challenging and complex time, including a global pandemic. Of the twenty-nine months I served in that leadership role, only nine of these months were not during a pandemic. So while we saw many wonderful things occur and a major Great Commission Vision adopted, I also felt God wanted me to depart from this significant leadership role in November 2021. We do not understand it all and probably never will. So we walk by faith day by day and night by night. Our times are in his hands. Our trust is only in our sovereign and providential God.

Oh, I love preaching, teaching, developing leaders, and mobilizing people, missionaries, churches, and finances to the Great Commission. I believe in the supernatural power of prayer and fasting. I love leadership in the good times and even through challenging times. Yet through it all, God is constantly humbling me, teaching me, using me, and preparing me for whatever may be in our future.

Read this carefully: all that God has deposited into me all these years through prayer and fasting, he continued to empower me with even during the most challenging times. Furthermore, God has seen me through this difficult season through prayer and fasting. Day by day and night by night, God has seen us through. We look for the cloud during the day and the fire at night. We live to experience the presence of God. Perhaps these words will minister to you today like they have ministered to us over this recent season. The Bible says, "With a pillar of cloud You led them by day, and with a pillar of fire by night to light for them the way in which they were to go" (Nehemiah 9:12).

It has been the supernatural power of prayer and fasting that has lifted us to meet the moments on the greatest of mountaintops. The supernatural power of prayer and fasting has also helped us through the deepest valleys. God will do the same for you. I am more convinced than ever that this miraculous gateway to God's supernatural intervention is not exclusively reserved for a select few. It is the supernatural power of God available to everyone who trusts Jesus. It is the supernatural power of God for anyone who desires to enter the gateway called prayer and fasting. You *will* experience God's supernatural power.

Revival Is Coming

God is at work in America and across the world. We need to be encouraged by all the Lord is doing. Even in this past year, our hearts should leap with joy and be filled with hope to hear of the accounts of revival on a few college campuses across America. We also have heard about some gatherings of believers and in some churches where the refreshing winds of God's Spirit appear to be blowing upon his people.

Simultaneously, whether it be through the popular multi-season series about the life of Jesus Christ and his followers called *The Chosen* or the movie called *The Jesus Revolution*—which is a movie about the Jesus Movement that is seeing many people come to Christ in response to it—indeed this is a special moment in history. Time will test these things, so leave it all with God.

What should move us with hope is that while darkness and danger are so apparent everywhere across our nation and world, God is also at work and is giving us refreshing hope about the days to come. Revival is the manifested presence of God in our lives. Do you believe this? I do. Let our generation become known as The Revival Generation!

God blessed me to experience revival in 1995 and

many times since then. He did the same in our church, which still impacts our church today with a great passion for Christ and a clear focus of reaching our region, state, nation, and world for Jesus Christ. What I said and wrote then in 1995, I still say today but in this newer way: God placed in my heart that he will bring a mighty spiritual revival to America that will transcend all denominational, generational, cultural, racial, and ethnic lines. Yes, I do believe this. I still pray for this daily, literally. I look for any hope, moment, or time when our God may decide to bring it to us. I believe in Jesus' name, another reason we need to experience the supernatural power of prayer and fasting: revival is coming!

God can take our lost generation in America and change us into The Revival Generation. Therefore, we must understand that this is only possible through God's supernatural power. I know this: without God's power, we do not have hope. But through prayer and fasting, we can see God's power like never before. This is what I need. This is what you need. This is what our churches need. This is what America and the world need.

It happened before. It can—and will—happen again. This spiritual revival and Great Awakening will break the mold of all preconceived notions. It will rekindle the spirits and ignite the hearts of God's people. It will be exciting and dynamic. This coming revival and awakening will result in thousands and even thousands upon thousands and millions upon millions responding to Jesus Christ positively. Yes, I believe this will occur before the Lord comes again. It will defy all human explanations. It will not be the exclusive product of any speaker, preacher, celebrity, or unknown person, nor will it be owned or controlled by any denomination, a self-appointed believer or group of believers, or anyone else. Nor will this revival and awakening be bound by international borders.

When it comes, we will know it because it will be authentic and spread like a raging fire in all directions. It could be as simple as a growing awareness of God's grace in our lives or as dramatic as a worldwide awakening. This true revival will result in countless thousands, perhaps millions of people saying yes to Jesus Christ. It will mobilize the church ultimately to advance the gospel of Jesus Christ to every person in every town, every city, every state, and every nation.

Revival is coming! Say it aloud. Preach it everywhere. Share it with others. Today, tell someone. Revival is coming!

Fasten Your Eyes on God

In the first chapter, I shared with you how King Jehoshaphat led the people to proclaim a period of prayer and fasting. Their desperation for God's intervention moved them to pursue God with great intentionality and focus. The Bible says, "Our God, will You not judge them? For we are powerless before this great multitude that is coming against us; nor do we know what to do, but our eyes are on You" (2 Chronicles 20:12).

We live in a season where the forces of hell are standing up in defiance of God as we have never seen before. It is time to admit our helplessness and turn in humility before God. As he called the people to fast, he called them to renounce their natural desires to pursue the God of heaven to do something supernatural around them. The days of self-gratification, self-worship, and self-exaltation must cease. If we desire revival to come and for the Holy Spirit to be poured out upon our generation in a way we may have never witnessed before, we must realize our great need to place our eyes on God and fasten them on him.

The calling of the fast was for them to see the face of God once again, fastening their eyes on him. God desires our undivided attention. We must always be hungry for God rather than always hungry for food. Since God is at work, we must trust him through it all. The Bible says, "This is what the LORD says to you: 'Do not fear or be dismayed because of this great multitude, for the battle is not yours but God's'" (v. 15).

The people prayed. The people fasted. The people put their eyes on God. The people trusted God. God prevailed! God gave the people a great victory. God answered their prayer and fasting with victory. This victory was their moment of experiencing the presence of God mightily. This changed their lives and their futures.

This was their revival, the moment when they saw and experienced the manifested presence of God. This is what we need to see and experience personally. This will change your life. This is revival.

It is time to put our eyes on God and experience him. Revival is coming!

3

Walking Humbly before God

Revival will not come from the next election. Revival will not come from your next career achievement. Revival will not come because of your next house purchase. Revival will come when you practice walking humbly before God. He determines where and with whom revival comes. God is likelier to be attracted to someone walking in humility before him. Are you doing this today?

Considering humility, have you heard the story of a man who supposedly wrote the book *Humility and How I Attained It?* It is now available in five volumes! I still smile when I share this verbally or mention it in writing. I learned several years ago that pride has the power to blind us from seeing ourselves as we are. God is never attracted to a proud heart, but pride does repel him. Our pride comes naturally to us, but walking in humility before God and others comes only supernaturally.

God speaks about each of these in this way: "You

younger men, likewise, be subject to your elders; and all of you, clothe yourselves with humility toward one another, because God is opposed to the proud, but He gives grace to the humble" (1 Peter 5:5). These words are not valuable just for younger men but for everyone. First, God encourages younger men to be submissive and subject to their elders. Then God instructs all people of all generations to put on humility toward one another. Even as one puts on an apron to prepare a meal for others, so God wants us to fasten humility into our lives.

Why is this important? When we continue reading the text, we see that Peter reminds us that God opposes the proud. This is a strong word about how God resists pride and that he even lines up against those who are proud. Then with compassion, God invites us into a life of grace whenever we humble ourselves before him. The word "humble" means to make yourself low before God. This call to action is to everyone everywhere.

In this section of Scripture, we are called upon to take the initiative to make ourselves low before God. The Bible says, "Humble yourselves under the mighty hand of God, so that He may exalt you at the proper time" (v. 6). Therefore, God's call to you is to humble yourselves before him who is strong and mighty. When you place yourself low before God, with his generous grace, he says that he will even exalt you at the proper time. When you go low before God, he will lift you up and exalt you in some way and in his time.

Walking humbly before God is an initiative you must take, but it is only possible by God's grace and through God's power working in you.

The Link Between

I believe there is a link between walking humbly before God and prayer and fasting. You are far more likely to walk before God humbly when practicing prayer and fasting. David declared, "I humbled my soul with fasting" (Psalm 35:13). David understood that if he was to walk humbly before God, he needed to take the initiative to pray and fast. Even as David did, you should be willing to also do. When you do, your life will change like never before! And one of the ways you will change is that you will begin to walk humbly before God.

Ezra 8 has a powerful story about God answering the prayer and fasting of God's people. The one point relating to this specific subject of walking humbly before God is recorded in this chapter. "I proclaimed a fast there at the river of Ahava, to humble ourselves before our God" (v. 21). To stay on this subject, I am quoting only one sentence in this verse, and in time, I will share it all with you.

It is more than clear: the fast was a call to fall before God in prayer. Ezra's people had a spiritual goal in mind, but they understood their first and greatest need was to humble themselves before God in prayer and fasting. In Jesus' time on this earth, he understood this. After his baptism and before his public ministry, he entered the wilderness for forty days of prayer and fasting. After the church's birth in Acts 2, we see this modeled before the world through the church at Antioch. In Acts 13, the Bible tells us that before they sent out Paul and Barnabas on their mission, this great church was practicing prayer and fasting.

I believe people in the Old and New Testaments understood and demonstrated this link and connection between walking humbly before God and practicing prayer with fasting. I have found that practicing prayer and fasting leads me to walk before God humbly and relate to other people with a genuine spirit of humility.

The Restless Night That Changed My Life

As a pastor, I often experienced a real challenge sleeping well on Saturday night. Usually, the burden of the message was so substantial and the desire to see God move in our midst was so great that this made me restless. The Sunday services were never something I dreaded because I had spent so much of my life preparing for the opportunity to open the Word of God and proclaim its truth to the church and the gospel to the whole world. However, these things together at times created a restlessness on Saturday nights.

One Saturday night and early Sunday morning I remember being in the latter part of my first forty-day fast in 1995. God had been speaking to me, breaking, stirring, and working in me. My heart was becoming more sensitive and softer toward God. After two hours of sleeplessness and extreme restlessness, I realized God wanted me to get up because he had something to say. I had learned already in this long-term fast to interpret sleeplessness and restlessness as a call from God to arise and be with him. Therefore, I got up, went to the living room, and lay before God on the floor with my Bible and journal, ready to listen and respond to his Spirit. So it was on this night and through this experience that God wanted to change my life.

As I was talking to God about our church, I felt the Holy Spirit put in my heart these words, *Ronnie, your church is not the problem, but you are the problem. You are full of pride and full of yourself.* So God took me to the spiritual woodshed on that early Sunday morning, just past midnight. I felt rebuked, deeply guilty, and very sinful because God was right; I was proud, arrogant, and full of myself. I also felt love and grace like never before. I felt like God was in the room.

I was broken and emptying myself to God in an unprecedented way. I confessed my pride and then repented immediately. The Holy Spirit rushed through me and into that room. Yes, God was there. But then, I felt God had led me to a passage of Scripture in the book of Isaiah. When I was reading and came across these words, I was crushed even more and broken repeatedly. The text verified God's rebuke of my life. "This is what the high and exalted One who lives forever, whose name is Holy, says: 'I dwell in a high and holy place, and also with the contrite and lowly of spirit in order to revive the spirit of the lowly and to revive the heart of the contrite'" (Isaiah 57:15). I want to share this with you.

Who is God, and what is God? Isaiah 57 says God is high, lofty, eternal, and holy. Furthermore, God is changeless, immovable, constant, and firm. We also learn in this Scripture passage that God dwells in heaven, a holy place. So then, we see God also dwelling and residing with the contrite, crushed, bruised, needy, troubled, and humbled. Then the text speaks of this great miracle: our God, who is high and holy and distant from us, then comes upon those who are humble and broken. So on that early Sunday morning, God came to me and upon me like never before. Then God fulfilled the Scripture verse because he revived me, all due to where I was with him at that moment. I was lowly, humble, and broken.

Dear friends, this is where God wants me to always be in my life. He also wants the same for you. Revival is the renewal of life and the spiritual awakening. Revival is the manifested presence of God. His presence became manifested in my life like never before. The God who comes upon the humble and broken is the same God who is distant to the proud and the sufficient. In that setting and through this experience on that early Sunday morning, while I was broken before God, he pressed upon me a statement I have never forgotten. When pride walks on the platform, God walks off.

Just imagine what could happen in our churches and across this nation and world if we began to believe this and refrain from letting pride enter the personalities, worship services, and ministries across the church and denominations. Then we would experience revival! Never forget this: when pride walks on the platform, God walks off. Therefore, we must put away our pride before revival ever begins. This was a watershed moment in my life and ministry, which eventually led to the day that revival came to our church on Sunday, June 4, 1995.

That morning, God placed in my heart that one day he would bring a mighty spiritual revival to America that would transcend all denominational, generational, cultural, racial, and ethnic lines. I still believe this and pray daily for this revival to come. Oh, how we need God to come upon us and revive us!

Pride and God's Word

You walk in pride when your life is mostly about you, your way, and your opinion. Pride is when you have an excessive obsession with yourself. Pride is when you feel you are sufficient and have no needs. It is almost like you say, "God, I got this one!"

Pride is about your status, influence, titles, awards, recognitions, accomplishments, and achievements. Each of these is a part of living; we should be grateful and thank God alone whenever we experience these blessings. But at the same time, we must be cautious and filled with wisdom. Walking humbly before God only happens honorably and effectively when we keep our eyes on Jesus, hold all these other things in our hands loosely, and know this world is not our home and that we are just passing through.

Sometimes we may be reading the Bible too selectively, and in the process, we forget what God's Word has to say to us about being humble before God. But when we take the time to search for God's truth in this matter, we read:

- "Gideon said to them, 'I will not rule over you, nor shall my son rule over you; the LORD shall rule over you.'" (Judges 8:23)
- "This is what the LORD says: 'Let no wise man boast of his wisdom, nor let the mighty man boast of his might, nor a rich man boast of his riches.'" (Jeremiah 9:23)
- "This is what the LORD says: 'To the same extent I will destroy the pride of Judah and the great pride of Jerusalem.'" (13:9)
- "Then David the king came in and sat before the LORD, and he said, 'Who am I, Lord GOD, and who are the members of my household, that You have brought me this far?'" (2 Samuel 7:18)

- "The LORD is near to the brokenhearted and saves those who are crushed in spirit." (Psalm 34:18)

- "Now I, Nebuchadnezzar, praise, exalt, and honor the King of heaven, for all His works are true and His ways just; and He is able to humble those who walk in pride." (Daniel 4:37)

- "When he became strong, his heart was so proud that he acted corruptly, and he was untrue to the LORD his God, for he entered the temple of the LORD to burn incense on the altar of incense." (2 Chronicles 26:16)

- "Whoever exalts himself shall be humbled, and whoever humbles himself shall be exalted." (Matthew 23:12)

- "Humble yourselves in the presence of the Lord, and He will exalt you." (James 4:10)

Walking humbly before God is one of the significant changes God makes in your life when you pray and fast. You begin knowing that we cannot simultaneously be filled with pride and with God. These two never fit together but are in continual contention for your heart. When God brought major revival to my life, he addressed my pride dramatically. He still does today. Each time God has moved powerfully in my life, I had to die to myself. I had to crucify myself before God. Pride is always in contention to rule my life.

Pride is the common and universal seed of sin in our

lives. Everyone who lived before us, and everyone who lives now and who will live after us will have the deep seed of pride that caused the fallenness of all humanity before God. The good news is that Jesus can create in us the kind of humility that crushes the wall of pride in our lives. Nothing is more deadly than pride in our lives, and the only cure for pride is humility and brokenness.

Humility destroys the wall of religious tradition. By the way, I have seen people fight for their religious traditions more than I have seen people fight for the truth. We also tend to fight over matters that preserve our ways when we are dead to all of them. This is not about us. It is all about God. Humility removes the wall of greed. Greed hoards the time, money, or possessions we have been entrusted with. Greed exists because of pride. For example, when followers of Jesus do not honor God with the first tenth of all God has given them in life, it is because of their pride. Pride leads to greed.

We demonstrate humility through our obedience to God's Word regarding generosity. We know giving removes the wall of greed. We can pray and fast for revival all day, but Christians must stop robbing God weekly. Many who are stealing from God still pastor churches, lead worship music, mentor adults and children, teach classes in our churches, and go on mission trips worldwide. May God help everyone get transparent before him, repenting from pride and greed. Only humility before God in giving removes the wall of greed.

Unforgiveness is prevalent in the lives of many Christians and most churches. Unforgiveness occurs because of pride. I believe unforgiveness is the major obstacle to revival in today's church. Pride is so powerful that unforgiveness has become the norm in most Christ followers and churches. This pride has built such callouses on the hearts of people that they are no longer bothered by having an unforgiving spirit toward others. This is so sad and should move everyone to repentance.

When our vertical relationship with God is right, our horizontal relationships with others will be right. Therefore, whatever it takes, each faithful Spirit-filled follower of Jesus must walk in harmony with others. It is essential to know that pride is powerful. Pride has destroyed men and women, teenagers, children, marriages, families, relationships, businesses, churches, and governments. Most of all, pride leads you to grieve the Holy Spirit. Are you grieving the Holy Spirit? Scripture urges us not to grieve the Holy Spirit of God.

The only thing that will crush and remove the spirit of pride is when we humble ourselves through prayer and fasting. When we humble ourselves before God with prayer and fasting, God will change our lives with his supernatural power.

The Urgency before Us

Our pride and self-sufficiency have created a national and international spiritual crisis. What we have sown for years, we are now reaping for generations. The urgency before us is undeniable. Yet while I could illustrate to you how serious this hour is in America and worldwide, things are changing so rapidly and degenerating minute by minute that my examples would be out of date by the time you read them.

Since the Bible is timeless and God always uses a crisis to create an urgent call to his people, I want to ask you to look at the crisis in Joel's Old Testament book. Of course, we must interpret this in the proper sequence biblically.

God Is Judging His People

In Joel 1:1–14, you read about the crisis occurring because God was judging the sinfulness of his people. In these verses, you will discover these things:

- God has taken away his provision to his people. (vv. 4–7).
- God has taken away the protection of his people. (vv. 8–12).
- God has taken away the joy of his people. (v. 12).

This crisis is severe and critical. Everyone was impacted by this spiritual crisis. While this may not be popular to hear, God was judging his people. It was a terrible season of judgment. But it was not over yet.

In Joel 1:15–2:11, Joel prophesied about a coming judgment that would occur apocalyptically at the end of time. Joel told them that if they thought this present judgment was difficult, it was nothing compared to the coming judgment, referred to as the day of the Lord. The coming judgment at the end of time will be so horrific that the Bible says these words about it: "The LORD utters His voice before His army; His camp is indeed very great, for mighty is one who carries out His word. The day of the LORD is indeed great and very awesome, and who can endure it?" (2:11). This warning states that the judgment, which will occur before the end of all time, will be so powerful and devastating that not one person will endure it.

Is God judging America today? Absolutely! Day by day, our nation is reaping what we have sown in sin for many years. The deterioration and degradation of our country are extensive, and we watch it daily. However, I believe this occurs because God is judging his people, the church. After all, we are not the salt, the light, and the bearers of the gospel as we should be. The church in America today is a pitiful representation of biblical unity. We limit our potential to be used by God because we prefer to fight with one another more than love one another. Humility is difficult to find while arrogance, haughtiness, and pride abound. This is not God's will or God's way for us. The church must lead the way by walking in humility toward one another because we are walking humbly before God. How is this possible?

God Is Calling His People

God appeals to his people to return to the Lord and even tells us how. The Bible says, "'Yet even now,' declares the LORD, 'Return to Me with all your heart, and with fasting, weeping, and mourning'" (Joel 2:12). The urgency and call from God were for his people to return to him in total surrender, complete humility, and a new attitude. God told them it was not good enough to rip their garments when something was wrong. God wants our hearts broken before him; he wants us to return to him in praying, fasting, weeping, and mourning. The call from God in the book of Joel was for his people to return to him now, and they would see God greet them with compassion and release them and the nation from the chastisement of God. God called them to fast, worship, and come together before him. The call was so urgent that even newlyweds were to leave their bridal chamber before they consummated their marriage so they could join everyone in repentance of sin and return to God.

God is calling each of us to return to him today. God is calling each local church in America and worldwide to return to him today. God calls every elder, every pastor, and every spiritual leader to return to him today. No one is exempt from this call, and anyone can make their way to return to God. So it is time for us to cease being prideful and selfish, making up our own rules, and giving our excuses before God.

The way of your return to God is clear: we must return to God with all our heart. We must return to God through prayer and fasting. We must weep and mourn before him over our spiritual condition, the condition of the church, and the entire world. Pastors, elders, spiritual leaders, and every follower of Jesus Christ, now is the time to lead the way personally and with your church and ministry to return to God.

The Bible tells us that the people returned to God, and when they did, God answered their prayer. Joel 2:18–27 tells us that when God witnessed this supernatural miracle in their attitude and lifestyle, God showered his mercy on them. Once again, God provided for them, protected them, and granted them joy. Our God is always faithful to do what he says he will do. God will do the same for you, your church, our nation, and the world.

The Outpouring of the Holy Spirit

Two critical words are found in Joel 2:28. The words are "after this." After what? After the people had returned to God in repentance, praying, fasting, weeping, and mourning and the hand of God was lifted, then we read these profound prophetic words and promise: "It will come about after this that I will pour out My Spirit on all mankind; and your sons and your daughters will prophesy, your old men will have dreams, your young men will see visions." I encourage you to take the time to look up and read Joel 2:28–32. God gave them a word about the Holy Spirit coming upon everyone everywhere. Joel prophesied there would come a day when the Holy Spirit would come upon all people and God would do supernatural and miraculous things in their midst. I believe this; do you?

The initial fulfillment of Joel 2:28–32 began on the day of Pentecost as recorded in Acts 2. Peter even quotes this prophecy in his sermon on the day of Pentecost when the Holy Spirit came upon the apostles miraculously and supernaturally. Furthermore, we must understand that the complete fulfillment of this will occur the nearer we are to the return of Jesus Christ.

God will pour out his Spirit today and even in the final days as we have never seen before. In "those days" before Jesus comes, an outpouring of the Spirit will be released, resulting in the gospel increasing to every corner of the globe before the second coming and the final judgment day. Therefore, be encouraged. When you and your church and your ministry return to God in prayer, fasting, weeping, and mourning, God will pour out his Spirit in an unprecedented supernatural way in your life, church, and ministry. I believe we are on the brink of the world's mightiest outpouring of the Holy Spirit.

Our brokenness precedes repentance. Our repentance precedes revival. Spiritual revival precedes the coming Great Awakening. This will usher in evangelism as we have never seen before, resulting in a supernatural gospel explosion, nationally and internationally, in our generation. God's invitation to every person in the world is, "It will come about that everyone who calls on the name of the LORD will be saved" (Acts 2:21; cf. Joel 2:32).

Respond to God Now

Take a few minutes before you turn the pages to the next chapter. Respond to God now! Let God destroy your pride today. The supernatural power of prayer and fasting cannot be denied or rationalized. What God led Joel to prophesy, God *will* do. He will do it with you or without you. Therefore, I do still believe and pray daily for what God put in my heart years ago that he is going to do one day soon: he will bring a mighty spiritual revival to America that will transcend all denominational, generational, cultural, racial, and ethnic lines. Prepare now!

Walking humbly before God is one of the profound ways God changes your life through the supernatural power of prayer and fasting. Will you pay the price?

4

Honoring the Holiness of God

In 1904–1905, God brought a mighty spiritual revival and awakening to Wales. The impact of God's presence and movement resulted in approximately one hundred thousand people coming to know Jesus Christ as their Lord and Savior. Just over two million people lived in Wales at this time, but God sovereignly chose to shake this nation in such a way that this movement impacted other parts of the world.

The holiness of God was honored in this movement of the Holy Spirit. As one example of this historic movement, these words give us insight into it: "It truly was a revival where God poured out His presence unilaterally and without focus on any man. It is a divine visitation in which God moves in answer to a praying people."[2]

God raised up a humble, praying young man named Evan Roberts to give a unique and supernatural leadership to this movement. I write this in such a manner because he would often enter and pray with the people for three hours in meetings and never speak. Yet the Spirit would come and fall upon the people. James A. Stewart emphasized this when he wrote, "Evan Roberts was not the author of the Welsh Revival. The author was none other than the Holy Spirit of God Himself."[3]

The power of the Holy Spirit became like a river running through various regions of Wales. The fire of God fell in such a way that dramatic meetings occurred, upon which men never placed time limits.

People of this movement, which even extended to the mission fields of India, learned and understood something about the Holy Spirit that the church of America must learn today. Stewart addressed this and wrote, "You cannot organize or control the fire of God."[4] When God comes upon his people and church, the Spirit's movement is never determined by our money, advertising, or organization. When God touches down in powerful moments in America and around the world today, often it comes under the scrutiny of modern-day Pharisees. Usually, criticism and skepticism abound. If people cannot understand or qualify why it is happening and whom it is happening through, they will attempt to extinguish it. It would do us all well to know we cannot organize or control the fire of God.

When we are walking humbly before God and honoring the holiness of God, we will receive and live by the watchword of Evan Roberts. Once again, James A. Stewart provides incredible insight into this when he writes: "'We must obey the Spirit' is the watchword of Evan Roberts, and he is as obedient as the humblest of his audience."[5]

Their meetings would close when God's Spirit directed them to close. What is remarkable and something only God can do is that, at times, their businesses and factories would close for a day or two or three so the people could attend the meetings and not miss one thing God was doing. Evan Roberts did not control these meetings; God did.

The holiness and presence of God were so honored through this movement that multiple well-known preachers would come and observe what God was doing. Men such as G. Campbell Morgan, Gypsy Rodney Smith, F. B. Meyer, and General Booth would visit, and if they did anything, they might pray publicly or give brief remarks and encouragement. They did not want to be in the way of what God was bringing about. They would sit humbly, listening, learning, and experiencing what God was doing.

"We must obey the Spirit" needs to become our watchword, even as it was for Evan Roberts. This is the spirit God wants to create in each of us as we live and honor the holiness of God in our lives. When we are broken and humble before God, we will learn that our most extraordinary preparation for the coming moves of God is in prayer coupled at times with fasting. This is when the anointing of the Spirit will become great upon us, and this is when the world's lostness will become our most significant life burden.

A Biblical Vision for Revival and Awakening

A biblical vision for revival and awakening is provided for us in the book of Isaiah. The people of God had wandered away from God and his will. Isaiah cried out to God for a mighty move of the Lord. Give careful attention to his prayer to God.

> Oh, that you would burst from the heavens and come down!
> How the mountains would quake in your presence!
> As fire causes wood to burn and water to boil,
> your coming would make the nations tremble.
> Then your enemies would learn the reason for your fame!
> When you came down long ago,
> you did awesome deeds beyond our highest expectations.
> And oh, how the mountains quaked!
> For since the world began,
> no ear has heard and no eye has seen a God like you,
> who works for those who wait for him!
> (Isaiah 64:1–4 NLT).

Pastors, ministers, church leaders, and all churches across America and the world need to pray the way Isaiah did in these verses. With a deep hunger for God and a desire to honor the holiness of God and see the Spirit come in ways as we have never seen before, we must pray with this kind of vision and intensity, with a biblical vision for spiritual revival and spiritual awakening.

Begins with a Burden

A biblical vision for revival and awakening always begins with a burden. With a thirst and intense desire, Isaiah cried out to God, with the intention to never let it go until God came upon the people. His powerful groaning in spirit expressed verbally as "Oh" indicates he was aching with a deep burden for God to come.

Isaiah wanted God to tear open the heavens and come down. With urgency, he desired for God to reveal to everyone everything that was concealed from them now. Look up in the sky now and imagine the heavens opening to you. This is what Isaiah saw and desired passionately when he cried out, "Come down!"

The manifested presence of God is what he wanted. Do you? When the Lord comes down among us and upon us, everything changes. Everything will shake, including the mountains. Can you imagine the Rocky Mountains shaking in the holy presence of God? The fire of God's presence is so powerful it can make the wood burn and the waters boil. Water images the Spirit, and the fire is one of the symbols of the Spirit as he came at Pentecost. The presence of God is so holy that even enemies will scatter because they fear God's wrath and judgment to come.

When we honor the holiness of God and his movement in our lives, we are burdened and know that we need God to arise and come down among us.

The Right View of God

A biblical vision for spiritual revival and awakening always begins with a burden. And a biblical vision for spiritual revival and awakening is always set on fire by the right view of God. In Isaiah 64:3, Isaiah prays, "When you came down long ago" (NLT). This chapter records how God saved his people and fought for them in Egypt, leading to their exodus, opening the Red Sea, placing his Spirit among them, guiding and protecting them. Yes, he came down among them. So then, God came down to Mary, giving us Jesus, and God came down at Pentecost, giving us the Spirit who always points us to Jesus.

When God comes down among us, he exceeds our expectations and blows our minds! We learn experientially that God is all-powerful. He can shake the unshakeable. God is limitless because he is not limited by time or space. He can do anything at any time with anyone. God is the one and only God. "No ear has heard and no eye has seen a God like you" (v. 4). Isaiah's vision and passion for revival and awakening were profound.

Confidence That God Is Always Working

A biblical vision for spiritual revival and awakening creates confidence that God is always working for our good and his glory since God works for those who wait for him. Always be confident: God *is* working. God *is* working. God *is* working.

Yes, God is always working for our good and his glory as we trust in him. Some view waiting on God like we are waiting on a stoplight to turn from red to green. This is not waiting on God. Passivity is not waiting on God. Please understand this in your life: waiting on God is trusting in God and looking eagerly for God to work in your life and future. I do not always understand what God is doing in my life. Do you? However, based on what I do know about him, I will confess this with confidence: God's work is sometimes mysterious, frequently unimaginable, usually incomprehensible, but always for our good and his glory.

Would you stop and reread this? God's work is sometimes mysterious, frequently unimaginable, usually incomprehensible, but always for our good and his glory. At times, God reveals what he is doing through his Word, the Bible. Sometimes God reveals what he is doing through his Spirit. And at other times, we will only know what God is doing when we go to heaven.

A biblical vision for spiritual revival and awakening is built upon the one and only God, who is holy, all-powerful, and all-knowing. This is the God we cry out to by pleading to him to open the heavens and come down. This God came upon Evan Roberts and all of Wales, resulting in a spiritual revival and awakening that touched the world. Therefore, Roberts lived by this watchword: we must obey the Spirit.

We need the fire of God to come down upon the church and our nation. Will we live with a passion and desire to follow Isaiah's vision for revival and awakening? Will we die to ourselves and stop restricting and legislating the Spirit's work? We must obey the Spirit.

I believe God honors everyone who stands in awe and lives honoring the holiness of God. Jonathan Edwards was a faithful servant of God in colonial New England. This godly man was a shining example of what God can do. Edwards believed deeply in the sovereignty of God, but he also believed significantly in the holiness of God. As Edwards preached, he held God high before the people and called upon them to respond in faith in Jesus Christ. As much as he believed in God's love and holiness, he also believed in the wrath of God. He never held back preaching on God's judgment, even urging people to follow Jesus Christ now.

Although his pulpit manner was not commanding, nor was he an extraordinary orator, many of his sermons overwhelmingly impacted the people who heard him. What may be his most well-known message, "Sinners in the Hands of an Angry God," moved many people to repentance from sin and turned them to personal faith in Jesus Christ. In the 1740s, God used Jonathan Edwards and his ministry to ignite a Great Awakening throughout Massachusetts and the early colonies.

This brilliant man, who would study the Scriptures for up to thirteen hours daily, was set on fire by the Holy Spirit of God. Jonathan Edwards was scholarship on fire. I am convinced that God built within him a healthy view of God's sovereign power and divine holiness that would come together through his preaching in his urgent plea to respond to God.

Edwards believed in the supernatural power of prayer and fasting. His preaching was so compelling and profound that people sensed they were falling into hell. With a deep burden, he pleaded with God and fellow ministers to fast and pray for God to move mightily in New England. Edwards prayed and fasted for a spiritual breakthrough in New England. God responded to his heart and his request.

At times, before he even began to speak, spiritual dread and the heaviness of the conviction of sin fell upon his audience. He was even known to hold his sermon notes so close that the audience could not see his face. He preached until the people in that crowded assembly were moved almost beyond control. One man jumped up and rushed down the aisle crying, "Mr. Edwards, have mercy!" Others clutched the backs of the pews for fear of falling into the fiery pit of hell itself. Most thought judgment day had dawned. Yet the life and preaching of Jonathan Edwards honored the holiness of God.

Prayer moves us into the greatest power the church has—the power of God. This is why we must prioritize prayer in the church and at times, elevate our prayers with fasting. A church committed to prayer will fight against Satan constantly. But when we pray, and at times fast, our God is able to move the church to experiencing victory over our enemy, Satan.

We are living in challenging and violent days of spiritual warfare. Gimmicks, games, and business as usual will only lead to defeat. To defeat the Enemy's strongholds, we come face-to-face with the holiness of God by entering his presence through fasting and praying with a humble and repentant heart. When we do, our lives will be changed indelibly because of our firm commitment and conviction to honoring God's holiness.

The Four Points of Evan Roberts' Message

In the small town of Loughor in South Wales is Moriah Chapel. It is known as the birthplace of the Welsh Revival. Worship still occurs there each Sunday. When you go to their official website, you will read a message from Evan Roberts in his handwriting and emphases. It says, "Dear Friend—God loves *you*. Therefore, Seek Him *diligently*; pray to Him *earnestly*. Read His Word *constantly*. Yours in the *Gospel*. Evan Roberts."[6]

In 1904, when Evan Roberts was twenty-six years

old, God raised him to shake Wales and the world for God. Compelled by God while being educated, Roberts felt the Lord directing him to a convention held in Blaenannerch, about eight miles from his school. In this gathering, Roberts believed the Spirit whispered to him, *Bend me, oh Lord*. The Spirit appropriated and applied this to Roberts supernaturally.

"I fell on my knees with my arms over the seat in front of me and the tears flowed freely. I cried, 'Bend me! Bend me! Bend me! Bend us.' What 'Bent me' was God commending his love and my not seeing anything in it to commend." With perspiration and tears pouring down his face, he heard the congregation sing, "I am coming, coming Lord, to Thee!" Then a significant burden for lost souls fell upon him.[7]

On that night and through this experience, Evan Roberts became convinced and testified that God would bring the most powerful spiritual movement Wales had ever seen. In that setting, God told him to return to Loughor to work with the young people at Moriah Chapel. God had been preparing him for this historic, unprecedented moment in his life, country, and even the world.[8]

In his book *Invasion of Wales by the Spirit through Evan Roberts*, James A. Stewart wrote that on November 2, 1904, Evan Roberts spoke for the first time on what he called The Four Great Tenets, which became the heartbeat of his message at the beginning of the revival. Later, they became known as The Four Points.

Did they desire an outpouring of the Spirit? Very well; four conditions must be observed, and they were essential:

I. *Is there any sin in your past that you have not confessed to God?* On your knees at once. Your past must be put away, and yourself cleansed.

II. *Is there anything in your life that is doubtful?* Anything that you cannot decide whether it is good or evil. Away with it! There must not be a cloud between you and God. Have you forgiven everybody, *everybody,* EVERYBODY? If not, don't expect forgiveness for your sins. You won't get it.

III. *Do what the Spirit prompts you to do.* Obedience—prompt, implicit, unquestioning, obedience to the Spirit.

IV. *A public confession of Christ as your Saviour.* There is a vast difference between profession and confession.[9]

These direct words from Evan Roberts would be great words to share with other followers of Jesus, so share them! These words are significant, whether with a small group of Christians or your entire church or ministry. He will bring spiritual revival and awakening when we answer them in obedience to God.

Bend Me, Oh Lord

This prayer of Evan Roberts became a prayer that dramatically changed his life and future trajectory. Overcome by the love of God, he was physically, emotionally, and spiritually stirred with a vision of one hundred thousand people coming to Christ, and the greatest movement of God was coming to Wales. So with a significant burden for the lost and a great vision of God's holiness, Roberts cried out to God, "Bend me, Lord!"

With total surrender to the Holy Spirit and complete availability for God to use him supernaturally, Evan Roberts knew he would have to let God bend him, shape him, and make him become the man and the vessel God wanted to use. This "Bend me, Lord" prayer became the impetus and watchword of Evan Roberts: "We must obey the Spirit." Therefore, from his four points, which became the heartbeat of his message, we need to evaluate our hearts, confess our sins, and repent from all sin, doubt, and unforgiveness. Then we must also commit to following the Spirit's promptings and declare Christ everywhere as Lord.

So I appeal to you now to put aside all distractions and earnestly pray through the remaining moments of the final section of this chapter. This will help you live out today, right now, what Evan Roberts urged the people to do when revival came to Wales. Now is the time for you to encounter God personally in your life, asking him to work in you extraordinarily and supernaturally. This is only possible when you address these matters persistently and seriously.

Examine Yourself

Examining your own heart is critical in your life. The following list of questions I have gone through during almost every time of prayer and fasting I have ever experienced. But there are also times when I pray like you are today, and I take a few minutes to work through each of them. Each time I find it to be beneficial to me. Each time, God has met with me powerfully.

Now take these questions alone and sit before God, letting him examine your life with you. May the searchlight of God's holiness reveal every reality to you as you do. Pray now: *Holy Spirit, speak to me and bend me, oh Lord.*

1. "In everything, give thanks; for this is the will of God in Christ Jesus for you" (1 Thessalonians 5:18 NKJV). Do we worry about anything? Have we forgotten to thank God for all things, the seemingly bad and the good? Do we neglect to thank him for our breath, health, and life?

2. "Now to Him who is able to do exceedingly abundantly above all that we ask or think, according to the power that works in us" (Ephesians 3:20 NKJV). Do we shy away from attempting things in our heavenly Father's name because we fear we are not talented enough? Do feelings of inferiority keep us from our desire to serve God? When we accomplish something of merit, do we choose to give ourselves, rather than God, the glory?

3. "You shall receive power when the Holy Spirit has come upon you; and you shall be witnesses to Me in Jerusalem, and in all Judea and Samaria, and to the end of the earth" (Acts 1:8 NKJV). Have we hesitated to thank God for the miracles he has performed? Have we believed it's good enough to live our Christianity casually and that sharing the good news of our deliverance with others is not all that important? Are we sharing the gospel? Are we involved in advancing the message of Christ in our region, in America, and across the world?

4. "I say...to everyone who is among you, not to think of himself more highly than he ought to think" (Romans 12:3 NKJV). Are we overly proud of our accomplishments, talents,

and families? Do we have difficulty putting the concerns of others first? Do we have a rebellious spirit at the thought that God may want to change us and rearrange our thinking? Do we brag or boast to others about what we have? Do we swell up with pride when we receive compliments?

5. "Let all bitterness, wrath, anger, clamor, and evil speaking be put away from you, with all malice" (Ephesians 4:31 NKJV). Do we complain, find fault, or argue? Do we nurse and delight in a critical spirit? Do we carry a grudge against believers of another group, denomination, or theological persuasion because they don't see the truth as we see it? Do we speak unkindly about people when they are not present? Do we find that we're often angry with ourselves? With others? With God? Are we in harmony in all our relationships? Are we right with everyone? Are we willing to let it go and start over again? Will we grieve the Holy Spirit with our unforgiveness toward others? Or will we make everything right with everyone, resulting in a greater anointing from God?

6. "Do you not know that your body is the temple of the Holy Spirit who is in you, whom you have from God, and you are not your own?"

(1 Corinthians 6:19 NKJV). Are we careless with our bodies? Do we defile our bodies with unholy sexual acts? Do we overeat? Do we consume food or drink we know is unhealthy? Do we desire to be physically fit?

7. "Let no corrupt word proceed out of your mouth" (Ephesians 4:29 NKJV). Do we use language that fails to edify others, tell off-color jokes or stories that demean another person's race, habits, or culture? Do we condone these comments when guests are at home or when our colleagues share them with us at work? Do we curse?

8. "Do not...give place to the devil" (vv. 26–27 NKJV). Do we close our eyes to the possibility that we may be a landing strip for Satan when we open our minds to him through ungodly practices, psychic predictions, occult literature, and violent, sex-driven, sexually perverted movies and DVDs? Do we seek counsel for daily living from horoscopes in the paper, on television, or the internet rather than relying on God, our faithful and ultimate source of living? Do we let Satan use us to set up barriers that inhibit the cause of Christ in our churches and our homes through criticism and gossip?

9. "Not slothful in business" (Romans 12:11 KJV). Are we chronically late in paying our debts, sometimes choosing not to pay them? Do we charge more on our credit cards than we can afford? Do we keep honest income tax records? Do we engage in shady business deals? Do we inflate our financial worth? Do we get into business partnerships with unbelievers?

10. "Beloved,…abstain from fleshly lusts which war against the soul" (1 Peter 2:11 NKJV). Are we guilty of a lustful eye toward the opposite sex? Do we fill our minds with sexually oriented internet sites, television programs, lewd movies, unsavory books, and magazines? Their covers? Centerfolds? Especially when we sense no one is watching? Do we indulge in lustful activities that God's Word condemns, such as fornication, adultery, or perversion? Do we have improper relationships through the internet? Do we enter "chat rooms" we should not be in? Are we engaged in pornography in any way? Are we practicing gambling or betting, or playing the lottery in any way?

11. "Bearing with one another, and forgiving one another, if anyone has a complaint against another; even as Christ forgave you, so you also must do" (Colossians 3:13 NKJV). Have

we failed to forgive those who may have said or done something to hurt us? Have we written off certain people as not worthy of our friendship?

12. "Even so you also outwardly appear righteous to men, but inside you are full of hypocrisy and lawlessness" (Matthew 23:28 NKJV). Do we know that we are often not what people see? Are we possibly using our involvement in our churches as a cover for our activities away from the body of Christ? Are we mimicking the Christian faith for social status and acceptance in our church or community? Are we real?

13. "Finally, brethren, whatever things are true, whatever things are noble, whatever things are just, whatever things are pure, whatever things are lovely, whatever things are of good report, if there is any virtue and if there is anything praiseworthy—meditate on these things" (Philippians 4:8 NKJV). Do we enjoy listening to conversations that hurt others? Do we pass it on? Do we believe rumors or partial truths, especially about an enemy or a competitor? Do we spend little or no time each day allowing God to speak to us through his Word?

How Did You Do?

God is calling Christians to be authentic and transparent. Did you answer these questions honestly before God and examine your heart purely? Honoring the holiness of God occurs in your life when you are seeking God, examining your life spiritually, and then positioning yourself to be used by God powerfully and supernaturally.

Bend me, oh Lord!

5

Abiding in Jesus Continually

In 1971, the First Baptist Church of Atlanta, Georgia, extended the call for Dr. Charles Stanley to become their senior pastor. He served in this role through September 13, 2020, and then was named pastor emeritus of the church. Upon this, the transition plan for succession was completed, and the church installed Dr. Anthony George as their new senior pastor.

On April 18, 2023, Charles Frazier Stanley left this earth to enter eternal life in the glory of heaven. Now he is abiding in the presence of Jesus Christ daily. While thousands of people heard him proclaim the Scriptures in person each week, Stanley also shared the good news of Jesus Christ with millions of people worldwide through In Touch Ministries radio and TV broadcasts.

When I sat in the worship center of the First Baptist Church of Atlanta on that Sunday night, April 23, 2023, for an extraordinary Legacy Celebration for Dr. Stanley, it was obvious that many would remember this man for being a Bible preacher and a man of God who had a deep, ongoing passionate and personal relationship with Jesus Christ. His intimacy with Jesus was nurtured and ignited daily in his prayer closet. While God used him so greatly in his life, Charles Stanley's influence will continue for generations until Jesus comes again.

But Charles Stanley was just a man. He was a sinful human being like all of us. Even in this Legacy Celebration shared by thousands of us who loved him, everyone recognized this reality about him. Yet there was something different about him. He was a man after God's own heart. His humility was obvious to everyone who met him. Ultimately, his desire was to abide in Jesus continually. This is what always drew me to him.

I was not his close friend and never had the privilege of having a single private conversation with him. Yet there was a day as a younger pastor when I was asked, along with fewer than ten of my older brothers in ministry, to come to Atlanta and spend a few hours in prayer together. Charles Stanley was part of this group of praying pastors, and prayer was our only agenda. I saw him on his knees with us and then on his face before God with us that day. To anyone who heard him pray and join others in prayer, it was more than obvious that this man had an intimate, abiding relationship with Jesus Christ. This experience made an indelible impact on my life.

Motivation

I believe the motivation to enter a time of prayer and fasting must be to glorify God by focusing on and continually abiding with his Son, Jesus Christ. If this is not your goal, then it is not time for you to enter a season of prayer and fasting. Prayer and fasting are not hoops you jump through to get God's attention or check a box to try to get into good standing with God. Just because you may have a need or you are in a crisis, it does not mean you need to pray and fast. This may become a supporting motive for doing it, but it is not the main motive for doing fasting.

I have learned so much through the years about prayer and fasting. One of the realities I have learned is that the purity of our motives does matter when we pray and fast. While the ongoing process of prayer and fasting will indeed purify your motives, it helps greatly if, from the beginning, you establish that your motivation is pure and right. The big picture of prayer and fasting must be that I want to glorify God by focusing on and continually abiding with his Son, Jesus Christ. This must be my main motivation as I submit to God's calling to pray and fast.

Let's imagine for a moment that you are facing a major decision in your life. You may have been given the opportunity to accept a new position that will require you to move to another location, but it will be a huge career move for you. As most people would do, you might seek counsel from others about this opportunity. This usually involves a private meeting in some location where you can state the details of the situation and what may be ahead of you. In other words, these kinds of conversations are important, one-on-one, and confidential.

As a follower of Jesus Christ, when you face critical life decisions like this, should you also consider prayer and fasting? Absolutely, but let me be very clear about this: your motivation still needs to be that you want this decision to glorify God; therefore, you must get into Jesus' presence powerfully through prayer and fasting so that you may hear what he wills for you to do. I think of it this way: If God gives me the go, I go. If God gives me the no, I do not go. It is not about decorating the decision I have already made by spiritualizing it with a little prayer and fasting so I will feel better about it. God sees right through this and may not bless this decision.

Here is what you must recognize: God knows your heart. He sees right through you. He knows you better than you know yourself. He is the one who has gifted you to even be considered for this career opportunity or whatever decision you are facing. He knows your motives for why you do what you do. You cannot con God. You cannot pull one over on him as if he does not know what is on your heart. Motive matters. Yes, your motivation in prayer and fasting matters.

What I want to make clear for you is that while any process of prayer and fasting has a purifying, cleansing effect on you, the greater impact is when you pray and fast in obedience to Jesus. The high view should be that you desire more than anything to glorify God by entering into the presence of Jesus continually through prayer and fasting so that you can really hear more clearly and confidently what God wills for you to do. This should always be your ultimate motivation when you enter a day or a season of prayer and fasting.

I can assure you, if your heart is even close to being right when you begin, the prayer and fasting process of really getting with God intimately will purify and cleanse anything in you that may not have been right initially. If this is the case, as it has been with me at times, repent, learn from it, and listen to God's voice and will for whatever your need may be.

Aspiration

Your aspiration for one day or a season of prayer and fasting should be to abide in Jesus continually. This will always glorify God and will impact your life extraordinarily. To be in the personal presence of Jesus is always best for you.

Prayer and fasting are nothing like walking through a department store saying I want this and do not want this. Your aspiration should be to abide in Jesus continually. When you start with this pure motivation, everything else will become clearer to you. Once you know what God wills, you can receive it and trust him through it all. Over the course of time, you will see why God wants you to do or not to do something. Then you will say, *Thank you, God! You cared for me when I did not know how to care for myself.*

So many times, I have had this kind of conversation with God. Through my prayer and fasting, he always builds in me a greater spirit to receive whatever he wills for me. I can readily receive it if I just know it is his will. The Bible says Jesus did only what he saw the Father doing. "Jesus answered and was saying to them, 'Truly, truly, I say to you, the Son can do nothing of Himself, unless it is something He sees the Father doing; for whatever the Father does, these things the Son also does in the same way. For the Father loves the Son and shows Him all things that He Himself is doing; and the Father will show Him greater works than these, so that you will be amazed'" (John 5:19–20).

In this section of Scripture, Jesus was making clear to everyone that he was doing what his Father wanted him to do. He had just healed a man on the Sabbath, which meant he had broken the Sabbath in the minds of the Jews. But this must have been the Father's will, or Jesus never would have healed him. "The Father will show Him greater works than these, so that you will be amazed" (v. 20). This is a profound insight into Jesus' relationship with his Father and the Father's relationship with Jesus, his Son. It also reveals the kind of relationship we should have with Jesus Christ. Jesus' aspiration was to see what the Father was doing and then do it. Jesus' aspiration was to do whatever the Father was doing and in the same way the Father was doing it. Jesus' aspiration was to see even greater works that the Father said he would do.

Through one day of fasting, several days of fasting, or a season of prayer and fasting, our aspiration should be to glorify God by entering in and abiding in Jesus continually in a greater way so we will know what he wills for us to do. In John 15, Jesus' words are insightful and very helpful to us. Jesus says, "Remain in Me, and I in you. Just as the branch cannot bear fruit of itself but must remain in the vine, so neither can you unless you remain in Me. I am the vine, you are the branches; the one who remains in Me, and I in him bears much fruit, for apart from Me you can do nothing" (vv. 4–5).

What is most important for you to know is that the word from the Greek text is translated as "abide," "continue," "stay," or "remain." Therefore, any of these are acceptable words. Ultimately, Jesus calls upon us to aspire to abide, remain, continue, or stay in Jesus because he is the vine and we are the branches. A branch cannot bear fruit of itself but must remain in the vine. Jesus was teaching us that he alone is the vine and we are the branches. We will bear much fruit only when we are willing to remain, abide, stay, or continue in Jesus.

Then Jesus takes up this significant point in a greater way than ever when he declares: "Apart from Me you can do nothing" (v. 5). In today's world, we would call this a "drop the mic moment" as Jesus puts a period on it all. None of us can do anything on our own. We must be connected to the vine, Jesus Christ, and be in fellowship with him continually so we can bear much fruit and so the fruit will remain. Abiding in Jesus, remaining in Jesus, staying in Jesus, or continuing in Jesus is imperative for Jesus' power to be our source of everything and so he can use us to bear much fruit.

Jesus later says that we glorify God when we are bearing fruit (v. 8), which also proves that we are Jesus' followers. Abiding in Jesus continually must become our aspiration. Jesus is where life is. Jesus is where the power is. Jesus is where the inspiration is. Jesus breathes into us through his Holy Spirit, and power ignites us to do what the Lord wills regardless of the impact or the cost that we would need to pay for obeying God's will.

Therefore, we must never lose this biblical aspiration, especially when we pray and fast. Praying and fasting should always be ultimately about bringing glory to God by abiding in Jesus continually. When you are with Jesus in deep, continuing fellowship, he will shape your perspective, change your heart, and set you on fire with the supernatural power of the Holy Spirit to do greater things.

Abiding in Jesus continually should always be your motivation and always be your aspiration. I say it again not to be redundant but to be clear: without living in, staying in, remaining in, continuing in, and abiding in Jesus, you can do nothing. Therefore, *with* Jesus, all is possible in your life. Jesus changes everything. When you pray and fast under the leadership of the Holy Spirit and experience being in Jesus' presence more meaningfully, you will move to an entirely new dimension spiritually.

What will happen, and what will this look like in your life?

A Greater Anointing

When I walked through my first forty-day season of prayer and fasting, something happened to me that I rarely share in any way. To this day, I still do not understand what occurred, but something happened that had never happened to me before.

In the latter part of May in 1995, I was in the final days of this first forty-day season of fasting. God was meeting with me in ways that are difficult for me to put into words. Since that transformational experience on that early Sunday morning, which I shared with you earlier in this book, heaven opened to me. In those final days of fasting, God poured into my life in an extraordinary way. I was set to conclude my fast on a Thursday evening. I was not longing to end it because each moment was so precious. I had been asked to attend a gathering of leaders in the city of Atlanta. The meeting was on a Friday, so I knew I would need to fly down on Thursday afternoon to be ready to meet on Friday. Furthermore, this meant that my fast would conclude alone in a restaurant in the hotel where I was staying.

All the way there, I was writing in my journal some of the insights God was continuing to give me. Additionally, I was reading through some of what I had written earlier. It was a meaningful time with Jesus and me. Of course, the plane was full, but to me, it was just Jesus and me.

It was sundown when I arrived, and I checked into the hotel, knowing soon this fast would conclude. I spent more time with Jesus before taking the elevator down to dinner. In the restaurant, I ordered a baked potato, and they also brought me a roll. After I thanked Jesus again for his sustaining power throughout these forty days, I ate some of the potato and a little of the bread. My body was lean, then, due to weight loss from the fast, so it did not take much to make me full, but I was humbled to know how God had sustained me and met with me in a gracious and transformational way. After talking with my wife on the phone, I went to sleep calmly and peacefully, resting in the confidence of our faithful God.

In the early morning, and I do get up early, the Lord woke me before my alarm, and I could not help walking around the room singing and rejoicing in loud praise and thanksgiving to God. I felt like the glory of God filled the room and enveloped my life in a way that I had never experienced before nor since then. My emotions were bursting forth with joy as I sensed a new, fresh, powerful anointing of God upon my life. I continued shouting and exclaiming praise to God. Then a deep sense of humility overcame me, and all became calm and peaceful. I began my quiet time with God.

Ever since that moment on that day, I have sensed a greater anointing upon my life, my family, my church, and my ministry. Nothing has ever been the same again. Ever since that day and that entire experience, I have discovered that God can do more in a moment than I could ever do in a lifetime.

The Bible says, "You have an anointing from the Holy One, and you all know" (1 John 2:20). Each Christ-follower has an anointing of the Spirit. While in the Old Testament, an anointing would come and go, that all changed in Acts 2 when the Holy Spirit came down to live within us, never leaving nor forsaking us. The Spirit of God dwells in each Christ-follower; therefore, we have an anointing. This anointing helps you know the difference between truth and error. Through salvation, you have been baptized by the Holy Spirit and placed into the body of Christ. Jesus is the Anointed One, and he has given to each of us a gift, the Holy Spirit, who anoints us.

First John then says in the same chapter, "As for you, the anointing which you received from Him remains in you, and you have no need for anyone to teach you; but as His anointing teaches you about all things, and is true and is not a lie, and just as it has taught you, you remain in Him" (v. 27). This anointing is a gift to you, and God gives you an anointing to grow you. The Scripture says, "As for you," which intentionally emphasizes the personal dynamic in the text, this anointing abides in you permanently. Jesus is living in you, and the Spirit is there to help you and teach you the Word of God. Biblically, the Spirit of God connects you to the Word of God. Through all of this, God grows you.

This anointing also guards you. The anointing helps you separate false teachers and all their teaching that undermines Jesus Christ as being God in the flesh. In today's world, where truth is minimized and conveniently redefined, you need the anointing of God to guard your life.

The Spirit's anointing teaches you, grows you, guards you, and it also guides you. He guides you into the truth of God's Word, and the Spirit reveals where he wants you to go and what he wants you to do in your life and future. The Scripture verse here even reaffirms the strong command to each of us, "You remain in Him." Abiding in Jesus is the key to all of this, and when ignited to a new level with prayer and fasting, you begin to experience a greater anointing, a supernatural anointing.

Jesus practiced prayer and fasting. Following his baptism and prior to the beginning of his public ministry, the Bible talks about forty defining days in the life of Jesus Christ. "Jesus, full of the Holy Spirit, returned from the Jordan and was led around by the Spirit in the wilderness for forty days, being tempted by the devil. And He ate nothing during those days, and when they had ended, He was hungry" (Luke 4:1–2). Authority came to Jesus Christ as he prayed and fasted. The Gospel of Luke says in the first verse that Jesus was full of the Holy Spirit and was then led around by the Spirit in the wilderness. It is interesting to notice that Jesus was full of the Spirit, and then the Spirit led him around in the wilderness. While he was there fasting for forty days, he encountered the devil and was tempted by him.

Then Luke gives us a keen insight further into the chapter. "Jesus returned to Galilee in the power of the Spirit, and news about Him spread through all the surrounding region" (v. 14). Following his forty days of fasting and overcoming the devil, Jesus was empowered by the Holy Spirit. The dynamite power of the Holy Spirit was upon him.

Therefore, Jesus was "full of the Spirit" and "led around by the Spirit" in the wilderness. Then several verses later, following the temptations from the devil, Jesus returned to Galilee in the "power of the Spirit." When you look through Luke 4 in its entirety, you will discover the following areas of extraordinary power that Jesus received through fasting, and he was doing these things with unique spiritual authority:

- In teaching
- In preaching
- In deliverance
- In ministry
- Over Satan and his demons
- Over sickness
- In spreading the gospel to the world

I believe deeply that there is a greater supernatural anointing upon those who pray and fast as they truly abide in Jesus continually.

A Personal Transformation

You can do nothing if you have seasons, days, or moments when you choose to live without abiding in Jesus. No spiritual power, force, or energy comes from living without continually abiding in Jesus. Jesus makes the difference! With Jesus and through Jesus, all is possible. The Bible says, "I can do everything through Christ, who gives me strength" (Philippians 4:13 NLT). Therefore, we must live with the confidence that God is able.

I wrote this earlier in this chapter, but I want to repeat it so you can see it and know it is possible: When you pray and fast under the leadership of the Holy Spirit and experience being in Jesus' presence more meaningfully, you will move to an entirely new dimension spiritually. You will receive a greater anointing of the Holy Spirit in your life. Furthermore, you will experience a personal transformation. Personally, over the years, I have seen God change me from the inside out. The genuine transformation has not only occurred but is still occurring in me.

Since my college days, I have had a strong desire to have a defining and powerful walk with Jesus daily. I cannot recall a day since that time when I did not begin my day with God by having a personal quiet time in the Word of God and prayer. This ongoing passion for abiding in Jesus continually inspired me to begin practicing prayer and fasting while I was in college. Then, because I have prayed and fasted throughout these years, my passion for abiding in Jesus has increased.

Therefore, Jesus is changing me from the inside out. I am not the man I was thirty years ago. I am not the man I was twenty years ago. I am not the man I was ten years ago. I am not the same man I was one year ago. From the inside out, Jesus is transforming me. My willing pursuit of Jesus Christ makes this possible. Additionally, my personal problems and transitions have contributed to this transformation.

When we walk through the fires of life, God uses them to build us more into the likeness of Jesus Christ. An inside-out transformation occurs. He knocks off us anything that does not look like Jesus and continually creates the person he wants us to become. Paul wrote of his desire, "that I may know Him and the power of His resurrection and the fellowship of His sufferings, being conformed to His death" (Philippians 3:10).

When we desire to abide in Jesus continually, get to know him, and experience his power, we join in the fellowship of his suffering, and God uses this suffering to conform us to his death. As we die to ourselves, Christ's power can live through us in a greater way. The transformation from the inside out is God's way to bring genuine change in and through us and bring himself glory as a testimony to the world. This new dimension spiritually leads us to higher ground with God.

The Lord wants to do something supernatural in each of our lives. I want to live and abide in Jesus continually and increasingly so I can experience God's supernatural power. I want to live and minister with a greater anointing of the Holy Spirit of God. Furthermore, I want to experience an ongoing personal transformation until Jesus takes me home to heaven. Do you?

Through the supernatural power of God, we can make a difference. Without it, our influence and impact are extremely limited or may even be non-existent. Therefore, we must choose to abide in, remain in, stay in, and always continue in Jesus. Jesus alone changes everything and everyone. With all I am and all I have been entrusted in my life, I believe strongly in this biblical reality: "Nothing will be impossible with God" (Luke 1:37).

6

Living in Obedience to God

When you follow the leadership of the Holy Spirit and enter a time of prayer and fasting, you are living in obedience to God. Walking through this door will lead you to experience the transforming power of God, which will then launch you into a future where obedience to God becomes your life. Through the supernatural power of prayer and fasting, God will change you so that living in obedience to him becomes part of who you are. This does not mean you will never wrestle again with matters of obedience because there will be times when you will. But now, things are different. Your faith has been enlarged, and your confidence in God has significantly increased. Therefore, you live believing and knowing that God will see you through whatever lies before you. This kind of supernatural power awaits anyone or any church practicing the faith experience of prayer and fasting.

One of these inspiring faith stories that God is writing is through the Liberty Live Church, which is based in Hampton, Virginia. This multi-campus church is exploding in health, growth, and influence because of the supernatural power of God. Under the leadership of their pastor, Grant Ethridge, God is raising up a mighty church to God's glory. Their pastor believes deeply that their decision a few years ago to practice twenty-one days of prayer and fasting each January and again in August has released a mighty movement of the Spirit of God upon their church. In each of these seasons of prayer, hundreds and hundreds of people in this metropolitan region gather for prayer in the early mornings before they go to work each day. Simultaneously, significant numbers of people join them online. Then when the church meets on Sunday, it is a powerful demonstration of God's mighty power.

I have personally witnessed what God is doing through this church. When I was invited to preach one Sunday during one of these seasons of prayer and fasting, it was a fantastic experience for Jeana and me. The presence of the supernatural power of the Holy Spirit was evident in God's people and each worship experience. God is moving powerfully in Pastor Grant and his wife, Tammy, their family, the staff team, and the entire church family.[10]

When followers of Jesus, pastors of churches, and even the members of the congregations are willing to enter seasons of prayer and fasting, God will release his supernatural power upon them. This is what awaits anyone or any church that is willing to live in obedience to God.

A Decision to Obey God

The eighth chapter of the Old Testament book of Ezra records a story about Ezra returning to Jerusalem. During Ezra's captivity in Babylon, the king of Persia determined to send Ezra back to Jerusalem. The Lord permitted Ezra to have great favor with the king, and Ezra was sent to Jerusalem to proclaim God's truth. Many others returned to Jerusalem with him.

Since Ezra had proclaimed to the king how great his God is, Ezra was ashamed to approach the king to request troops to accompany them through enemy territory. How could Ezra have testified to the king about how great and mighty God is and simultaneously ask the king to send his troops to protect the Israelites as they traveled through enemy territory? Ezra had a decision to make, and he decided to obey God. The Bible records this short story for us:

> Then I proclaimed a fast there at the river of
> Ahava, to humble ourselves before our God,
> to seek from Him a safe journey for us, our
> little ones, and all our possessions. For I was
> ashamed to request from the king troops
> and horsemen to protect us from the enemy
> on the way, because we had said to the king,
> "The hand of our God is favorably disposed

to all who seek Him, but His power and His anger are against all those who abandon Him." So we fasted and sought our God concerning this matter, and He listened to our pleading. (Ezra 8:21–23)

Ezra halted the travelers to seek God's protection during their return to their homeland in Jerusalem. They were about to enter enemy territory and needed a miracle to see them through. Ezra and the people were in a crisis. Nevertheless, Ezra and the people decided to obey God. Let me tell you what they did.

While the overarching decision was to obey God, I want to show you how they did it biblically and practically. What you are about to read summarizes any experience you will have through prayer and fasting. Therefore, anytime you choose to enter a season of prayer with fasting, you will learn it is a decision that is spiritual, humble, specific, trusting, and powerful.

Spiritual Decision

"Then I proclaimed a fast" (v. 21).

Ezra needed an intervention from God. He knew that if God did not show up and protect the people, the enemies might destroy them. The crisis was so real to Ezra that he saw it as a life-or-death decision. He knew that God had opened the king's heart and given Ezra favor with the king, so obviously, God must be up to something extraordinary.

Ezra did not appoint a task force to create a strategy for how they could do this. Nor did he ask for help from his denomination. Nor did he turn around and go back to Babylon. What Ezra did was to proclaim a fast. Ezra knew fasting was abstinence from food with a spiritual goal in mind. He knew he was asking the people to abstain from one of the most natural things their bodies craved—food—to entreat the God of heaven to do something supernatural among them. Ezra made a spiritual decision to proclaim a fast.

Humble Decision

"To humble ourselves before our God" (v. 21).

Ezra proclaimed a fast for the people to humble themselves before God. There is a correlation between fasting and humbling yourself before God. When you humble yourself before God, you are making yourself flat and putting yourself underneath him. As you lie low before God in prayer and fasting, God gives you his grace to see you through.

God can and will humble you, but the better way is when you take the initiative to humble yourself before God. Scripture is clear: "Humble yourselves" (1 Peter 5:6). Therefore, Ezra and the people prayed and fasted, humbling themselves before God. They made a spiritual decision and a humble decision.

Specific Decision

"To seek from Him a safe journey for us" (v. 21).

These are simple but profound insights from Scripture about prayer and fasting. Remember what I have shared with you already. Fasting is abstinence from food with a spiritual goal in mind. Ezra and the people of Israel had a specific and spiritual goal in mind: a safe journey. Not only for the people but even for the little ones and their possessions.

Anytime you enter a season of prayer and fasting, you must be specific about what you ask God to do. Ezra was transparent with God and the people: "To seek from Him a safe journey for us, our little ones, and all our possessions." While his request was specific, it was a big request. But Ezra knew he could ask God to do it because God is big and can do anything he chooses to do.

Trusting Decision

"So we fasted and sought our God concerning this matter" (v. 23).

The fast had now begun. They were humbling themselves before God in prayer and fasting. They asked God for a safe journey for everyone, including all their possessions. So now, they trusted God and believed God would answer their prayer.

In simplicity, they had a need and humbled themselves through prayer and fasting to talk to God about it. Now, they were on the fast and seeking God about their request. They put their trust in God and believed God to answer their prayer.

Powerful Decision

> "He listened to our pleading…and He
> rescued us from the hand of the enemy and
> the ambushes along the way" (vv. 23, 31).

While their overarching decision was to walk in obedience to God, they made a spiritual decision, a humble decision, a specific decision, a trusting decision, and a powerful decision. When we pray and fast, God listens to our pleading. God also rescues us from the hand of the Enemy and the ambushes along the way. God answered Israel's plea through prayer and fasting. They experienced the supernatural power of prayer and fasting because they were living in obedience to God. They obeyed God, and now they will be launched into a fresh new commitment to living in obedience to God in the future.

The Bible says, "We journeyed from the river Ahava on the twelfth of the first month to go to Jerusalem;

and the hand of our God was upon us, and He rescued us from the hand of the enemy and the ambushes by the road" (v. 31). What a decisive outcome occurred because God's hand was upon them, and in answer to their humble pleas through prayer and fasting, God rescued them from their enemy and ambushes along the way. As a result, they arrived in Jerusalem safely. This is the supernatural power of prayer and fasting.

Whenever you consider or pray about entering a day or a season of prayer and fasting, remember Ezra 8:21–23, 31. Do the same as they did. They made a spiritual decision, a humble decision, a specific decision, a trusting decision, and a powerful decision. These insights are profound. Experience them. Share them with others. This is living in obedience to God, one of the supernatural ways God changes your life.

Opening Your Eyes

Living in obedience to God will open your eyes. The holy presence of God is real, and anyone who chooses to embrace the biblical teachings and realities of prayer and fasting can experience them. These truths from God are not for a few people only but for all of God's people. Our desire to experience the manifested presence of God is made possible when we are living in obedience to God. This life of obedience may sometimes involve practicing prayer and fasting.

Opening your eyes to see what God may want to

do in you and through you may lead you into experiencing the supernatural power of prayer and fasting. Life is much more than just the everyday busy matters of your family, job, or church. We must encounter God and experience God himself along the way. If we quiet ourselves before the Lord, we may hear his whisper. We may even hear Jesus saying, *There is a better way. Come into my presence. I will give you rest. Trust me and obey.*

Throughout history, many have been willing to open their eyes. They have discovered that opening their eyes would give them a fresh vision of God and lead them to experience the supernatural power of God. Many of these world changers have also testified to the necessity of fasting in their lives. For example, John Wesley instructed his followers to fast twice weekly and would not ordain a man to the Methodist ministry if he didn't embrace this fast.

Others who recognized the importance of prayer with fasting as their spiritual worship and discipline included Martin Luther, John Calvin, John Knox, Matthew Henry, Jonathan Edwards, Charles Finney, David Brainerd, Andrew Murray, and D. Martyn Lloyd-Jones. This list could go on and on.

When we are willing to obey the biblical call to prayer and fasting, we are opening our eyes to experience a more significant vision from God and to receive a greater power to live for Jesus and make a difference in this world.

The Kind of Fast God Chooses

There is a right way and a wrong way to practice prayer and fasting. While opening our eyes will help us to see what God wants us to see, learning to listen to God's voice in this noisy world will keep us on God's path to living the way God wants us to live. This is why there is great value in sitting in quietness before the Lord.

Isaiah 58:1–5 informs us about fasting that does *not* please God. Living and abiding in sin, speaking wickedness, and living in deceit, along with quarreling, strife, and fighting will never result in God hearing your prayer and answering it. Just because you put on sackcloth and appear to have humility does not mean your fast is pleasing to God.

This is not what God has chosen. The kind of fast God has chosen for us to experience is written about in Isaiah 58:6–12. The following words should captivate you because they overflow with promise. Try to read these verses alone and listen to the Holy Spirit when you do. The Bible says:

> "Is this not the fast that I choose:
> To release the bonds of wickedness,
> To undo the ropes of the yoke,
> And to let the oppressed go free,
> And break every yoke?
> Is it not to break your bread with the hungry
> And bring the homeless poor into the house;
> When you see the naked, to cover him;

And not to hide yourself from your own flesh?
Then your light will break out like the dawn,
And your recovery will spring up quickly;
And your righteousness will go before you;
The glory of the LORD will be your rear guard.
Then you will call, and the LORD will answer;
You will cry for help, and He will say, 'Here I am.'
If you remove the yoke from your midst,
The pointing of the finger and speaking wickedness,
And if you offer yourself to the hungry
And satisfy the need of the afflicted,
Then your light will rise in darkness,
And your gloom will become like midday.
And the LORD will continually guide you,
And satisfy your desire in scorched places,
And give strength to your bones;
And you will be like a watered garden,
And like a spring of water whose waters do not fail.
Those from among you will rebuild the ancient ruins;
You will raise up the age-old foundations;
And you will be called the repairer of the breach,
The restorer of the streets in which to dwell."
(Isaiah 58:6–12)

This kind of fast honors and pleases God. This fast helps us live for Jesus and inspires us to live a Christian life. This fast leads us to experience multiple promises from God that can become living realities in our lives. If you are struggling with physical challenges, dealing with mental or emotional pain, or walking through a financial crisis, what you are about to read will inspire you greatly. Whatever your problem may be or whatever you are facing in your life, whatever it is, God can make a way.

God's Promises When You Pray and Fast

Consider how blessed we are that God has provided us with twenty-two promises through the prophet Isaiah when we fast like God desires for us to fast. The inseparable twins of prayer and fasting assist in ushering us into a God-sized moment. I have experienced these promises personally. I am confident that when we fast the way God desires, these promises will occur in God's way and God's timing.

I want to focus on seven of these promises and give you a few thoughts about them. May God inspire you to believe that he will bring them to reality when you obey God through prayer and fasting.

Promise 1: Set Free

When you practice prayer and fasting, God will set you free. God can set you free from the chains of injustice. The most oppressed can be set free. God can untie the cords of the yoke. Our God is even able to set free those who are in bondage.

God cares so much for you that he can free you from the comparisons game where you always feel like you do not measure up. When you fast and pray, God steps in and sets you free from any perceived separation you may have with him. God can even set you free from Satan, who tries to immobilize, paralyze, and keep you bound up in fear and hopelessness.

God can set you free even when you feel guilty. Since he has forgiven you, you can forgive yourself. Freedom means you do not have to commit the same sins again and again. Being set free even means that you do not have to go to God and keep confessing the same tired old sins that you have been confessing for many years.

When you consider responding positively to God's call to prayer and fasting, you may start slowly, fasting and praying for only one day. Perhaps you may decide to fast and pray one day each week throughout the year, during which you declare that specific twenty-four hours as your time of obedience to be alone in the intimate presence of God. If you do, I suggest you begin your fast at six o'clock in the evening by writing down one, two, or three specific things you will focus on talking to God about over a twenty-four-hour period. As you do, God will give you grace, leadership, comfort, and perhaps even a new direction in your Christian walk. In the end, he will set you free.

I have heard multiple stories about how God has set people free from many sins and strongholds through prayer and fasting. God can do everything, so trust him and ask him for the miraculous to occur in and through you. Stand on this invaluable word from God's holy Word. Jesus said, "You will know the truth, and the truth will set you free" (John 8:32).

Promise 2: Oppressed No More

God promises you he can break every yoke of oppression that crushes you. What is it like to be oppressed? When you are so low and feel so beaten down that you doubt it is possible for you to rise again. Fears, anxieties, and even hostilities overcome you as you feel you are targeted by Satan and perhaps others.

Oppression is the burdensome and unjust exercise of authority or power over you. Sometimes, even your body and your spirit are weighed down into the depths of discouragement and depression. Almost all people deal with this kind of oppression at some point.

Do you feel that you struggle with oppression? Are you struggling right now? Prayer and fasting can unlock those prison doors in your mind, heart, or lifestyle. There is hope. When you become willing to pray and fast, set your goal: *I do not want to be oppressed anymore*. Denounce these spiritual authorities and powers that you feel are over you and crushing you. Call out to Jesus and plead with him to set you free.

You will begin to hear and receive his generous promises in life. Freedom awaits. Oppression no more! Guilt about the past and a negative mindset will be no more. You will take it to the cross and leave it there. Jesus died for all sins. We are free, even from oppression.

Unfortunately, too many of Jesus' followers settle for staying where they are. God can set them free from the burden of oppression. All is possible through God's power; often, that kind of supernatural power only comes when we pray and fast.

Promise 3: Becoming Generous

When we fast and pray, God teaches us how to become generous with others who have physical and spiritual needs. The Bible says, "Is it not to break your bread with the hungry and bring the homeless poor into the house; when you see the naked, to cover him; and not to hide yourself from your own flesh?" (Isaiah 58:7). The book of Proverbs complements this passage by reminding us that when we give to the poor, we lend to the Lord (19:17). Some may think this is unnecessary, but the Lord blesses those who do.

The needs across our nation and world are significant. Feeding the poor, caring for the widow, and fostering or adopting a child are each important to God and should be to us. Are you practicing generosity with those who have physical and emotional needs? We need to live out what we believe. Each time we practice prayer and fasting, our generosity becomes more genuine. Giving and sharing become the natural things to do. Prayer and fasting also put our selfish lives into perspective as God teaches us through it all. So put the self-life into perspective. You are never more like the Father in heaven than when you are generous with other people.

Promise 4: Shining Light

God uses prayer and fasting to ignite your light to shine more brightly. The Bible says, "Your light will break out like the dawn" (Isaiah 58:8). There is nothing more blinding than the sun coming up on a brilliantly sunny day. God says that the fast he has chosen for you will result in a light beaming through you that will break out like the dawn. He is making us a promise that this will happen to our lights when we come to him in fasting and prayer. The darker the day, the brighter our lights will become when we fast and pray.

As I observe those who have fasted and prayed over an extended period, I can always see that the light from the spirit of their inner person glows more brilliantly than ever before. That's because death to self is profound; then we experience an awakening to who we are in Jesus Christ. This brings a glow that God alone can give people when they fast and pray. It's what brought such a radiance to the face of Moses when, on the mountain with God, he came face-to-face with his Creator. When we fast and pray, we, too, will begin to experience the glow of God that comes only when we go one-on-one with him. As a result, your countenance will reflect the glory of God.

Promise 5: Healing for Body, Soul, and Spirit

Scripture states, "Your healing will quickly appear" (v. 8 NIV). God is our healer. Your body, soul, and spirit can become robust and healthy when you pray and fast. The world wants freedom from all pain and anything that will help them feel and look healthier. The Bible says that your healing will quickly appear.

Prayer and fasting activate a divine force within us. Through prayer and fasting, I have seen the Lord heal various medical challenges I have had. Since fasting has become integral to my spiritual worship, I have been delivered many times. Was it the fasting that gave me relief? Did the elimination of poisons and toxins from my body bring on my healing? I don't have any idea, and it doesn't matter. I believe that there are occasions when God heals me. All I can do is trust God and always believe he can heal.

Promise 6: Divine Protection

Look at this promise from God when we pray and fast: "Your righteousness will go before you; the glory of the Lord will be your rear guard" (v. 8). When we come humbly into the presence of God in prayer and fasting, God promises us protection. Protection from the front and the rear. God literally has us covered.

God is our shield and protector. He can crush the Enemy and shield us from all demonic forces. This is important because you will face major spiritual warfare when you pray and fast. Therefore, you need to remember that God is covering you. God is protecting you. And always stand upon these words: "Greater is He who is in you than he who is in the world" (1 John 4:4).

Promise 7: Answered Prayers

As you pray and fast, you will call on God, who can answer your prayer. Answered prayer is the quintessence of praying and fasting. If I were to share some of the pages of my daily prayer journals I have recorded since 1990 and then walk you back through my journals following each short or long-term fast, you would see one thing: my prayers were answered.

There *is* something to the disciplines of prayer and fasting. When God has led me to fast and I have put food aside to seek God more fully and completely, without exception, God answered prayer. It may not have been what I desired, but he did answer it. The answer may come later, and many times it does, but God uses this time to prepare me for whatever he wills.

Nothing ushers you into the throne room more than prayer and fasting. It is so supernatural that regardless of how God answers a prayer or even if he answers it in a way that I did not prefer, it still builds confidence and greater faith within me because I am more readily accepting that God is working and he is in control. He will do what he wants to do. He is God; I am not.

When I leave a season or day of prayer and fasting, I

have one primary goal: living in obedience to God. This is one of the ways God changes our lives through prayer and fasting.

7

Surrendering All to Jesus

Since 1865, The Salvation Army has been committed to transforming lives. Joining a group of Christian businessmen who were burdened for those in their London community who were poor and disadvantaged, William Booth began preaching to people gathered outside the Blind Beggar pub. After that, William and his wife Catherine started doing everything possible to take the good news of Jesus to impoverished and disadvantaged people.

Therefore, The Christian Mission began in 1865 and bore that name until 1878, when Booth stated, "The Christian Mission…is a Volunteer Army." From then on, the word "Volunteer" was changed to "Salvation." The Christian Mission organization has held its new name high even to this day, The Salvation Army. Beginning on a humble street corner over a century and a half ago, The Salvation Army now spreads the love of Jesus in over 130 countries across the world.[11]

When someone asked William Booth, the founder of The Salvation Army, the secret of his enormous success, Booth remained silent for several moments. Finally, with tear-filled eyes, he said, "There have been men with greater brains or opportunities than I, but I made up my mind that God would have all of William Booth there was."[12] Several years later, when General Booth's daughter heard about her father's comment regarding his full surrender to God, she said, "That wasn't really his secret—his secret was that he never took it back."[13]

This powerful testimony illustrates the theme of this chapter, "Surrendering All to Jesus." Look what God is still doing through the ministry of one man who said that he made up his mind that God would have all of him there was. Even as I write this, I am overcome with conviction from the Holy Spirit. I must right now pause here and pray, *Father, there are others who are smarter than me, have greater gifts than me, and have much greater opportunities than me, but on this day, I declare that from this day forward, Lord Jesus Christ, you will have all of Ronnie Floyd there is. I surrender all to Jesus again, wholly, fully, today. Amen.*

You may need to do just as I did. Simply pray the prayer I just prayed, delete my name, and insert your name. We often forget that the men and women God has used providentially and historically lived a life surrendered to Jesus Christ.

Please do not read so fast that you miss what Booth's

daughter said about his comments. She said that once her dad prayed to God and surrendered himself fully to Jesus, he never took his own life back because it was God's. What a testimony! May our children, grandchildren, and others look at us like this one day.

God Will Change Your Life

When you practice prayer and fasting and begin to experience God's supernatural power through it, surrendering all to Jesus will be one of the ways God will change your life. You will never be content to live your life again or to take it back for your use and pleasure only.

Prayer and fasting can lead you to this kind of surrender, where you are poured out daily to Jesus first and only. Whether you fast for one day, three days, seven days, ten days, twenty-one days, or even forty days, prayer with fasting does something that you cannot do on your own. God uses it to set you free, to open your hands, to allow you to give yourself all to Jesus, and to position you to hear God's voice like never before. Just one short season of fasting may have a long-term effect on your entire life.

There is something extraordinary about praying and fasting to the Lord. For some reason—perhaps it is obedience to God, denial of self, humility before God, surrendering all to Jesus, or all these things together—but for some reason, God is drawn to those who pray and fast, giving them unusual favor and extraordinary blessing. We will only comprehend matters like these once we get to heaven. Yet the Lord and his power supernaturally come upon anyone who prays and fasts with pure motives before the Lord.

Surrendering all to Jesus is pivotal in our daily walk with God. God uses surrendered men and women, surrendered teenagers and children. To the level of our understanding and spiritual maturity, surrendering our all to Jesus is spiritually significant.

Poured Out to Jesus

Surrendering all to Jesus leads me to think of many people in the Bible, throughout history, and even today. One verse of Scripture that captivates my heart and illustrates surrendering all to Jesus is recorded in 2 Timothy.

When the apostle Paul, under the leadership of the Holy Spirit, wrote these profound words just before his death, they became like handwriting on the wall for each of us to see. Paul's words should arrest us. They should call us to personal spiritual examination. They should move us to repentance. Then, if all of this has occurred, they should lead us to surrender all to Jesus in a more extraordinary way than ever before.

This Christian persecutor and killer, who was radically transformed by Jesus himself on the Road to Damascus and whom then God used to shake the world for Christ even to this day, in his final letter to Timothy before his looming death said, "I am already being poured out as a drink offering, and the time of my departure has come" (2 Timothy 4:6).

Knowing death was soon ahead of him, whether he lived or died, whether in prison or on a missionary journey, the apostle emulated for us what it means to surrender all to Jesus. He knew Jesus and wanted more than anything to be like Jesus. Paul understood total surrender and the cost of living this way. This time, he would not be rescued from a lion's mouth or the devastation of stoning, but he would face death. Just before AD 68 and prior to Nero's escape from Rome, Paul was taken away and beheaded for Jesus Christ.

When Paul wrote the words of 2 Timothy 4:6, he knew the picture he was painting for us of his life. It represented where he had been, was now, and was about to be, even through death. He would be "poured out as a drink offering." Surrendering all to Jesus is what this is all about.

Let me explain in a different way. Paul was using some Old Testament language, referring to being "poured out as a drink offering." In ancient rites, before the sacrifice of Christ, the priest would pour wine onto the altar after having sacrificed the burnt offering. Paul was saying, "I am that offering." Urgency and finality rang loud and clear through that declaration. I believe Paul was saying, "I am pouring myself out slowly, and I willingly will shed my blood as a way to give myself all to God, even in death." Paul was moving toward his death, and he knew it. Once Jesus changed Paul's life, Paul began pouring out, moment by moment, his vision, energy, heart, passion, and all he had to live 24/7, surrendering his all to Jesus.

Paul also refers to his departure, knowing his days and hours were limited because soon he would be martyred for his faith in Jesus Christ. This word "departure" gives us a couple of word pictures. First, its usage illustrates a ship lifting its anchor to leave. It also illustrates soldiers who were breaking their camp. Both word pictures illustrate going home. In other words, Paul informed us that he was setting sail for his eternal home with Jesus Christ. He was taking his tent down and preparing to be with his Savior.

From the moment Paul came to Christ until the day of his martyrdom, he poured his life out as a drink offering. The present tense used here means "being poured out as a drink offering" occurred continually until his final breath. Paul knew Nero was not the one who would take his life because Paul was surrendering his all to Jesus already, even unto his death.

The apostle Paul's perspective was set several years earlier when he wrote, "To me, to live is Christ, and to die is gain" (Philippians 1:21). Paul never saw himself losing either way. Instead, his life was all about Jesus on this earth, and when he died, he saw his death as gain because he would be with Jesus personally. Living on this earth, all for Jesus! Dying for Jesus, all for Jesus!

Giving his life in death was gain. This is the way Paul lived, and this is the way he died.

Are you surrendering all to Jesus like this in your life each day? Until we die, we should be like Paul, being poured out as a drink offering to God. God is calling us to surrender all to Jesus 24/7. It never ends until our final breath in this world. Whether we walk in days of blessing or times of trouble, surrendering all to Jesus is necessary. This alters our perspectives and changes our lives. This is an outcome of the supernatural power of prayer and fasting, so I am calling you to commit to practicing prayer and fasting in your life, church, and nation.

Denial of yourself and surrendering all to Jesus will never come naturally to any of us but only supernaturally. Our minds and wills will usually only be ordered into submission to Jesus when the Holy Spirit directs us through prayer and fasting. If this does not occur, we open ourselves to Satan, his demonic forces, mindsets, philosophies, and ideas. None of this will lead to God, but away from God and his supernatural power.

Therefore, we must lift our hands in complete and total surrender to Jesus. We need God to work in our lives, both inside of us and through us. When we practice prayer and fasting, we will see God's supernatural hand leading us daily to surrender our all to Jesus.

Weakness versus Strength

Surrendering all to Jesus involves the daily battle between our weaknesses and strengths. Which one would you say that God is drawn to the most: weakness or strength? Over twenty-five years ago, a book called *Fresh Wind, Fresh Fire,* was published and became widely read by the church in America and beyond. Many things were special about the book, but one of the profound and significant insights for me as I read it still rebukes me regularly and inspires me daily.

What do you think about these words written by the book's author and the Brooklyn Tabernacle's pastor, Jim Cymbala? He writes these powerful and profound words: "God is attracted to weakness." Now read and notice the framework for these words. Jim Cymbala writes: "I discovered an astonishing truth; God is attracted to weakness. He can't resist those humbly and honestly admitting how desperately they need him. Our weakness, in fact, makes room for his power."[14]

When I read those words decades ago, my eyes opened. I saw that being strong is not my strength. God wants my weakness. He wants my desperation. God is attracted to weakness so he can exhibit his strength and power through us. He wants us out of the way. When I am weak, this makes room for God's power. When I am weak, God is strong!

This is why God works in us supernaturally when we enter days or seasons of prayer and fasting. In our humility and weakness from not eating food, we are drawn to God, and God is drawn to us in our weakness. When we are weak, God is strong. Therefore, we are able to surrender all to Jesus. We need him! When we surrender to Jesus, we are emptying ourselves before God so that God can fill us with his supernatural power. We must die to live; we must give it all up to gain.

No great work anywhere by anyone at any time has ever come about without surrender. For God's kingdom to come, our kingdom must go. This is where we experience the supernatural power of God. When we surrender to Jesus, we become better fathers, better mothers, better husbands, and better wives, better children, better students, better employees, better leaders because we have transferred our lives, our ideas, our plans over to our heavenly Father.

It's the transfer of our bodies (our physical being), our minds (how we think), our spirits (where God lives), our tongues (every word we say), our attitudes (the way we respond to others), and our motives (the reality of who we are). All that God has given us, we must transfer, give over, and surrender all to Jesus. We surrender all for God's great purposes and no longer keep anything for ourselves. The more we live in God's holy presence, staying focused on God and what he says to us in the Bible, the more the Holy Spirit will grant us joy in prayer and fasting.

We also discover in these days or seasons of fasting

that no one has ever made more promises than God. No one has ever kept more promises than God, and no one has ever been more faithful than God. God will be faithful to answer all his promises to those who pray and fast. God is the Promise Keeper!

God knows each of us, our families, and our churches are engaged in the battle of our lives. God tells us in the Scriptures: "Our struggle is not against flesh and blood, but against the rulers, against the powers, against the world forces of this darkness, against the spiritual forces of wickedness in the heavenly places. Therefore, take up the full armor of God, so that you will be able to resist on the evil day, and having done everything, to stand firm" (Ephesians 6:12–13).

Every mom and dad must understand that their marriage and family are in a war against Satan. Every pastor and church leader must know that their church is in a war against Satan. Every schoolteacher and administrator must understand that their children and students are in a war against Satan. Every local, state, and national politician must know that our towns, cities, states, and nation are at war with Satan. He comes to steal, kill, and destroy (see John 10:10). He hates God's truth and despises God's people. He wants to captivate our ideologies and philosophies, to deceive us from believing God's truth in the Bible.

Therefore, Jesus' followers should seriously accept the call to pray and fast as they live life, do family, work in their jobs, and surrender daily to Jesus. When we pray and fast, walking in the power of our weaknesses, we will be strengthened and ignited by God, who is all-powerful.

We are facing intense spiritual warfare daily. Consider opening your eyes to see what it is: Satan is our enemy and wants to destroy all of us. This is another reason we must discover the supernatural power of prayer and fasting. When we are living life surrendering all to Jesus each day, we will win in the end.

We Need Revival

Revival is the manifested presence of God in our lives. How can we live surrendering all to Jesus daily if we do not experience the manifested presence of God? We cannot! Therefore, we need to deal honestly with our sins and unforgiveness. We must confess them to God and others if an offense is against someone. We need to make restitution to others and do everything we can do to be clean before God and to walk in harmony in our relationships. Surrendering all to Jesus places us in a position to experience the manifested presence of God in our lives. This is revival! I firmly believe this is why we need to pray and fast.

When we humble ourselves before God and begin to see ourselves the way God sees us, we are like dry wood ready to be ignited. When we are weak but ready, humble but hungry for God, breakthrough, revival, and awakening are near. Consequently, I still pray for, believe God for, and fast for revival. God placed in my heart that he will bring a mighty spiritual revival to America that will transcend all denominational, generational, cultural, racial, and ethnic lines. We need an outpouring of the Holy Spirit like this. So catch this vision and carry it as a prayer burden that you lay before God daily. This is our hope.

Surrendering all to Jesus will lead you to experience some great moments and movements of God. Surrendering all to Jesus is living your life while releasing all to God continually. Grabbing for this and that in your life will cease. The genuine humility and willingness that releases everything to God will replace it. No longer will you live with your hands in a fist, but your hands will be open. No longer will you choose to hold on to all you think you have or own now, but you will release it all to Jesus continually. Yes, you will release your desires, dreams, and even the secret sins you hold on to that you think no one knows. God knows about each of them.

Revival requires surrendering all to Jesus. God desires us to surrender our minds to him (the way we think); our wills (what we're convinced we should be or do); our emotions (how we feel); our bodies (our physical being) our talents (the natural abilities we have); our gifts (the supernatural gifts of the Holy Spirit); our attitudes (our often selfish responses to others); our motives (what really drives us to succeed); our careers (the business of life that too often becomes our purpose in life). Once again, revival requires surrendering all to Jesus.

When we pray and fast, surrendering all to Jesus is one of the outcomes and transforming realities in our lives. We learn the value of transferring everything to Jesus daily. We discover the power of exchanging our life for Jesus' life.

Whenever God calls me to fast, in which I deny myself the natural act of eating to focus on specific spiritual goals God has put in my heart, I ask God to show me those areas in my life that I may still be keeping for Ronnie Floyd and perhaps am not even aware of it. I do not want to live like many in spiritual deception, but I want to live in God's light by God's power. I do not want to be blinded spiritually. I want to be all Jesus wants me to be. I want to live each day surrendering my all to Jesus. Moment by moment, day by day, and night by night, surrendered.

I appeal to you to release it all to Jesus. Pour yourself out to Jesus. Hold nothing back. Surrender it all. Everything! Prayer and fasting can lead you to this kind of total surrender. It sets your heart free, opens your hands to release, and positions you to hear the voice of God like never before.

The Fasting Team Needs You

I have discovered through the years that God has an army of his people worldwide who are practicing prayer and fasting. Often, their anonymity exists by conviction or choice, or perhaps they fear the looks they will receive if others knew they were fasting.

Let's face what I perceive to be the truth. Anecdotally, most pastors and churches across America do not practice prayer and fasting. Nor do they teach it or preach it. I have heard hundreds of sermons in churches, conferences, seminars, and online. It is rare, and I mean very rare, to hear prayer and fasting mentioned briefly or even extremely rare to hear a full message about it. Thankfully, this is improving across America, and a few more voices are beginning to address this subject positively.

None of these observations I have made are to cast judgment or criticism on anyone or any group. It is a simple observation of the realities of the church today. If we keep praying about it, the perceptions about fasting will continue to change positively and increase in visibility and practice. Therefore, I do appeal to you to consider joining the fasting team.

Now there is not a formal team that I am aware of, as we would imagine the word "team," but let me assure you that we need more people on the fasting team. Start where you are. Perhaps you have never fasted before. All is well. Learn what you can from my book and other resources available. But sooner or later, you must jump into the water and begin to fast.

Knowledge is essential when you fast. I am not a medical doctor. This book does not exist to advise you on the physical or medical aspects of fasting. I have written this book from a spiritual perspective based first on what the Bible says and then on some insights from my own experiences in prayer and fasting. Because of medical conditions, there are some individuals for whom a fast would not be safe. Anyone considering a fast should assess their physical situation and consult a physician familiar with fasting before beginning.

Your heart is also essential when you fast. I am not speaking of your heart in your physical body because I have addressed physical and medical matters in the above paragraph. I am talking here about your spiritual heart, your depth, and your desire to be all God wants you to be. Each of us experiences decisive moments in life; perhaps this is one for you. When you decide to fast, jump on in there and see what God wants you to be and do with your life. For example, consider these questions:

- Are you uncertain what God is doing in your life right now?
- Are you unhappy with where you are in your spiritual progress?
- Do you want God to do something specific in your life this year?

- Are you carrying a significant burden in your life right now?
- Are you aware of a sin that you want to overcome?
- Do you have a bad habit that you need to be set free from?
- Is there a spiritual stronghold from which you need God to set you free?
- Do you need a miracle in your life, marriage, family, finances, or health?
- Do you need a breakthrough?
- Has your passion for Jesus diminished some?
- Do you need to get more serious about your spiritual life?
- Do you need to develop your spiritual life and grow spiritually?

If you have answered "yes" or "maybe" to any of these questions, you need to pray about and consider entering a day or season of fasting. Join the fasting team! God wants to do great things *in* you so that he can do greater things *through* you. This is why you cannot delegate your spiritual life and growth to anyone else.

So stop imagining your spiritual life as just one of the many compartments in your life or just another box to check. Jesus is to be the center of your life. Everything else orbits around Jesus and your spiritual walk with him. This means Jesus is greater than yourself, greater than your marriage, greater than your parenting, greater than your entertainment, greater than your career, and greater than your money and possessions. Each one of these has a place in your life. However, they are to orbit around Jesus and your spiritual walk with him. Jesus Christ is Lord! Surrendering all to Jesus will change everything else in your life, including you and your priorities.

8

Adjusting to God's Will

Many who follow Jesus are on a sincere quest to discover the will of God for their lives. This occurs because the deeper their walk with Christ is, the more they desire to please him. They realize that discovering, knowing, and living in God's will is the safest and greatest place to be in their life.

We desire to know God's will because we love him and want to become all God has created us to be. While I do not believe God is concealing his will from us, I do think there is a mystery at times in God revealing his will to us. It is not a mystery for him because he already knows his will for us. But it is a mystery to us sometimes because we do not always know where the journey will lead us.

The Scriptures always remind us of the importance of faith in our lives. One example that is short in length but deep in content is found in these significant words, "We walk by faith, not by sight" (2 Corinthians 5:7).

While the context of this verse is comparing the temporal and the eternal, this universal principle about life in this text is clear, succinct, and profound: "We walk by faith, not by sight." As long as we live on this earth and journey toward our eternal home in heaven, we cannot live the Christian life by what we see but by our faith in the Son of God, Jesus Christ our Lord.

Walking by faith means my faith is ultimately in God himself; it is not in me trying to navigate and understand the will of God on my own. God is perfect, but I am not. My ultimate confidence is in our sovereign and providential God. My confidence is not in my quest to always understand his will and path for me.

Therefore, I have come to believe that the will of God is as much about our providential journey with God through life as it is about a destination we reach where we deeply sense, *I am in the center of God's will for my life.* Of course, this is a special prize to reach a destination like I just described. But our life journey is also important because it calls upon us to live by faith and place our trust in God's providential care for us even if we do not always know where this is leading us.

The supernatural power of prayer and fasting leads us to have a spiritual fluidity in life, where we are always willing to adjust to the will of God. It creates agility in our walk with Christ so that we can more readily go where the Spirit of God is leading us and adapt to what God is doing in us, through us, and around us.

My Journey

Recently, after entering a significant professional transition, I had no idea what I was about to go through personally. Quite honestly, it devastated me. Before this time, God had placed before me all kinds of opportunities for leadership and influence in an above-and-beyond way, speaking, writing, encouraging, and providing leadership. Yet within months of this transition journey, God took me to a new level of humbling me and teaching me to walk with him day by day and night by night, experiencing the presence of God. Each day I looked for the cloud, and each night I looked for the pillar of fire. The pillar of cloud during the day and the pillar of fire by night represented God's ongoing presence and guidance for his people.

Listen, friends, I have walked with God for years and have been a passionate follower of Jesus. While I longed to be "in a destination" within months of my transition, I know now that if God had done this, I may have missed one of the greatest lessons I have ever learned in following Jesus.

Once Moses had built the tabernacle, the cloud, the presence of God, covered it and filled it, and even Moses could not enter it at times. The Bible says, "Throughout their journeys, whenever the cloud was taken up from over the tabernacle, the sons of Israel would set out; but if the cloud was not taken up, then they did not set out until the day when it was taken up" (Exodus 40:36–37).

Notice in the text how the people adjusted to what God was doing. They followed the cloud when it lifted, but when the cloud stayed, they stayed. For even greater clarity, when the cloud stopped, they stopped. When the cloud moved, they moved. The cloud and the fire represented God's ongoing presence and guidance for his people.

Even as they were learning to adjust to what God was doing and where God wanted them to be, we must do the same. When God and his presence are known, we must join him wherever he is. Today, we have the Holy Spirit of God living in us. He never leaves us or forsakes us. When we sense he is moving us, we need to move. When we sense he desires us to stay, we need to stay. This is regarding God's will and the spiritual journey God has each of us on each day.

I was a happy, fulfilled, and content senior pastor of a large, growing, multi-campus church for almost thirty-three years. Then, about two years before I left this assignment, I felt deeply in my time with God that I needed to begin praying words from this verse daily: "Then I heard the voice of the Lord, saying, 'Whom shall I send, and who will go for Us?' Then I said, 'Here am I. Send me!'" (Isaiah 6:8). Therefore, while not understanding, I just began praying these words daily in my quiet time: *Here am I. Send me!*

I willingly did this because I have always believed that regardless of where I am, I must be willing to follow

God's leadership. Additionally, I thought and still believe that my comfort and preferences must die to the will of God. When I daily prayed this verse from Isaiah, I felt God wanting to keep my heart agile to him. That was it! I never believed it would result in God calling me away from our church.

Well, surprising to me, I sensed God's call upon my life. Yes, after all those incredible years of serving this great church where we had raised our family and had lifetime friendships, I entered a season away from the pastorate. I began serving in a significant national ministry executive leadership position. Jeana and I willingly followed what we believed was the will of God and adjusted our entire lives to do it. We moved away to a fantastic city, zealous and sold out to this calling.

After twenty-nine months of serving in this role, twenty of which were in a global pandemic, we came to believe God was leading us to depart. Therefore, I announced my resignation and worked another two and one-half weeks helping prepare them for the transition. Consequently and subsequently, we entered a season in life we had never experienced before or would have imagined ourselves ever to be. Yet God is still seeing us through.

God is humbling me, teaching me, using me as he chooses, and preparing me for whatever future he has for me. Through this season, God has taught us to live day by day and night by night. Experiencing the presence of God and trusting him 24/7 for each day and for our future has been quite a journey. We are learning so much about walking with Jesus daily, moment by moment, day by day, and night by night.

In May 2024, a 365-day morning and evening devotional book that I had written months before called *Day By Day and Night By Night* was released. I encourage you to get it for yourself, your friends, family, church, and colleagues and share it with them. It will inspire you and help guide you each day and each night. I promise you, these 365 morning and evening devotions will invest in your life, inspire you daily, and will influence your life in a positive manner.

Let me be so open that it may make you feel somewhat uncomfortable: I do not have it all figured out! Yet I know that I need to walk so close to Jesus Christ each day that I adjust as necessary to follow and do the will of God. When the cloud and the fire stop, I stop. When the cloud and the fire move, I move. Just as God has been faithful throughout history to reveal himself to his people and clarify his way and will for their lives, he will do the same for you and me. God is with us always! Look for him today.

Whether you are in business, government, finance, law, politics, education, sports, healthcare, the military, media, or ministry, you need to know God is with you, and your greatest need today is to experience God's presence day by day and night by night. God says in the

Scriptures, "With a pillar of cloud You led them by day, and with a pillar of fire by night to light for them the way in which they were to go" (Nehemiah 9:12). Just as God wanted his people to adjust to his will and direction for them, so he wants the same for you and me.

God was going *before* the people to show them the way and even seeking a place to camp for the night. All the people needed to do was to follow the fire by night and the cloud by day. The Scriptures become like the fire and the cloud for us today. His cloud, God's presence, never leaves you. His fire, God's presence, never goes out. As a follower of Jesus, you have the Holy Spirit living in you now, and as you search the Scriptures daily, he will show you the way forward each day and night.

This transition in my career path and journey has been significant for Jeana and me. While many of our days have been low emotionally, challenging personally, and even lonely, we realize God is with us and is teaching us day by day and night by night. Furthermore and most importantly, we realize there are people with real-life challenges much more significant and life-altering than ours. I would rather walk our journey right now than deal with what some others are dealing with, like a terminal illness, a child away from God, the loss of a spouse or a child to death, a divorce, or an upcoming surgery that may physically impair them for the rest of their life.

What I have come to realize is that sooner or later,

regardless of the problem or challenge I face, will I live out the Christian faith or not? Or am I just going to preach, teach, sing, and never live it out personally? God wants me to live out my faith even when it is somewhat challenging. Even when no one is looking at me or checking on me, I want to be faithful. This calls upon me to align my attitude, thoughts, words, feelings, and actions with God's Word and will for my life.

We must periodically experience days or seasons of God's supernatural power through prayer and fasting. Throughout the years, God has used these experiences to call my life into order, physically and spiritually. Times like this affirm that God is still building a man, and this man is me. If I have breath to breathe and a life to live, God shapes me into being what he wills me to be. He has not given up on me or tossed me aside. His path is unique for each of us, including me. Therefore, I trust him.

I do know that God wants me to experience him, and I want to experience him not only periodically but day by day, night by night, and even moment by moment. I need him desperately and always. Without him, I am nothing. I also know I need God to lead me. While I have learned so much from my past, my focus is on today and God's future for me. I cannot live looking backward, but I must live my life going forward. As I go forward, I know God is with me each day along the way.

Throughout this transition, Jesus and I have spent more time together than ever before.

Habakkuk the prophet asked God several questions. God was faithful to answer his questions, pointing him mainly to two realities. First, the just shall live by faith. Second, God is on the throne.

For me—and I trust that you know it to be true for you also—I must resolve to live by faith and to be comforted by realizing God is on the throne. Yes, God is in control. Over this past year, I have completed my daily prayer time in the same way that Habakkuk closed his book. Read this slowly and prayerfully:

> Even if the fig tree does not blossom,
> And there is no fruit on the vines,
> If the yield of the olive fails,
> And the fields produce no food,
> Even if the flock disappears from the fold,
> And there are no cattle in the stalls,
> Yet I will triumph in the LORD,
> I will rejoice in the God of my salvation.
> The Lord GOD is my strength,
> And He has made my feet like deer's feet,
> And has me walk on my high places.
> (Habakkuk 3:17–19)

Sometimes life does not make sense. At times, it may not be fair. There are even times we feel that God is silent. Yet God's Word roars with profound words like this from Habakkuk 3:17–19. Therefore, I choose to believe God. I choose to trust God. I choose to adjust to God's will wherever he leads. When the cloud and the fire stop, I want to stop. When the cloud and the fire move, I want to move, knowing always that I will experience God in this process, follow his lead, and walk in confidence. God is with me through it all.

Four Positive Responses to Adjusting to God's Will

When you practice prayer and fasting, one of the dynamic ways God will change your life is to lead you and teach you to adjust to the will of God. Therefore, I want you to notice these four positive responses to adjusting to God's will. Of course, each condition and situation is different, but each is also a positive way to adjust to where God is leading you. Are you ready? Let's begin!

When You Don't Know Where You're Headed

Abraham is regarded as the Father of the Faith. The story of Abraham and Sarah is one of the great stories of walking by faith in all the Scriptures. God called Abraham, whose name was Abram at that time, to leave his family and go to a land that God would show him. The Bible says, "By faith Abraham, when he was called, obeyed by going out to a place which he was to receive for an inheritance; and he left, not knowing where he was going" (Hebrews 11:8).

One of the remarkable things about this story is that Abram was seventy-five years old at that time. Yet God called him to go. Abram adjusted everything and followed God even though he did not know where he was going. Can you imagine what that conversation with his wife, Sarai, must have been like?

Let's imagine this conversation that may have occurred between them. Abram goes home one day and says to Sarai, "Sweetheart, I believe God has called us to move." Sarai says, "Really? Where?" Abram looks at her and says, "Well, honey, I am not sure yet." She says, "What do you mean, you do not know where?" He says, "Well, I do not know now, but surely God will show us."

I am not trying to make light of their spiritual maturity, but it would have been an interesting conversation. Regardless of any supposed conversation we could imagine, here is the reality. Abram and Sarai adjusted to God's will even when they did not know where they were going. Can you do this? Would you do this? Are you willing to do this? We need to be willing to go anywhere before God calls us somewhere. Regardless of age, stage, or vocation, we must do whatever God calls us to do.

Our geographical preferences or personal desires must die. Sometimes we do not have all the answers or fully understand everything. We walk by faith, not by sight. Think about it this way. If Abram had tried to negotiate with God or disobeyed him completely, we would not know him as the Father of the Faith. But Abram and Sarai adjusted to the will of God even when they did not know where they were going. It may not have made sense to do what they did, but they did what God wanted.

I have learned that obedience to God does not always make sense, but regardless, I try to follow God always. We must be willing to adjust to God's will even when we do not know where we are going.

Wherever God Leads

Joshua surrendered to God's calling to lead the people into the promised land. Few were as courageous and strong as Joshua. He could be strong and courageous because he knew God was with him and would lead him wherever God wanted him to go. The people had the faith to follow God wherever he led them. They were faithful to follow the ark of the covenant. Out of reverence for God and the great miracles God had done for them, they knew God would direct them wherever he willed them to go. Even though they had not been this way before, they believed "wherever" meant "wherever."

Question: Will you follow God wherever he leads you today and in the future? Since you belong to him, I pray you will. Only God can lead you and give you the faith to go forward wherever he wants you to go. Just because you have never been there before should not limit or stop what God may choose to do with you in the future.

Never let your preferences for a certain geographic location or even the influence of other people determine where you may go. Ask the Holy Spirit to give you the power to adjust to God's will wherever you go. Furthermore, be willing to adjust to God's will by asking God to show you his way.

Show Me Your Way

I pray that this entire chapter about adjusting to the will of God will inspire you to a greater willingness to be all God wants you to be and to go wherever he wills for you to go. Ask God faithfully and daily, *Lord, show me your way*. I am confident that most people who read this book want to be what God wants them to be and to go wherever God wants them to go. I encourage you to be willing to do God's will, whatever it may be.

As we adjust to God's will, we will also learn that sometimes, God's will may never require changing our geographical location or entering a new vocation. However, for some of us, it will. Life is full of transitions. We will go through transitions personally, as a family, and sometimes even in our job and career. Therefore, we must have the heart and the will to pray repeatedly throughout each day, *Lord, show me your way*.

I believe it is healthy spiritually and personally to pray to God: *Lord, tell me what you want me to do and where you want me to go*. You have nothing to lose praying like this; it will build your faith and vision. Even as I sit here today and write, I still believe and testify that I am willing to go and do whatever God wills for my life. Are you? If so, tell him today. Pray it today.

Even when you do not know where you are going, you must adjust to God's will. Wherever you go in your life, God may call upon you to adjust to his will. So even when you ask God to show you his way, it requires you to adjust to God's will. Furthermore, adjusting to God's will is even necessary when you are already giving your all to the Lord.

Following the Lord Fully

One of the most incredible and inspiring people in Scriptures was Caleb. Of the twelve spies Moses sent into the promised land, only Caleb and Joshua wanted to go then and possess the land. But they were outvoted as the other ten spies were paralyzed with fear. The Bible says, "Nevertheless my brothers who went up with me made the heart of the people melt with fear; but I followed the Lord my God fully" (Joshua 14:8).

Fast forward forty-five years later, only Caleb and Joshua lived long enough to go into possessing the promised land. At eighty-five years of age, Caleb told Joshua that he had the same strength he had at forty, and his commitment to war and possessing the land was just as significant. Therefore, Caleb possessed the land.

Three times, Joshua 14 gives a powerful testimony saying that Caleb followed the Lord his God fully. Therefore, God let him possess the land at eighty-five years of age. He was sold out for God even during those forty-five years he had to wait to fulfill God's promise, declaring, "I followed the Lord my God fully" (v. 8).

I hope you understand the value of being willing to adjust to God's will. Caleb adjusted for forty-five years, waiting and trusting God in his timing. When you follow God fully, anything is possible! The Lord will do it when he puts his vision in your heart. Never let your age limit you or determine what God may want to do through you. Whether you are fifteen, fifty, or eighty-five, if you have breath to breathe, God wants to use you. Whatever God is doing, join him in it. Adjust your life and future to his activity. Be assured he is with you. Never limit what God may want to do through you when you are following the Lord fully.

Remember, when the cloud and the fire stop, you stop. When the cloud and the fire move, you move. Adjusting to God's will is one of the ways God will change your life when you experience the supernatural power of prayer and fasting.

9

Following the Holy Spirit

Arguably, today's most forgotten of God's commands in Christianity is to be filled with the Holy Spirit. Therefore, one of the most consequential decisions you will make each day is to be filled with the Holy Spirit of God. When we place our faith and trust in Jesus Christ and him alone for our salvation, the Holy Spirit enters our lives simultaneously. Our relationship with the Spirit is significant. It cannot be denied, ignored, minimized, or dismissed as irrelevant. If one thinks it is, it is very doubtful that authentic personal salvation has occurred in that person.

Living a Christian life without an ongoing relationship with the Holy Spirit is impossible. So likewise, one cannot follow biblical principles consistently without this ongoing relationship. Furthermore, it is impossible to relate to others properly without a meaningful, ongoing relationship with the Spirit of God. Therefore, we must know what it means to follow the Holy Spirit.

This biblical principle is essential and must be taught today. Following the Holy Spirit is one of the most profound ways God will bring life change to you when you practice prayer and fasting. The supernatural power of prayer and fasting will awaken, instruct, guide, and lead you to follow the Holy Spirit.

In the last chapter, I shared what it means to adjust to God's will in your life. When the people of God experienced their exodus from Egypt and wandered in the wilderness for forty years, God in his love and mercy provided them with his presence and guidance through the pillar of cloud during the day and the pillar of fire by night.

But now, as followers of Jesus Christ, we have the Holy Spirit living *in* us. As we search the Scriptures daily, the supernatural power of the Holy Spirit will show us the way forward each day and night. Furthermore, the Spirit can empower you to live for Jesus and be everything God created you to be.

The Holy Spirit

The Bible teaches us many things about the Holy Spirit. In this brief section, I want us to know these realities about the Holy Spirit. First, the Holy Spirit is God. The Bible teaches us there is only one God, and he reveals himself to us as Father, Son, and Holy Spirit. As followers of Jesus, we call this the doctrine of the

Trinity, which means there is only one God who is three Persons, the Father, Son, and Holy Spirit.

The Lord Jesus Christ, in his Great Commission to us as recorded in the Gospel of Matthew, reaffirms this doctrine of the Trinity. Jesus said, "Go, therefore, and make disciples of all the nations, baptizing them in the name of the Father and the Son and the Holy Spirit" (Matthew 28:19). The apostle Paul affirms this belief in his second letter to the Christians in Corinth. He writes, "The grace of the Lord Jesus Christ, and the love of God, and the fellowship of the Holy Spirit, be with you all" (2 Corinthians 13:14). Since the beginning of creation, God has been clear in the Scriptures about this truth. The Bible says, "God said, 'Let Us make mankind in Our image, according to Our likeness'" (Genesis 1:26). God shares with us this insight about the Trinity when describing himself in this manner throughout the Scriptures.

The Holy Spirit is active throughout the Scriptures, including being the one who breathed with divine inspiration, insight, and illumination upon the writers of the Scriptures. When we are born again by the Spirit in what we call "salvation," the Bible says the Spirit baptizes us into the family of God. "By one Spirit we were all baptized into one body, whether Jews or Greeks, whether slaves or free, and we were all made to drink of one Spirit" (1 Corinthians 12:13). This Spirit is the Holy Spirit of God.

His entrance into our lives at our spiritual conversion results in him distributing spiritual gifts to each of us. As our helper through life, the Spirit also walks alongside us. Through the Holy Spirit, we are empowered to live the Christian life, becoming more like Jesus daily and taking the good news of Jesus Christ to the whole world. Jesus said, "You will receive power when the Holy Spirit has come upon you; and you shall be My witnesses both in Jerusalem and in all Judea, and Samaria, and as far as the remotest part of the earth" (Acts 1:8). Therefore, ten days following Jesus' ascension into heaven, on the day of Pentecost, the Holy Spirit came in great power and the initial three thousand persons who believed on that day were not only baptized in water as a testimony to the world, but they also received the Holy Spirit to live for Jesus. From that day until eternity, the Holy Spirit immediately enters everyone who follows Jesus Christ.

From the moment you began your faith experience with Jesus, the Spirit, God himself, came to live within you. He is there to walk with you, comfort you, inspire you, and empower you. We need to recognize the Holy Spirit as God and as a person and develop a relationship with him daily.

While the Bible reveals so much more about the Holy Spirit, with this general understanding of him, we will now discuss following the Holy Spirit, one of the significant outcomes you will experience from the supernatural power of prayer and fasting. This personal change will come from the inside, from who you are and who you will become.

Your daily choices regarding how you relate to the Holy Spirit personally will either help ascend your spiritual life or result in a descent in your spiritual life. If you make the right choices relating to the Holy Spirit, you will grow, develop, and flourish. If you make the wrong choices relating to the Holy Spirit, you will stop growing, decline in your walk with Christ, and live in spiritual defeat. How you relate to the person of the Holy Spirit will impact your life and everyone you relate to daily.

What I am about to share with you are some of the most significant insights God has taught me throughout my life but even in a much greater way in recent years. Your relationship with the Holy Spirit moment by moment and day by day will depend on your sensitivity and your response to him. You will respond to the Holy Spirit in any of these three ways:

- Quenching the Holy Spirit
- Grieving the Holy Spirit
- Following the Holy Spirit

I want to unpack each of these for you biblically and practically. Ask God to teach you and provide insight into your life over these next few pages.

Quenching the Holy Spirit

Quenching the Holy Spirit means trying to extinguish the fire. The Holy Spirit is a holy fire; therefore, wherever he is, he burns. Anytime you extinguish his fire, stifle his fire, or smother his fire, you are quenching the Holy Spirit.

The Bible says, "Do not quench the Spirit" (1 Thessalonians 5:19). The word for "Spirit" means "breath" and "wind." Fire is an emblem of the Spirit since he is ablaze. As we stated earlier, the Holy Spirit is a person. Therefore, how do you think the Holy Spirit will respond when you ignore him, attempt to control him, or withdraw from him? How would you respond if someone treated you this way? You would feel disregarded and unimportant, and the Spirit feels the same way.

Those who go camping know what it is like when the wind blows. Safety calls you to protect the fire, or disaster can occur. But this is not true for the Holy Spirit because he does not want you to try to control him. Since revival is the manifested presence of the Holy Spirit, quenching the Spirit would be to try to stop revival. The Holy Spirit does not want to be quenched but to be released.

We quench the Spirit anytime we do not rely on the Holy Spirit. Do you rely on the Holy Spirit each day? Are you counting on him helping you today? We also quench the Spirit anytime we attempt to legislate or restrict the Holy Spirit. We do not have the privilege or responsibility to do either of these. Shame on us if we ever try to do either one! The Bible is our guide in teaching us the role of the Holy Spirit. When someone is pontificating on what God can or cannot do in their opinion, their ego and pride are going up against God. We do not tell God anything like this. God is the only one who tells us what to do and how to do it.

Quenching the Holy Spirit also takes place when we refuse to let the Holy Spirit have complete liberty in our lives and our midst. Again, the Scriptures give us keen insight into the Spirit of God. It says, "The Lord is the Spirit, and where the Spirit of the Lord is, there is freedom" (2 Corinthians 3:17). Since the Lord is the Spirit and anywhere the Spirit is, there is freedom, then who are we to think we have the power to shut down God? We do not.

If we pray for revival and God's manifest presence comes down upon us, then we have no business trying to restrict what he does or restrain him from being who he is. Pastors and church leaders need to release the Holy Spirit among the body of Christ, not shut him down.

We must stop quenching the Holy Spirit before revival can ever begin in our lives or in our churches. Therefore, we must obey God's command, "Do not quench the Spirit" (1 Thessalonians 5:19).

Grieving the Holy Spirit

Grieving the Holy Spirit makes God feel tremendous sadness, pain, and sorrow. The Scriptures declare, "Do not grieve the Holy Spirit of God, by whom you were sealed for the day of redemption" (Ephesians 4:30). Remember, the Holy Spirit is a person.

I have studied this multiple times but most specifically in these recent years and seasons in life. I am convinced that grieving the Holy Spirit is even more personal and prominent in the lives of Jesus' followers than for those who are not Christians. I believe you will agree when you finish reading this chapter.

When you study this passage, you must understand that there is a relationship between grief and love. I have also discovered that the level of our love determines the level of our grief. We know God loves us so much. The Bible says, "God so loved the world, that He gave His only Son, so that everyone who believes in Him will not perish, but have eternal life" (John 3:16). Why is this important to know? Because God loves us so much that he becomes deeply grieved when we do things that hurt ourselves or hurt others or hurt him and his work around the world. Therefore, if we love our holy God, we should do everything we can to never grieve the Holy Spirit.

Ephesians 4:30 also teaches us that the Holy Spirit seals us for the day of redemption. To understand this, we must answer the questions, "What is a seal, and what does this mean?" As an illustration, when you purchase a new home, money must be transferred from the financial institution to pay for the home. Whether you pay for the home in cash or with a loan, you must sign documents that a certified notary then stamps with a seal to protect all parties from fraud. When the financial institutions see this seal, they know they can safely transfer the monies to pay for the home.

Biblically and spiritually, a seal signifies a completed transaction that protects us from the loss of everything God has promised us. The Holy Spirit is the seal and guarantees our future in heaven. Therefore, since the Holy Spirit lives in you and wants to live through you, why would you ever want to offend the Holy Spirit of God? It makes no sense to offend or grieve him since he is God's gift to help and protect you.

We cannot overstate the depth of offense that occurs when we grieve the Holy Spirit because of our actions. Knowing we have offended and grieved the Holy Spirit of God should break our heart. So what is it that grieves the Holy Spirit?

The Bible is clear about what grieves the Spirit. There are six ways the Holy Spirit is grieved, according to Ephesians 4:31: "All bitterness, wrath, anger, clamor, and slander must be removed from you, along with all malice." I want to discuss each these briefly, but I appeal to you to seriously consider each one in accordance with your relationship with the Holy Spirit.

(1) Bitterness

The Holy Spirit wants to be your spiritual fire, spiritual power, and your ever-flowing life. Whenever you become bitter toward someone or something in life, you are causing great pain to the Holy Spirit. Even the pronunciation of the Greek word for bitterness gives us a feeling of pain. The word is *pikria*, which refers to an "irritable state of mind that keeps a man in perpetual animosity—that inclines him to harsh and uncharitable opinions of men and things—that make him sour, crabby, and repulsive in his general demeanor."[15]

Therefore, whenever we become bitter toward someone or about something that has occurred in our life, the above definition happens in and through us. Unforgiveness is bitterness. Anytime our heart is hard toward others or we are cynical, hateful, and harsh with our words and actions, it becomes evident that our life has perpetual animosity.

Bitterness is like a rattlesnake in public conversations today. Bitterness poisons one's personality and oozes through relationships. When we recognize it in ourselves, we need to stop and repent. The anointing of the Holy Spirit upon your life will not occur when you have bitterness. Which one would you rather have? Anointing from God or bitterness?

Are you bitter about something that has happened to you or someone you love? Are you bitter toward another person because of an action they have taken against you? If so, confess it to God as a sin and repent from it. Bitterness grieves the Holy Spirit.

(2) Wrath

Wrath is like a deeply flowing anger inside a person. While bitterness smolders, and anger escalates to a boil, wrath rages. Someone with wrath in their hearts quickly loses their temper, and suddenly, a stream of venomous and poisonous words rolls out of their mouth. The wrathful person can burst into a rage or at least harbor the desire to hurt others. This creates fear in others that leads to grieving the Holy Spirit of God.

Do you ever lose your temper and explode emotionally, allowing matters to escalate to sudden rage? If so, always remember that what is in you will come out of you. Whenever wrath occurs in us, we need to move to deep repentance. There is not one of us who does not struggle with this at times. Ask God for his forgiveness and freedom from your wrath.

(3) Anger

Anger grieves the Holy Spirit. Anger is personal and passionate, and Ephesians 4 tells us we should never let the sun go down with anger in our hearts. Anger opens the door for Satan to gain a footstool in our hearts.

Usually, anger is something we hold on to over a period, and the longer we hold on to it, the more painful and personal it becomes. This sad public reality results in negative personal relationships. No one wins when anger wins. Anger hurts us, hurts the person we are angry toward, and of course, hurts and grieves the Holy Spirit.

Anger is more evident than ever before. Angry Christians, angry churches, and angry denominations and networks are plentiful. This vile anger grieves the Holy Spirit. He is never drawn to angry people, churches, denominations, or networks. So why should we be surprised by the anger level in America when God's people lead the way with indignation and offense about the smallest things? It is time to turn from anger and turn to God, asking him for forgiveness of this sin. If we want the fullness of the Spirit, then we must first repent of the evil of anger.

(4) Clamor

Some Scripture translations interpret clamor as making noise, shouting angrily, insulting others, arguing, and holding nothing back in your words and actions. Strife and conflict resulting from yelling at someone and crying out against them do not honor God. On the contrary, clamor grieves the Spirit of God.

Clamor divides relationships and can lead to their destruction. Sadly, this happens in marriages, between parents and their children, in the workplace, in places of education and healthcare, as well as in the church and among relationships with believers.

I realize that clamor is not a word we often use, but a good way to understand it is that it is the opposite of self-control, which we know is a fruit of the Spirit. When we shout someone down or embarrass them or demean them privately or publicly in any way, we are sinning against the Holy Spirit and tearing others down, which leads them to feel worthless, humiliated, and defeated. None of this glorifies God.

Refuse to live and act this way. We cannot be what God wants us to be if we act like this. We must repent of this, ask God for forgiveness, ask others to forgive us when we act with clamor, and cease grieving the Holy Spirit. We must guard our words, watch our tone, and work toward healthy relationships.

(5) Slander

We live in an era when slandering others seems as acceptable as drinking water. Whenever someone speaks evil about someone else, the Holy Spirit is grieved and saddened. Slandering someone else is never acceptable. It is a grievous sin. Gossip and spreading rumors can injure people's reputations and destroy their lives. Slander slithers like a poisonous snake seeking to strike its next victim. When slander is happening, you can be assured that the person doing it is filled with the sins of bitterness, wrath, anger, and clamor.

This evil conduct occurs privately and publicly. Most people know what it is like to be slandered. As a Christian, I am amazed at what I have witnessed in the professing church of Jesus Christ. The online world has taken slander and destruction to an entirely new level. Christian leaders slander other Christian leaders; pastors slander other pastors, Christ-followers slander leaders in the workplace, which fuels the fires of sin and evil. Slandering others grieves the Holy Spirit. It is a terrible witness for Jesus Christ; thus it bears the fruit of sin, evil, destruction, and Satan.

Every follower of Jesus and every Christian leader must understand that when we slander others, we will not be anointed by the Holy Spirit of God. Anointing by the Spirit does not occur when we are also grieving the Holy Spirit. Grieving the Holy Spirit and the anointing of the Holy Spirit never happen simultaneously. If we act as though it does, we are being deceived. We must repent from these sins and come back to God today. We must ask ourselves if we would rather hold a grudge and slander someone else or have the touch of the Spirit, the anointing of the Spirit, and walk in the supernatural power of God.

(6) Malice

The Holy Spirit is grieved when bitterness, wrath, anger, clamor, and slander occur, singularly or simultaneously. God desires his people to always walk in holiness. Sins like these, as noted in Ephesians 4:31, occur due to a depraved and evil heart. Therefore, malice is used in this same verse as one of these sins that grieve the

Holy Spirit. "Malice is the general Gr. term for evil, the root of all vices."[16]

Malice, or the depravity of the human heart, grieves the Spirit of God. Turn away from all malice. Repent from it. Receive God's forgiveness and cleansing power of the blood of Jesus Christ.

Remove These Sins

This convicting text calls us to immediate action to remove these sins from our lives. Often, these sins are so deeply rooted that only the supernatural power of prayer and fasting can effectively uproot them. Therefore, we must beg the Lord Jesus to pick up these sins and carry them away from us, as he did on the cross for us. We must remove each of these sins individually and all of them collectively so we will cease grieving the Holy Spirit of God. Then the Holy Spirit will bring his refreshing winds of anointing into our lives.

Kindness, Compassion, and Forgiveness

Whenever these sins that are grieving the Holy Spirit are removed from our life, then we must develop kindness, compassion, and forgiveness to take their place. When these virtues are grafted into your spiritual life, the Holy Spirit will be pleased and even attracted to do great things in and through your life. Imagine what can happen when we respond to others and situations with kindness, tenderhearted compassion, and unconditional forgiveness instead of with bitterness, wrath, anger, clamor, slander, and malice.

For the past two decades, I have believed that the wall of unforgiveness is the number one obstacle to spiritual revival. I believe it more today than ever before. Releasing our offenses, letting them go, and giving people the same grace Jesus gives to everyone is the way of biblical Christianity. The supernatural power of God through prayer and fasting will eliminate sins that grieve the Holy Spirit and then replace them with kindness, tenderhearted compassion, and unconditional forgiveness toward everyone.

Filled with the Spirit

We must remember our need to be filled with the Holy Spirit. The Bible counsels us strongly when it says, "Do not get drunk with wine, in which there is debauchery, but be filled with the Spirit" (Ephesians 5:18). The subsequent chapter in Ephesians that calls us to cease grieving the Holy Spirit commands us strongly to be filled with the Spirit.

When we live with wisdom, we will seize every opportunity to understand and follow the Lord's will each day. The Lord's will is not for us to become controlled by a substance like drugs or alcohol or anything else because we will squander our life away. Therefore, we must stop allowing anything unwise, wasteful, and foolish to control us. Instead, we should be filled with the Holy Spirit. Is there a more critical verse for followers of Jesus than Ephesians 5:18? If we fail to obey this command to be filled with the Spirit daily—and even throughout each day—we will struggle to live the Christian life the way God wills for us to live.

Let me ask you this personal question: How much of you is the Holy Spirit controlling today? Only you can answer this question for yourself. Therefore, I encourage you to ask yourself this question each day. *How much of me will I release to the control of the Holy Spirit today?* Then, prayerfully, you will release yourself to Jesus each day, 100 percent!

This imperative to be filled with the Spirit means to be flooded by, directed by, and controlled by the Holy Spirit of God. Being filled with the Spirit is a continual and ongoing action in your life. Repeatedly, moment by moment, day by day, and night by night, we are to be filled with the Spirit regardless of our age, stage, or vocation. The Spirit wants to control and influence your life continually. You can only bear the fruit of the Spirit and be led by the Spirit if you are being filled with the Spirit repeatedly. So practice this daily: ask God to fill you with the Holy Spirit. Discipline yourself daily and throughout the day to ask God to fill, control, flood, and direct you by the Holy Spirit. The following three words may help you when you ask the Holy Spirit to fill you each day:

- Confess: Confess your sinfulness and sinful actions, receiving God's forgiveness and cleansing power as referred to in 1 John 1:7–9.
- Surrender: Surrender your mind, will, emotions, body, spirit, tongue, attitude, actions, and all relationships, as well as your past, present, and future. Yes, surrender each and all of these to the Lord continually.
- Fill: By faith, stand on Ephesians 5:18 and ask the Lord to fill you with his Holy Spirit. This means you want God's Holy Spirit to flood over you, dominate you, direct you, fill you, and control you.

When you follow the Holy Spirit like this, you can live life by the power of God. The Holy Spirit is the power of God. Therefore, repeatedly ask God to fill you with the Holy Spirit. Following the Holy Spirit is one of the most significant things you can do for God to change your life through the supernatural power of prayer and fasting. Being filled with the Spirit repeatedly will keep you from quenching and grieving the Holy Spirit. Therefore, being filled with the Spirit repeatedly and following him is God's will for your life and is one of the consequential decisions you must make each day and throughout the day.

10

Preparing You for What Is Next

God is always preparing you for what is next. I have learned over the past two years that God is constantly humbling me, teaching me, using me, and training me for whatever is next in the future that God has prepared for me.

"Just. Keep. Walking. You see, what to do next requires movement, change, and for you to fill a larger space than where you are right now."[17] These words of counsel from Jeff Henderson's helpful book, *What to Do Next,* encourages everyone about the future God has for them. Then, he strengthens these words with his testimony by writing, "If you'll do the work, keep walking, show up each day, eventually, inevitably, not only will you find what to do next. What to do next will find you."[18]

Through the years of walking with God and practicing prayer and fasting, I am convinced that every journey in prayer and fasting is about preparing for what is next. Most often, when we seek God through prayer and fasting, we may need God to speak to us about a decision we must make. Whenever the fast concludes, we can become discouraged if we do not have the exact answer. However, refuse to do this!

The reason I do not want you to become discouraged if you do not get the exact answer you were hoping for is that you will discover eventually that for your entire journey of prayer and fasting, whether it is for a day, a few days, or a long-term fasting journey, God was readying you, freeing you from that which binds you, and creating in you an open heart and an agile willingness to respond to God and do whatever he wills for you to do.

Furthermore, when we are talking about God preparing you for what is next, this may mean a decision concerning your family, the purchase of a new home, taking a promotion in your company, or even something more dramatic, such as retirement or even perhaps a career move and transition to a new city for your entire family.

Then, there are the realities of life that we go through that we did not see coming or have knowledge about. This could involve you or someone close to you receiving a frightening medical diagnosis. Or perhaps your family suffers a severe financial loss due to the economy turning downward. Or, out of the blue, someone may offer you something that is so significant you cannot pass it up. But all along, God was preparing you through your prayer and fasting. So when one of these events occurs, you may receive spiritual enlightenment immediately as the Spirit of God takes you back to that recent journey of fasting to remind you of some spiritual insight you received. Perhaps you didn't understand its significance then, but in light of your current situation, it becomes evident that God was preparing you for something you did not know was ahead of you. One outcome that emerges through the supernatural power of prayer and fasting is that God is preparing you for what is ahead. Fasting always builds readiness in us.

The apostle Paul told his protégé, Timothy, some very helpful words about the future. "Preach the word; be ready in season and out of season" (2 Timothy 4:2). The admonition is not only about the priority of preaching God's Word. Paul's urgent message to Timothy was also to tell him that regardless of whether it is convenient or inconvenient, servant leadership is about availability, willingness, and readiness. So we should always be ready to preach the Word.

There is a correlation between prayer and fasting and a ready willingness and availability to do whatever is next. Regardless of what it may be, wherever it may be, and even however difficult or impossible the next thing may seem, prayer and fasting prepares us for what is next. Furthermore, it may be a good reminder that soon after this letter, Paul was beheaded. His "next" was not the kind of success that some imagine the future will always be when you live for God. Whatever may be next is not always a promise or guarantee of success. Yet our success is that God will be with us. Therefore, when we imagine what is next, we must always be cognizant of these words of Paul: "Most gladly, therefore, I will rather boast about my weaknesses, so that the power of Christ may dwell in me. Therefore I delight in weaknesses, in insults, in distresses, in persecutions, in difficulties, in behalf of Christ; for when I am weak, then I am strong" (2 Corinthians 12:9–10).

You see, God is always preparing us for whatever is next even if it involves insults, distress, persecution, and difficulties. For the cause of Christ, we may be weak when we face these, but God will make us strong. Therefore, we must be ready in season and out of season. This is possible because God always prepares us for whatever is next, especially when we periodically or seasonally experience the supernatural power of God through prayer and fasting.

Ready in and Out of Season

I will never forget one of the most significant opportunities of my lifetime. The ministry of prayer and fasting united me with Dr. Bill Bright in the 1990s. Dr. Bright was the esteemed and internationally known founder and leader of Campus Crusade for Christ, today known as CRU. Dr. Bright had become aware of my life-changing forty-day fast in 1995; therefore, soon after, he asked me to join him in a couple of conferences on prayer and fasting that he was doing across the country. Then Dr. Bill Bright invited me to Fort Collins, Colorado, to preach to thousands of their leaders from across the world. I remember seeing him in his hotel room just hours before I was to speak, and he said to me, "Ronnie, challenge them to fast and pray for forty days for the nation they are serving and wanting to reach for Christ." While overwhelmed by his specific request, I was ready to do it.

I will never forget walking into an arena located on the campus of Colorado State University. The hall was packed with thousands of ministers, evangelists, and missionaries connected to the phenomenal ministry of Campus Crusade for Christ. When I stood up to preach God's Word, I challenged them to pray and fast for their nation, the nation they were serving, to win people to Christ. It was a powerful experience for me, and I know from reports sent to me later that it seemed to be a powerful visionary experience for those who were present.

Sometime afterward, I saw some people who were a part of that experience, and they informed me they did just what they felt God was calling them to do: pray and fast for forty days for their nation, the nation they were serving to win to Christ. These missionaries, ministers, and evangelists—Christians—were all trying to engage their future ministries in their respective countries. They were there in that arena for the conference in order to be launched out to their future in the power of the

Holy Spirit. Through the calling of God, it was apparent in that meeting that God wanted to do a new thing in the future of those leaders.

The Spirit's call to pray and fast for their nation radically altered their agenda but significantly strengthened it. I am convinced—partly by testimonies back to me but mostly by just knowing that God does mighty things in the lives and ministries of those who fast—that the Lord was calling every one of us, including me, to a new future. Little did I know in my journeys in prayer and fasting that God would open doors for me to preach the Word of God to thousands and call them to pray and fast for forty days for their nation to come to Christ.

A few years later, a similar event occurred. I was in Thailand at a regional meeting of missionaries of the International Mission Board, supported by the churches of the Southern Baptist Convention. These missionaries served the nations of China, Taiwan, and others in that part of the world. In that week as I preached daily to these missionaries, I sensed God wanted me to preach on prayer and fasting, calling them to pray and fast for the nation and the specific people group they were serving, intending to win them to Jesus Christ. Again, there was a great response to the call of God to pray and fast for their nation to come to Christ.

Fewer than one thousand missionaries were in that setting, but what a decisive moment as those godly, hungry missionaries committed to God to do just that.

Moreover, these men and women of God were connected to a global force of missionaries committed to the advancement of the gospel of Jesus Christ to the whole world.

At times through the years, I think about how difficult it must be for those missionaries. Even though they are called by God and compelled to go and serve, they wake up initially in a new and strange culture and are unable to communicate in it effectively until they have served for a while. After a few weeks, perhaps just days, the missionaries would have to come to the end of themselves about their future. Soon they may discover, in a way most people never do, that all they have left is God. This is not a wrong place to be because God will be strong in their weakness. He will see them through.

Whether it be missionaries across the globe or you, wherever you may be in your life, when everything we do is "all on God," we are strong. Weak people will become very strong when coupled with prayer and fasting. This will result in God preparing us for what is next. He always is and always does but never more than we pray and fast. Whenever we come to the end of ourselves, God is ready to step in powerfully and supernaturally with spiritual breakthroughs beyond our imagination. Therefore, it is incumbent on us, as followers of Jesus, to always be ready in and out of season. When we are, God will use us extraordinarily and supernaturally.

Preparing for What's Next

God is in the process of getting you ready for whatever is next in your life. However significant or insignificant it may be, God is calling you to be willing. It may pertain to something personal or something professional. It may be something life-changing or simply a part of life. Rest assured with great confidence in the Lord that God is always preparing you for what is next in your life.

Prayer and fasting may be a continual part of your spiritual discipline, such as doing this one day a week. Or it may be something you practice periodically throughout the year as you sense God is leading you. Or you may practice prayer and fasting once a year with your church with a particular spiritual emphasis for seven or twenty-one days. Then for many of you, prayer and fasting are new to you, and perhaps you have never done it. Regardless of where you are in your knowledge and practice, I pray God will give you the spiritual conviction to adapt prayer and fasting into your life as you sense God is leading you to do.

Fasting is abstaining from food with a spiritual goal in mind. It is when you neglect one of the most powerful desires within you, which is for food, to pursue the God of heaven to do something in your life. God will use your prayer and fasting to awaken your relationship and deepen your spiritual intimacy with him. God will use your prayer and fasting to get you ready for what is next in your life. What does this mean, and what may it look like?

Humility

As I have written, there is a correlation in Scripture between humility, prayer, and fasting. Taking the initiative to pray and fast will help build a spirit of humility as you humble yourself before God. Within the context of calling us to clothe ourselves in humility by refusing to be proud, the Scripture is clear when it says, "Therefore humble yourselves under the mighty hand of God, so that He may exalt you at the proper time" (1 Peter 5:6). The responsibility is on us to humble ourselves.

This call from God concerning humility means we are to lay ourselves low before God and become insignificant and weak. We do that through prayer and fasting. Therefore, deciding to fast is to humble yourself before God. I have found that when I fast, God builds within me a desire for holiness as I humble myself before him. This entire experience prepares me for whatever may be next in my life.

The following about humility is attributed to A. W. Tozer: "Humility is as scarce as an albino robin." How many albino robins have you ever seen in your life? Probably none. In our American culture, humility and humbling yourself through prayer and fasting are rare.

Desperation

When God creates spiritual desperation within us, he prepares us for what may be next. Our next may be in the now or in the future. Earlier in this book, I shared the story of Ezra as recorded in Ezra 8:21–23. When Ezra and some of the Israelites were at the Ahava River, Ezra became desperate for God's intervention and protection. Therefore, he proclaimed a fast. They fasted, and the Bible says that God listened to their pleading and answered their prayer.

In Daniel 1, desperation moved Daniel and his companions to prayer and fasting. So likewise, in Nehemiah 1, desperation moved Nehemiah to fast before God. When we get desperate, we take radical action. At times, this action is to pray and fast before God. Therefore, when we humble ourselves in desperation before God and join our prayers with a season of fasting, God uses this in multiple ways and, at times, to transform situations and circumstances, shaping the future.

God did this through King Jehoshaphat in 2 Chronicles 20 when several nations banded together to attack the land of Judah and the king became desperate before God. Jehoshaphat proclaimed a fast so that the people would seek the Lord for guidance, direction, and most of all, protection. God answered them miraculously and supernaturally.

There are moments or seasons when we need to follow the lead of Ezra, Daniel, Nehemiah, Jehoshaphat, and others, including David. Remember this powerful testimony from David about prayer and fasting: "I humbled my soul with fasting" (Psalm 35:13). There are times when we need to combine our desperation for God's intervention with humbling ourselves before God through prayer and fasting. You will discover that when you do this, God will do something fresh and powerful to prepare you for whatever is next. If you are a pastor and church leader in these desperate and unprecedented times, God will do the same for your church. Consider proclaiming a fast!

Inspiration

Throughout history, God has done great things in other people's lives. When we become aware of this, God uses it to inspire us greatly. If you need inspiration and motivation to enter a season of prayer and fasting, let this speak to you. You are in good company, so join the fasting team.

- King David fasted. God filled him with hope.
- Jonah fasted. God gave Nineveh a revival.
- Queen Esther fasted. The Lord used this moment in her life to save the Jewish people.
- John the Baptist fasted. He preached with power and fire.
- Jesus fasted. Everywhere he went and everyone he touched experienced profound change.

- The apostle Paul fasted. No one other than Jesus had a more significant influence on the church of Jesus Christ than Paul, not only in his generation but in the generations following.

What more do I need to say? Since prayer and fasting were good enough for them, let them inspire you to follow in their steps. You cannot biblically, historically, or personally dismiss prayer and fasting. God calls everyone to practice prayer and fasting. Do not forfeit this vision of God working, getting lost in "should I" or "how long." God wants us to pray and fast.

Power

There *is* supernatural power through prayer and fasting. God empowers us to do great things when we pray and fast. Believe it. Practice it. Begin it. Yes, he is always getting us ready for whatever may be next.

In 1996, I was a guest on the highly influential program, Dr. James Dobson's *Focus on the Family* broadcast. He was interviewing me about prayer and fasting. This interview was transcribed, and I want to share part of this conversation with you. I do so because it happened so close to the time when God had so changed my life through prayer and fasting.

Dr. Dobson asked, "Did He reward you with His presence during that time?" In this interview, I responded,

Like never before. Nothing happens any greater

when you pray and fast than to be aware of the incredible presence of God. The holiness of God comes to be more real than ever before, and the exceeding sinfulness of your own life is revealed. God did some things in me that needed to be done. I was a proud, arrogant pastor, and I needed God to break the mold and give me a fresh anointing where I would love people the way I needed to love them. Be the man of God I needed to be. Be the daddy I needed to be. Be the husband I needed to be. I am not there, but I guarantee it, I'm a lot further along in that journey.

I have prayed and fasted consistently numerous times throughout all these years. Each time I pray and fast, whether for a day, several days, twenty-one days, or forty days, God's presence is more evident in my life than ever. I believe spiritual power awaits you, too, if you pray and fast. You will never be the same—never.

Will You Pay the Price?

Are you willing to pay the price in your life, family, church, or nation to practice prayer and fasting? Will you be that man? Will you be that woman? Will you be that pastor or spiritual leader in your church?

There is always a price to pay to be all God wants you to be. When you fast, it is a call to deny yourself that which is normal, ordinary, and necessary—abstaining from food with a spiritual goal in mind. When you do, God will sharpen your mind, soften your heart, and alert your spirit to receive whatever God brings. The price is great but worth it. Be willing to pay the price. When you do, when you accept the call to pray and fast, God will change your life.

Record What God Does in Your Life

Since January 1, 1990, I have written a one-page prayer to God daily. This written prayer occurs at the end of my quiet time with God, which involves prayer, Bible reading, and journaling. This one-page prayer serves as documentation for my spiritual life because I write down what God has on my heart and what God is doing in my life. It is the story God has created in me all these years. Yes, to this day, and to God's glory alone, I have done this consistently since January 1, 1990.

Before I go on a long-term fast, I ask God to give me his plan that he wants me to pray through or to pray about during those days. These things become the prayer list I take to God daily, and they adjust along the way. They are specific and spiritually energized with the Scriptures that I stand upon while I pray and fast. It is the Bible, the Word of God, that the Holy Spirit uses to sanctify us and our prayers.

While on a long-term fast and through the entire fast, I spend extra time with God, withdrawing to be with him. My standard practice, even while not on a fast, is to spend the first ninety minutes to two hours each day with God alone, which is my personal daily devotion time. While on a long-term fast, this will expand so I can focus on him and what he wants to say.

After a long-term fast, I go back through my journaling, lift some key things God said to me, and then add them to my daily prayer list that I keep in the Notes app on my i-Pad. I hope you will follow a similar practice in some way. This takes the entire experience of fasting to a new level. I promise you that God will nourish these insights in your heart, and there is no telling what he may choose to do with you and the graces he gives you during your time of fasting. God may even release you to share some of your journey with others. If so, do it humbly but honestly. God will use your experience in the lives of others who hear you speak about what God did in your life through prayer and fasting.

As I have discovered—and you will find this also through prayer and fasting—God can do more in a moment than you can ever do in a lifetime. When you experience his manifested presence, your life will never be the same again.

Greatness

The key to greatness in the kingdom of God is neither your power nor your position. Greatness is being conformed to the image of Jesus Christ. If we want to identify with Jesus in his glory, we must also identify with him in his humility.

A faithful servant looks for legitimate needs, whether at home or across the ocean, ministering to others with joy and understanding. Through the supernatural power of prayer and fasting, God will reorder our priorities, reschedule our commitments, and revise our minuscule and artificial plans by reviving our hearts when we spend time with him. When the Old Testament saints took God seriously, see what occurred:

- Abraham rose early to stand before the Lord (Genesis 19:27).
- Jacob rose early to worship the Lord (28:18).
- Hannah and Elkanah rose early to worship God (1 Samuel 1:9).
- Moses rose early to give God's message to Pharaoh (Exodus 8:20).
- Joshua rose early to capture Jericho (Joshua 6:12).
- Gideon rose early to examine the fleece (Judges 6:38).

What are we willing to do to come into God's holy presence? Are we willing to

- Cease complaining and instead begin to praise the Lord Jesus Christ daily?
- Live beyond our feelings and walk by faith?
- Forgive others and release our bitterness and anger?

- Ask God to bring the next Great Awakening?
- Pay the price through prayer and fasting to experience personal spiritual revival?
- Pay the price through prayer and fasting to reach our town and city for Jesus Christ?

Perhaps you feel there is little hope because you sometimes feel lonely following the Lord and not sure the Lord can intervene. If so, let me remind you:

- When Noah was building the ark, he was in the minority, but he followed his God, who blessed Noah and his family.
- When Joseph was sold into Egypt by his brothers, he was in the minority, and even though his brothers meant it for evil, God meant it for good.
- When Gideon and his three hundred followers, with their broken pitchers and lamps, put the Midianites to flight, they were in the minority, but the battle was won, and God was honored.
- When Elijah faced the prophets of Baal, he was in the minority, but he prayed down fire from heaven and put the false prophets to shame.
- When David, ridiculed by his brothers, went out to meet the giant Goliath, young David was in a decided minority, but God ruled that day, and David easily defeated the enemy.

- When Jesus was crucified by Roman soldiers, by all appearances, he seemed to be in a conspicuous minority, but Jesus didn't stay on the cross or remain in the tomb. Instead, he arose and lives today for you, me, and a world waiting for a reason to face whatever is next for them.

With God as the source of our power, we will never be in the minority, and we will never be alone. The secret to greatness is to humble ourselves before God in days or seasons of prayer and fasting. This will result in us experiencing the supernatural power of God.

An Insightful Discovery

It took at least two forty-day fasts for me to discover that I had only four problems in my life. In fact, now, after many more years, days, and seasons of fasting, I still only have four problems in my life. I believe you will discover the same. So let me share with you what these problems are:

- Problem 1: My mind.
- Problem 2: My will.
- Problem 3: My emotions.
- Problem 4: My body.

I have a mind that wants to think about all kinds of things, and I sometimes struggle with where it wants to go. I have a will that is so strong and, at times, opposes God's will. I have a set of emotions that are up and down, almost uncontrollable sometimes. Furthermore, on top of all of that, I also inhabit a body that is decaying regardless of how much I attempt to train it. Oh, you have the same problems? Are you relieved to discover that you only have four problems too?

Scripture teaches that you are body, soul, and spirit. This is what you are comprised of, according to 1 Thessalonians 5:23: "May the God of peace Himself sanctify you completely; and may your whole spirit, soul, and body be preserved blameless at the coming of our Lord Jesus Christ" (NKJV).

God is in the process of sanctifying us, setting us apart toward holiness. Since we are comprised of body, soul, and spirit, let me tell you what I believe. If you know Jesus personally, he lives within your spirit. Your heart with the Spirit of Jesus is always right with God, always in oneness and complete fellowship. The Bible says, "He who joins himself to the Lord is one spirit with Him" (1 Corinthians 6:17). The soul is comprised of the mind, the will, and the emotions. So, yes, the soul comprises three of your biggest problems: Your mind, will, and emotions. But then, your body is breaking down daily regardless of how you work to fight the effects of aging.

We sometimes have difficulty seeing Jesus living through us or others because of what I just described. The spirit, which is in complete oneness with Jesus and always right with him, has a hard time ever getting to and through the surface of our lives. To live through or shine through us, our spirit must get through the challenges of the mind, the will, the emotions, and the body.

The Holy Spirit serves like an orchestra conductor in our lives. When conductors raise their hands to conduct symphonies, the players, with precision, lift their instruments. While individually, each instrument may sound weak or even strange, as they follow the conductor together, they make a beautiful symphony of music we enjoy. Remember, the conductor calls them to order and directs them together.

The Holy Spirit in your spirit is the conductor. I have discovered that when you pray and fast, your spirit, which struggles to surface, suddenly begins to stand at attention and alert to the Holy Spirit of God. As your prayer and fasting journey matures, God's Spirit stands up in and through your spirit, and your spirit which is joined with God's, is empowered anew by the power of the Holy Spirit of God. Then the Holy Spirit through your spirit begins to call the mind, will, emotions, and body into order. *Mind, get in order, and get focused. Will, submit to the will of God. Emotions, follow suit and come into the heart of God and feel what he feels. Body, submit to the Lord right now.*

This spiritual phenomenon happens when you experience the supernatural power of prayer and fasting. Then your life "gets it together" even during enormous challenges. All of you (mind, will, emotions, and body) become subject to the Spirit's leadership, making your spirit more alive than ever.

Again, prayer and fasting call these into order and awaken your spirit supernaturally. God does the work, but your submission to him through prayer and fasting sanctifies you through the power of God's Word igniting you by the Holy Spirit to become more like Jesus. Now you are ready for whatever may be next for you, your family, your church, and your entire future.

11

Believing God for Your Family

Praying and fasting for your family may be the most profound spiritual investment in them you will ever make. Each time you do this, you are planting seeds into their lives spiritually and eternally. This investment will outlive your days on this earth because God is faithful to answer prayer, and the Holy Spirit is always interceding for us according to the will of God.

Therefore, believing God for your family is one of the twelve ways God will change your life when you experience the supernatural power of prayer and fasting. Daily, periodically, and seasonally, I believe God for my family. Additionally, there are times when I join this act of faith in God and intercession for them with days of prayer and fasting.

Even if you never practice fasting along with prayer, you should become a committed intercessor for your family. Everyone can pray, and whatever situation or circumstance you find in your life or family today, you can pray. Prayer is faith, which will build greater confidence that God can answer your prayers for your family.

The Bible says, "Finally, be strong in the Lord and in the strength of His might" (Ephesians 6:10). Because of who you are in Christ and the presence and work of the supernatural power of the Holy Spirit in your life, God is strong in you and will be strong through you. This is true for you and all of Jesus' followers.

Believing God for my family enters a greater dimension of faith when I join it with prayer and fasting. Since the early days of our marriage and family life, I have practiced prayer and fasting. It often becomes focused solely on my family and their specific needs.

Anytime I write about this subject, I feel very vulnerable because I do not want to sound like I'm putting myself up as a perfect example for anyone. Yet the only thing I know is to be honest with you about my own life and practices. So with humility and giving all the glory to God, here are some ways I have prayed and fasted through the years for my family:

- When Jeana was diagnosed with cancer, I prayed and fasted one day a week for one year, asking God to heal her.

- Through a couple of years when Josh and Nick were growing up, I prayed and fasted one day a week for them to live for Christ, love him, and love the church.

- Each time I have prayed and fasted for a day or several days or during seasons of fasting, I always day by day make one of my significant requests about the members of my immediate family, and I still do this today.
- When Josh and Kate were considering marriage and Nick and Meredith were considering marriage, I prayed and fasted for each of them.
- When significant decisions about college, career, and future were before our children, I prayed and fasted for them.
- When Josh was diagnosed with multiple sclerosis a few years ago, through the initial weeks and months, there were days when I prayed and fasted for healing and wisdom in decision-making.
- Through all the stages of our family, I have prayed and fasted multiple times for them individually and collectively. There are thirteen of us today: Jeana, Josh, Kate, Peyton, Parker, Jack, Nick, Meredith, Reese, Beckham, Norah, and Maya. As I stated earlier, anytime I enter a series of days or seasons of fasting, I include praying and fasting for each family member.
- Through the years, as future opportunities came, I would enter prayer and fasting for our family to have clarity, wisdom, and discernment relating to the will of God. Now this is not only

associated with Jeana and me but also with Josh and Kate, as well as Nick and Meredith. Ten years ago, we were before the Lord when Josh and Kate departed with our grandsons for an incredible coaching opportunity in a large Alabama public high school. Then, we sensed that God was calling us away from service as pastor of Cross Church family, after almost thirty-three years, to a new ministry position in Nashville, Tennessee. Our leaders and I had a succession plan in place, and this involved my son Nick taking my place in the case of my death, retirement, or departure to another ministry, the latter of which not one of us thought would ever happen. So these were deep days before the Lord, not only relating to my calling away but even more so relating to Nick succeeding me upon my final day as pastor of Cross Church. We knew the implications were significant for the church and Nick and Meredith because their lives would change dramatically. But, to God's glory and all praise to him alone, the leadership succession at Cross Church has been very successful. Through our prayer and fasting, God has done great things.

While I could fill additional pages with examples, I will limit it to these. I pray they will encourage and inspire you to believe God daily for your family.

When we experience the supernatural power of prayer and fasting for our families, God will elevate our faith and expectations relating to our family members. I pray God gives me a very long life to one day witness my grandchildren and their families flourishing. When they do, whether I am here to see it or not, seeds of prayer and fasting have been planted before the Father in heaven on behalf of each of them and their future families.

Daily Needs of Your Family

Whether you only pray for your family or join your prayers with fasting for your family, I want to share with you some general daily prayer needs for all families. Of course, any member of the family can pray for these needs. Therefore, I will mention these needs briefly:

- Spiritual and Physical Protection: We should feel a deep sense of responsibility to pray for each family member about the spiritual and physical protection of their lives. Never in our generation has this need for spiritual and physical protection been any greater. Each of us should be on the alert for everyone in our family. I will share more with you about these matters later in this chapter.

- Personal Walk with God: From childhood to adolescence and adulthood, each family member should grow in their faith and walk with Jesus Christ daily. We should pray for one another to grow in our daily personal walk with Christ.

- Future Opportunities: Each family member will be presented with plentiful opportunities, such as jobs, investments, buying a home, or choosing a spouse. Just because these offers come, does not mean they are right or best. Therefore, we must pray for wisdom and discernment in all our decision-making.

- Specific Needs of Individuals: We need to pray for one another and our family members' specific needs. These needs could be regarding their health, salvation, growth in Christ, friendships, decisions they are facing, or personal choices relating to godliness. It could be related to their opportunities to compete in a sport, academia, or other matters.

- Praying Together: Families do need to pray together. We practiced this with our sons, even during their high school years. Our sons never went to school one day from kindergarten through senior high school without one or both of us praying with them. Find a way to pray daily with your family. Even now, with just Jeana and me at home, each evening, we pray together.

If you have ever said, "I do not know what to pray about for my family," the list above could become your daily prayer list for your family. Praying for your family's general and specific needs will encourage you and bless the entire family.

Your Family's Enemy

There is strong evidence of evil and sin throughout America today. I am astounded by how solid and mighty this evil is standing up in defiance against our God and his holy Word, the Bible. While we might point our fingers in blame toward people and, at times, processes, make no mistake about it and do not miss this: your family has an enemy!

The Bible says, "Put on the full armor of God, so that you will be able to stand firm against the schemes of the devil. For our struggle is not against flesh and blood, but against the rulers, against the powers, against the world forces of this darkness, against the spiritual forces of wickedness in the heavenly places" (Ephesians 6:11–12). We must stop underestimating our enemy and his power. We are in a war and should always know who our enemy is and his position.

This enemy engages with us in hand-to-hand combat. He and his forces are strong and authoritative, revolting against God and his plan. His army is not made of flesh and blood—that is, people, as we would understand it—but his is an army of demonic spirits inhabiting and combating in the heavenly places. The schemes are wicked, evil, and strategic.

In my book, *How to Pray*, I discuss what you need to know about your enemy.[19] I am convinced that every family must understand these things. As we experience a day or season of prayer and fasting for our families, we must see how serious these matters are. Your family has an enemy! Here are some facts about this enemy. We must understand these because so much is at stake.

Fact #1: You Are at War with Satan

You do not fight against people, situations, and circumstances. Therefore, stop trying to do so. The reality of this spiritual war with Satan is undeniable, both biblically and practically. To achieve victory and cease experiencing defeat, change your focus and clarify your understanding. You are in a spiritual war with Satan.

Fact #2: Satan Is Your Only Enemy

I encourage you to stop seeing people, institutions, systems, and circumstances as your enemies. Unquestionably, Satan can operate through any of these, but the essence of the battle is with the forces of spiritual darkness and evil. Begin to see what God sees. Put on your biblical lens. *Satan is your enemy, not people, situations, or circumstances.* Pray for God to give you insight into seeing these things.

Fact #3: Satan Wants to Destroy

Satan tears down; he never builds up. Satan divides; he never unites. Satan destroys; he never gives life. Satan wants to destroy your marriage. Satan wants to kill your children. Satan wants to destroy your grandchildren. Satan wants to kill every Christian. The more you love and serve God, the more Satan will want to take you out.

Satan also wants to destroy your church. When he does this, it will impact your family. Remember that he hates you and your family. He will do anything he can to disrupt God's work around the world. He will get God's people chasing good issues or secondary things if he can take their focus away from God's primary agenda of advancing the gospel to the world. Satan even uses scandal to turn people away from the church and Christ's message.

You are his target. Your marriage is his target. Your children and grandchildren are his targets. He wants to kill. Look what he is doing today. He wants to steal. Look what he is doing today. He wants to destroy. Look what he is doing today. He plays for keeps. His wins are not just short-term wins. Many times, his wins are eternal.

Fact #4: Satan Is Doomed

Satan is wreaking havoc upon our culture. He appears to have the upper hand in people's lives everywhere. He is tearing up and wrecking lives. Family and relational dysfunction abounds because he is the manipulator of all these things. Satan deceives, divides, and destroys. Satan is alive and well.

But please get this and never forget it: Satan's doom is certain. One day God will throw him and all his demonic forces into hell once and for all. The next time Satan points you to your past, which may be filled with defeat and despair, you should point him to his future, which will be finalized with guaranteed defeat. Satan *will* lose eternally. His doom is sure.

Friends, always remember that your family has an enemy. Live with your biblical and spiritual glasses on and see things as they are. Share these with your family members. This truth should call each of us to believe in the power of prayer. It should also call us periodically to pray and fast for our family if possible. Then we are more readily prepared to believe God for our family.

The Spiritual Battle for Your Family

Today's world does not encourage you ever to leave the front door of your home open. In most communities and all cities, you would never leave home, even for minutes, without locking the doors behind you. Then, if you have an alarm system in your home, you usually set it whether you are going on vacation or just out running errands.

While you may be diligent and intentional in closing and locking the doors in your home, are you as diligent and intentional in your spiritual life in this spiritual battle for your family? Are you leaving this front door open and letting your enemy into your life and family?

This reminds me of the story of Hezekiah, as recorded in Isaiah 39. Hezekiah had been sick and was now recovered. Marduk-Baladan, the son of the king of Babylon, heard this news and sent Hezekiah letters and a gift. Hezekiah was so pleased that when Marduk-Baladan's envoys arrived, Hezekiah opened all his storehouses and showed them everything, all his silver, gold, and other treasures. When Isaiah the prophet asked King Hezekiah about it, the king told him the men were from Babylon. Isaiah wanted to know what the envoys saw, and Hezekiah proudly told Isaiah that he had shown them everything, including the weapons in his armory.

Then Isaiah told Hezekiah that the day would come when everything in his house and all he had stored in it would be taken to Babylon. Even some of Hezekiah's sons would be taken away and become eunuchs in the palace of Babylon. Understand clearly and do not make this same kind of mistake by leaving the door to your family wide open for Satan to come and captivate their minds and steal their hearts from you. Shut the door and keep out the devil!

You are in a spiritual battle for your family. Therefore, be on the alert! Do not put your head down or turn away or go to sleep spiritually. On the contrary, you should always be highly alert for your family and their spiritual life and vitality.

You must be prepared for this battle. While never underestimating the power and position of your enemy, never overestimate your ability to win these battles. This is not a time for winging it or hoping it all works out. Hope is not a strategy. Instead, you need to take decisive steps to prepare for this battle. You cannot just think it will be okay, or this may lead you to defeat. You may even lose your family. Satan plays for keeps! Therefore, you must participate in this action daily by becoming prepared to fight this daily battle for your family.

Arming Your Family for Battle

One of the decisions I made decades ago that I still make today is to put the armor of God on my family each day in my daily prayer time. What is the armor of God? The Bible says,

> Take up the full armor of God, so that you will be able to resist on the evil day, and having done everything, to stand firm. Stand firm therefore, having belted your waist with truth, and having put on the breastplate of righteousness, and having strapped on your feet the preparation of the gospel of peace; in addition to all, taking up the shield of faith with which you will be able to extinguish all the flaming arrows of the evil one. And take the helmet of salvation and the sword of the Spirit, which is the word of God. With every prayer and request, pray at all times in the Spirit, and with this

in view, be alert with all perseverance and every request for all the saints, and pray in my behalf, that speech may be given to me in the opening of my mouth, to make known with boldness the mystery of the gospel, for which I am an ambassador in chains; that in proclaiming it I may speak boldly, as I ought to speak. (Ephesians 6:13–20)

We are told in this passage to put on the full armor of God because we must resist these evil days and vicious attacks from Satan. Evil days indicate the attacks from Satan and the trials of life. We are seeing today, more clearly than ever, the evil attacks of Satan before our eyes. We could fill paragraphs and pages with traumatic stories about the killing of children and families in mass shootings in schools, shopping malls, churches, and other public settings. It is all horrible and evil, and it proves that the demonic spirits in this world are alive and among us.

Therefore, we must be diligent and intentional about putting on the armor of God daily. Not only for ourselves but also for the members of our family. We are told in these verses to

- Belt your waist with truth: The armor did not need to be loose; therefore, the belt would cinch up the loose hanging material. The belt that pulls the loose ends of a family is truth, the truth of God's Word. We must do away with anything that takes away from truth. We must pursue truth everywhere, including, in this text, covering the loins. This mention may be a strong call to sexual purity and truthfulness.

- Put on the breastplate of righteousness: The breastplate protected the body from the shoulders to the loins. This protected the heart and the vital organs. God's righteousness and holiness are distinctive features and attributes of God. Our righteousness is Jesus Christ, and he is our breastplate.

- Strap on your feet the preparation of the gospel of peace: These Roman soldiers wore boots with nails on the soles to grip the ground when they were in combat. As we stand in spiritual battles, we must stand in the gospel of Jesus Christ. This good news is what brings peace to everyone, including ourselves. When we are in spiritual battles, we need God's peace. Jesus is our Prince of Peace and is with us.

- Take up the shield of faith: The Roman soldiers fought with a large shield that was 2.5 feet by 4.5 feet in dimension. They could kneel behind it to protect themselves. Our shield is all the truths of God found in his Word, the Bible. Even the devil's flaming arrows cannot get us as we take up the shield of faith which protects us from Satan.

- Take the helmet of salvation: This protects our head, our mind, which is always the target of the Enemy. He does all he can to defeat us with discouraging thoughts. But our helmet is our hope of salvation, which protects our minds in every way. Since our salvation is secure, the Enemy can never take it away from us.

- Take the sword of the Spirit: The only weapon of the soldier was his sword. It was his only offensive weapon. God's Word, the Bible, is the sword of the Spirit. God's truth and God's Word are eternal. There is nothing like the power of Scripture.

- Pray at all times in the Spirit: Prayer is how we stand against the Enemy with the Word of God in our hands, in our hearts, in our minds, and on our lips. Praying in the Spirit is submitting ourselves to the Spirit of God and lining up with his will continually. Prayer is where the battles are won against the Enemy. Pray for your family. Pray for the saints of God everywhere. Prayer is the key to the power of God. Pray with spiritual power. When you periodically couple prayer with fasting, everything ascends!

- We must put the armor of God on ourselves and our families through prayer each day. We need to be strong. We need to be aware. We need to be on the alert. We need to be prepared. Therefore, put this armor of God on your family each day.

Standing Together with God

I believe God for my family in times of prayer and fasting, but also, each day, I call their names out to God, asking him to clothe them in the armor of God. I stand upon the Scriptures as found in Ephesians 6:10–20, and I acknowledge that Satan is our only enemy as a family. For example, right now, from my existing prayer list as it is today, I pray like this:

> God, I stand upon Ephesians 6:10–20, asking you to protect and bless each member of my family. I recognize Satan as our only enemy, not people, situations, and circumstances. Father, put on Jeana and me, Josh, Kate, Peyton, Parker, Jack, Nick, Meredith, Reese, Beckham, Norah, and Maya the full armor of God. Lord, please put on our heads the helmet of salvation so our minds will be like Christ, and on our breasts, we ask you to place the breastplate of the righteousness of Jesus Christ, on our loins God's truth, and on our feet the preparation of the gospel of peace. Place in our right hand the sword of the Spirit, which is God's Word, and in our left the shield of faith to extinguish the flaming arrows of the evil one. Finally, Lord, we always pray in the Spirit with every prayer and request, persevering and interceding for one another and all the saints of God.
>
> Oh God, upon the authority of your Word, the blood of Jesus, and the name of Jesus, I submit my

all to you, Lord, and simultaneously recognize Satan as my enemy. I refuse to give up any ground to him, and in Jesus' name, I resist Satan and his demonic forces in every way. Please, God, protect the schools, churches, airports, and all public and private places where our family will be today and secure them with your protection because we know you alone are our shield of protection.

So, Lord, be our Shield. We drive all over our regions today or fly across the world, so be with Josh, Kate, Peyton, Parker, and Jack, with Nick, Meredith, Reese, Beckham, Norah, Maya, as well as with Jeana and me. Be a shield over us, underneath us, and all around us, to the right and left of us, in front of and behind us. God, we appeal to you in Jesus' name, shield us from all harm and evil. Please command your blessing upon each of us and all of us as a family. Protect us from viruses, illnesses, pain, and evil. We believe God for our family in every way, in Jesus' name, Amen.

Then, additionally, I enter a time of praying specifically for our grandchildren, Jeana and Josh, Kate, Nick, and Meredith, if I am aware of their specific needs. I share this with you in a general manner to show you how I am doing it presently.

Believing God for my family also occurs in special moments and periodic times when I go on a journey of prayer and fasting. I take all their needs very seriously and pray and fast for them with great intentionality and intensity.

I believe deeply that the ministry of prayer and fasting for your family is one of the greatest things you can ever do for them. This is one of your mightiest defenses to resist Satan and his influence over your family as well as one of your greatest offensive weapons as you stand on the promises of the Bible, claiming God's ground for the members of your family.

More Weapons in Your Arsenal

Along with the supernatural weapon of prayer and fasting, I believe there are other supernatural weapons to use when you are believing God for your family. These weapons are

- The name of Jesus: This is the mightiest name under heaven. In Jesus' name, you resist your enemy, Satan. When we use Jesus' name, strongholds can be obliterated, and walls will come down. Activate the power of God in the name of Jesus Christ.

- The blood of Jesus: When Jesus died on the cross in your place, his blood atoned for your sins, and his blood covered all your sins. Jesus is the perfect and once-and-for-all sacrifice for your sins. Call upon the blood of Jesus, sing about the blood of Jesus, and speak the name of

Jesus and his blood over everything, and God's power will fall upon your family.

- The Word of God: The major offensive weapon, and the only offensive weapon you have in Ephesians 6:10–20, is the Bible, the Word of God. Speak the Word, hear the Word, read the Word, stand upon the Word, grow in the Word, and preach the Word of God. This Word of God is eternal; one day, Jesus will come again.

- The word of your testimony: Satan hates it when Jesus changes your life and you talk about it to others. He does not want to hear about anything Jesus has ever done for you. Your testimony is powerful, so tell the story!

- A love for God greater than the desire to live: When you love your life and always want to preserve your reputation and claim your rights, these things do not honor God. The Bible tells you not to love your life, for he calls upon you to deny yourself, take up his cross, and follow Jesus.

Therefore, God has given you multiple supernatural weapons that will equip and empower you to believing God for your family. And here's a passage that will give you support as well: "They overcame him [the Accuser, Satan] because of the blood of the Lamb and because of the word of their testimony, and they did not love their life even when faced with death" (Revelation 12:11).

12

Seeing Your Church
Experience the Impossible

Extraordinary prayer always precedes every great movement of God. The prayer may be extraordinary in time, days, commitment, or focus. But when it occurs, a great movement of the Holy Spirit and the advance of the good news of Jesus Christ happens.

You can see the impossible happen. Your church can see the impossible happen. The Scripture encourages us to trust God and see his mighty power. The Bible says, "Call to Me and I will answer you, and I will tell you great and mighty things, which you do not know" (Jeremiah 33:3). When you pray personally and when your church calls out to God collectively, God will show you and tell you great and mighty things you have never known or experienced before.

This goes to a new spiritual level when churches within a community or city come together to pray in unity about something deep in their hearts. Through the extraordinary prayer of God's people, the impossible happened deep in the heart of Texas. Only God could do this. Here is the story recorded about *Prayer That Ended a Drought in Texas*:

It is common to hear news outlets report about drought in hot, dry Central Texas, but it is almost impossible to hear the news media reporting anything about a prayer meeting for rain—but it happened in 2014. When one thousand believers in Austin, Texas, gathered to pray for rain at the height of a drought, even the ordinarily skeptical local news shows were paying attention.

The drastic need was undeniable. We were in the midst of the worst drought in Austin's history, and the demand for water had never been greater. The unprecedented lack of rainfall and the taxing needs of a rapidly expanding population made the impossible situation worse.

Austin's drought was the worst on record and spurred lawmakers to consider multiple options, none of which promised rain. The primary water source for our city is Lake Travis, fed by the Colorado River. Austin had endured months with virtually no rain and daily temperatures of over 100 degrees almost every day in the summer of 2014.

One August morning at 6 am, a small group of about a dozen pastors and intercessors from the Unceasing Prayer Movement in our city gathered to pray and fast at Hyde Park Baptist Church. After praying for a couple of hours, one of the prayer warriors announced she sensed the Lord wanted us to call a city-wide prayer meeting for rain. Another intercessor said he got the same impression while he was praying.

A month later, in September 2014, a little over one thousand believers from churches around the city gathered at Hyde Park Baptist Church. We prayed and worshipped for about two hours, trusting God for rain. We needed a miracle. Lake Travis is "full" at a surface elevation of 681 feet, but it had dropped to less than 618 feet. Lake Travis covers almost nineteen thousand acres. Increasing the depth of the lake by "one-acre foot" requires at least 325,851 gallons of water. The amount of water needed to fill Lake Travis is astounding. We needed twenty-two million gallons of rain and runoff to fill our lake.

About two days after the prayer meeting, unexpected rains and flash floods covered

Austin. It was the start of a nature miracle. The rains were merciless for weeks, and against all predictions, the Lake started to fill up. The prayer movement that prayed for rain, and the prayer meeting we led, were even covered by a national news service.

Unseasonably heavy thunderstorms continued for months. We kept praying, and we watched God answer prayer with a modern-day miracle of epic proportions. Finally, the millions of gallons of water needed to fill Lake Travis pushed the levels to 681 feet. The drought was over. Rain filled the lake, and God answered our prayers in one of the most awe-inspiring ways imaginable.[20]

This is one of modern history's most remarkable stories I have ever heard about or read regarding God answering his people's extraordinary prayer and fasting. I know Trey Kent and Kie Bowman personally. Together these two pastors and men of God have led and are still leading the Unceasing Prayer Movement in Austin, Texas. Their book, *City of Prayer,* will build great faith and hope among churches, pastors, and Christian leaders in any community or city across the world. I have been with these two men, assisting and helping them lead a couple of these great city-wide prayer meetings in Austin, Texas.

There is nothing our God cannot do. The supernatural power of prayer and fasting will change your life, and you will see that even your church can experience the impossible. Never give up on Jesus' church. The gates of hell will not prevail against the church! Therefore, churches must come together periodically and experience a day of prayer and fasting for their town or city. Something about prayer and fasting sharpens our lives and accelerates our spiritual growth.

One day a young lumberjack challenged an older coworker to a contest. Both wanted to see which man could cut down the most trees in a single day. By sundown, the older lumberjack had won, hands down. The younger man could not figure out what happened. He had chopped nonstop all day while the older lumberjack had stopped every hour. He asked the older man how he had won the contest, and the older man explained, "Every time I sat down, I sharpened my ax."

Just as we cannot cut down trees with dull axes, so we will never be the men and women God created us to be if our spirits are not alert and daily sharpened by the Holy Spirit. I do not know of anything more capable of spiritually sharpening your life and church than a day or season of prayer and fasting.

If you want to see and experience the impossible, prayer and fasting need to become a part of your life personally and in the life of your church. Prayer and fasting will accelerate your spiritual growth exponentially.

God Does the Impossible

Even in my early years as a local church pastor, I taught about prayer and fasting and led the church to practice it together. Then, in the early 1980s, I served as the pastor in a coastal town on the Gulf of Mexico between Houston and Corpus Christi, Texas. We saw the power of God demonstrated during these three years of serving the First Baptist Church in Palacios, Texas. I wanted that small community of just over four thousand people to come to Jesus Christ. Through prayer and fasting, we saw many people come to know Jesus Christ, and the church more than tripled its attendance during those three years.

In one of those years, God put the vision in my heart to rent a tent to hold a city-wide evangelistic crusade. Our church leaders agreed, so we did it, but just before we had the event in March of that year, I shared this with the people:

> I am asking you to pray and fast as a church from Tuesday evening, March 12, beginning at 5:30 p.m., until Wednesday evening, March 13, at 5:30 p.m. The fast will be for twenty-four hours. It will culminate in a prayer rally here at the church at 7:30 p.m. on Wednesday evening.
>
> The purpose will be to petition God for one hundred souls to be saved in this crusade. Every time you are supposed to eat,

get alone for thirty minutes and pray. When you get hungry, read your Bible, pray, and ask God to control your appetite. It will be basically a food fast. Drink water, coffee, tea, or juices. That is all! Twenty-four hours for God and the souls of Palacios! Be quiet about the fast. Do not complain about it.

Our church saw the impossible! God answered our prayer and fasting. We saw over one hundred people come to Jesus Christ as Lord and Savior through that evangelistic crusade we held in a tent downtown. I am convinced God heard our pleas as we prayed and fasted. God does the impossible when the church practices prayer and fasting. And yes, he will do the same in your church.

Through the years, including almost thirty-three years as the pastor of Cross Church in Northwest Arkansas, I led congregations to experience prayer and fasting individually and together. We saw God do amazing things. God's movement among his people is inexplicable and amazing! God responds powerfully when he sees his church pursue him through prayer and fasting.

Through those years I served, we reached over twenty-five thousand people and saw them baptized to God's glory. Through evangelistic movements, we saw five hundred people come to Christ one night and over two thousand people come to Christ in a week. I could go on and on about the hand of God, but my point is to bring your attention to one biblical reality: when the church prays and fasts, God does great things. Yes, what some would call impossible things! Yet we know this biblical reality, and we should never forget it, "Nothing will be impossible with God" (Luke 1:37).

Cross Church still practices 21 Days of Prayer every January; fasting is encouraged at some level throughout that journey. The church has been doing great in the five years since my departure as senior pastor. They have continued with strong, healthy, biblical unity and experiencing a very special and wonderful season of God-sized growth. They will reach and baptize over eleven hundred people for Jesus Christ this year. The church's continued spiritual health has led to significant financial health. Cross Church is debt-free and positioned to respond to incredible opportunities for expanding space to accommodate the growing needs of the church. Our church's succession plan has been successful to God's glory; my successor, Dr. Nick Floyd, is leading the church exceptionally. The Cross Church staff team is strong, and God is using them greatly. The lay leaders are terrific. God is moving. To Him be the glory! God does the impossible when the church practices prayer and fasting.

I would be remiss if I did not tell you about another miracle that continues to happen through Cross Church. For the past thirty years, Doug Sarver has served as the Global Missions Pastor of Cross Church. Over these years, at least 173 churches have been planted across

America and the world. By the time this story is published, that number will continue to climb.

Reaching Northwest Arkansas, America, and the world for Jesus Christ has been and is the missional vision for Cross Church. Doug, a fellow prayer and fasting brother, has seen God do great things here on the ground in Northwest Arkansas and across America and the world. On May 9, 2023, Doug texted me these words relating to our conversation about prayer, fasting, and planting gospel churches: "Far too many people think that church planting is glamorous. But most don't realize that it's literally a boxing match with the devil every day to plant churches. And then, when you consider church planting internationally and cross-culturally, it brings a whole new dynamic of spiritual warfare in readiness, process, and everything else."

The advance of the gospel regionally, statewide, nationally, and globally is challenging in every way, but it is not impossible! On the contrary, I am convinced that prayer and fasting lead individuals and churches to see God do the impossible. God does the impossible when the church practices prayer and fasting.

Ten Ways Your Church Will Experience God

I pray and hope you will share this book with your church members and the churches and Christians in your community and city. While each church, town, city, and nation is different and, in its own way, difficult, we know that prayer and fasting are biblical principles and are relevant during all times throughout all peoples and places. Our God can do anything! Therefore, pray through and share these ten ways that your church can experience God when you pray and fast.

Focus

When your church prays and fasts together, God will clarify your focus on your church's mission. I trust your church's mission is built upon Acts 1:8 and Matthew 28:18–20. We must be moved to present the gospel to every person in the world and to make disciples of all nations. Each of us should realize that we need a vision to reach every person in every town, every city, every state, and every nation for Jesus Christ.

Prayer and fasting will wipe away the smudges on your spiritual glasses. Your vision will cease being blurred, and your heart will be moved with a desire to see Acts 1:8 and Matthew 28:18–20 fulfilled. When you pray and fast, the Holy Spirit will call your church into order. You will stop chasing after the cultural winds or desiring the world's approval. Instead, you will rise with mighty courage and focus on your church's mission.

Just as the lumberjack took the time to sit down and focus on sharpening the ax, the church today needs to slow down and become honed through the spiritual crucible of prayer and fasting. Churches are made up of people. People can get busy, operate in extreme distraction, and lose their effectiveness. Prayer and fasting call the church to refocus.

Extraordinary

It is extraordinary when a church prays and fasts. As the church does this, the church will begin to experience the extraordinary work of the Holy Spirit. The church will discover that God is who he says he is and can do what he says he can do. The people will experience genuine change through the manifested presence of God.

They will begin to revere the holiness of God and know of his great wonders. Prayer and fasting make the church more aware of the Lord and his wondrous works. Prayer and fasting will make you more aware of God's holiness, will open your eyes to his extraordinary person, and will lead you to experience God's astonishing power. Your church will never be the same again when you begin to pray and fast together.

Sensitivity

When your church prays and fasts together, an unusual spiritual sensitivity occurs. Your church will become sensitive to God and the leadership of his Spirit. You will desire to experience his filling and anointing, refusing to quench or grieve his Holy Spirit. Can you imagine your church being led by the Holy Spirit of God and you responding accordingly? Prayer and fasting will give your church a special sensitivity to the Holy Spirit.

There is nothing like being a part of a church in which the Spirit is so active that you leave the worship service saying, "I believe the Lord was with us today in a special way." As your church prays and fasts together, sensitivity to the Holy Spirit will increase.

Speaking of sensitivity, have you ever felt God put someone on your heart in such a way that you knew they needed immediate prayer? This happened to our friends David and Teresa Ferguson. Their close friend, Kay Horner, is one of their faithful intercessors and serves as the executive director of Awakening America Alliance. Kay works with David to make this ministry what they believe God wills for it to be. David wrote this testimony about being sensitive to the Holy Spirit and shared it with me in May 2023. It is truly a remarkable story. David permitted me to share it with you. In his words,

> "Though you have not seen Him, you love Him, and though you do not see Him now, but believe in Him, you greatly rejoice with joy inexpressible and full of glory" (1 Peter 1:8). During a recent trip my wife, Teresa, and I took to Northwest Arkansas, we spent time with Ronnie and Jeana. First, we enjoyed a wonderful dinner in their home. The next morning, we guys were on track for a meeting, and of course, the ladies were going shopping! As Teresa and I finished getting ready in our nearby hotel, a text at

exactly 9:07 a.m. interrupted my last cup of coffee. Noticing it was from Kay, our ministry team's intercessor, I read it between sips of coffee.

"How are you doing, my friend? You're on my mind…any specific prayer points you want me to target?"

Later, we learned that Kay felt such an intense burden to pray for us that she parked her car and texted immediately before entering her office.

Curious about Kay's burden, I reflected for a few minutes on what "specifics" we needed her to intercede for. Lacking much clarity, I walked into where Teresa was getting ready for the day to share the text and seek her input. As I walked into the room, Teresa was having a phone conversation with Terry, our next-door neighbor in Texas. Teresa repeated Terry's words with alarm. "Lightning struck our house, and it's on fire!" The call came at exactly 9:15 a.m.—eight minutes after Kay's text.

Even before the call was finished, I felt impressed to put my phone where Teresa could read it, and as she did, unexplainable peace flooded over both of us. God had gone ahead of us, and intercession was underway.

The house and almost everything inside was a total loss. Only the exterior rock walls remained and, hopefully, are secure enough for a 12- to 15-month rebuild.

Yet thanks be to Jehovah Jireh, who first provided intercession and then unexplainable peace! He has now brought "inexpressible joy." Yes, Teresa and I are being loved well!

I can assure you that Jeana and Teresa went on to shop some that day while David and I attended an important meeting plus our Businesspersons Summit. God intervened miraculously due to Kay's sensitivity to the Holy Spirit. Kay is a devoted prayer warrior and practices the power of prayer and fasting. Do what she did the next time you have someone on your heart. She prayed. She sought the person out to ask about them. Then she prayed more. All of us need sensitivity to the Holy Spirit in life.

Unity

Jesus prayed, "That they may all be one; just as You, Father, are in Me and I in You, that they also may be in Us, so that the world may believe that You sent Me" (John 17:21). Jesus prayed for the unity of the church. He wanted his followers to be as one so the world would be drawn to the love of Jesus.

When the church prays and fasts together, unity will

occur. Those who cannot or do not choose to participate in a fasting journey with you will still sense the unifying effect of your prayer and fasting. We must become a visible, undeniable answer to Jesus' prayer in John 17. Only through prayer with fasting will the church be as one. Then, as one body of Christ, the church will prevail against the gates of hell.

Churches, denominations, and networks all over our country and world are divided. Church bullies are tearing up many churches as they exert their carnal power. Division within churches, denominations, and networks, occurs over tribalism, territorialism, and power. None of this is from God, nor does it honor God. However, demonic influence is apparent in these situations, so we must practice prayer and fasting. Scripture says to be "diligent to keep the unity of the Spirit in the bond of peace" (Ephesians 4:3).

God desires the church to be as one. If your church is not living in unity, your church needs to get right with God and then get right with one another. The Holy Spirit brings unity to the church. Therefore, pray and fast. Prayer and fasting can provide the spiritual breakthrough to move the people of God toward unity.

Health

So when your church experiences God through prayer and fasting, you will begin to focus on the mission, experience the extraordinary work of God, develop a special sensitivity to the Holy Spirit, achieve unity together, and move toward becoming spiritually healthier in every way.

Prayer and fasting move Christians and churches toward having a healthy culture together. Healthy churches grow. When a church has an unhealthy culture, it is because there are spiritually unhealthy followers of Jesus in the church. As your spiritual life goes, so goes your church's spiritual life. When you are spiritually healthy before God and experience healthy relationships within the church, the church will be healthy.

The Bible says, "The churches were being strengthened in the faith, and were increasing in number daily" (Acts 16:5). This is a powerful testimony because as we become stronger in Jesus, stronger in the faith, stronger in the Scriptures, and stronger in our spiritual lives, the church will grow and be effective in reaching more people with the good news of Jesus. I believe that when the church prays and fasts together, the church will be healthier in every way.

Growth

When your church prays and fasts together, growth occurs. Growth follows health; prayer and fasting contribute to the health and culture of your church. Prayer and fasting grow Christians and grow churches. Let me share a fantastic testimony from Pastor John Cope of Metro Philadelphia. Cross Church helped him launch

Keystone Fellowship church over two decades ago. I asked him to update his story about how God has grown him, his church, their vision, and their family. John writes:

> From the day I gave my life to Christ as a senior in high school, prayer has been an intimate joy in my life. In my twenties, I began fasting, but not regularly. I lacked discipline because I lacked understanding. Then, in my early thirties, I served as student pastor under Dr. Floyd when fasting became a real breakthrough in my life. I could see the power of fasting modeled in Dr. Floyd's life and the fruit it produced within him and the church. Since then, I have seen hundreds of breakthroughs through the desperate humbling act of fasting—and they have come in all forms and sizes.
>
> Twenty-one years ago, not knowing a soul in the area, our family followed God's call to move to Philadelphia, Pennsylvania, to start a new church, Keystone Fellowship. We had two supportive sponsoring churches over nine hundred miles away but no local sponsoring churches. God moved in what sometimes seemed like impossibly hard circumstances, allowing us to continue to reach people and giving us a big vision for

starting new churches. We are now training up two new church plant pastors, bringing us to nine church plants!

My prayer, fasting, and Bible reading increased greatly during this uncomfortable move to the Northeast. I found that my greatest source of peaceful strength is hearing, believing, and obeying the voice of God. Teaching this to be a lifestyle to our church body has allowed us to raise up to fifteen of our current ministerial staff from within our church.

Through our intense prayer, God has given us a heart and has opened doors for international ministry. Keystone Fellowship has been blessed to train hundreds of pastors in Africa and South Asia over the past twenty years. We recently built a five-story facility in a large South Asian city where multiple churches can gather to worship. This facility has rooms to house over seventy orphans and is also used as a training center.

In 2009 during a season when I was praying and fasting, God spoke to me about a future opportunity. He said that I would be asked to lead a network that would see spiritual transformation in our state. Fast forward to March of 2023, when I joined the staff of the largest church plant network in the United States as the director of the PA/SJ Send Network while continuing to give oversight to our Keystone churches. Only God can speak this to fruition!

On a more personal family level, prayer and fasting have impacted our three sons and their families. Recently our oldest planted a church in Orlando, Florida. Our middle son and his family live and plant churches in the Middle East. Our youngest son planted a new Keystone church in the Philadelphia area. We are so proud of these guys and thankful for the prayers answered by a mighty, intimate God.

There is nothing our God cannot do! Through prayer and fasting growing us personally, God works mightily in and through people, churches, and families.

Anticipation

There is spiritual and holy anticipation when the church prays and fasts together. People look forward to seeing what God is going to do. They anticipate the Lord working powerfully. They cannot wait to be with God's people in a worship service because they know God will meet with them. They anticipate their experience with the church worshiping the Lord and listening to the preaching of God's Word.

When people have experienced God personally during the week, they anticipate what God will do on Sunday. Due to their spiritual sensitivity increasing, they excitedly anticipate what God will do in their lives and church. If you or your church has lost its anticipation, pray and fast.

Vision

When the church prays and fasts together, the church's vision will become enlarged and flourish in the future. The church will not talk about what they cannot do because God is speaking to them about what he wants them to do. Instead, they talk about what they will do to God's glory.

When a church struggles with its vision or direction in the future, they need to pray and fast. The vision will become clarified, and the Holy Spirit will energize the church toward the future God has for them. As he reveals his desire for your church, you will begin to see it from God's perspective and enter a season of experiencing the manifested power of the Holy Spirit upon the church.

Engagement

When the church prays and fasts together, ministry happens more in the community than ever before. First, God's people begin to see others the way Jesus sees them, to feel their pain and struggles as Jesus feels for them. Then the church begins to listen to what people are saying like Jesus is listening to them. As a church engages its community, the church feels the pain, illness, hurt, disappointment, discouragement, and even joy. All of these exist within a community.

Prayer and fasting result in your church engaging those around you. For example, many years ago, the Lord placed upon our hearts to begin our Cross Church Compassion Center, which is now a flourishing ministry that helps people with their needs. From this, so many powerful things have occurred, such as Feed the 479, a ministry that provides food for the entire 479 area code in this region.

When a church prays and fasts, it will more readily and eagerly engage the community. The needs of your community are screaming for your attention, and, perhaps for the first time, you are not only hearing them, but you are also going to answer their cries. This is what Jesus would do. We must engage our communities.

Advancement

As the church practices prayer and fasting, we advance toward fulfilling the Great Commission more than ever. We desire to see people come to Christ, be baptized, and be discipled in their faith. We see the need to do this regionally, statewide, nationally, and globally.

I have found through the years that the more Cross Church encountered God through prayer and fasting, the more intentional we became about reaching Northwest Arkansas, America, and the world for Jesus Christ. Additionally, more doors opened that were only possible because of God's supernatural power.

Cross Church is a multi-church. What does this mean? Cross Church is a multi-campus, multi-ministry, multi-generational, multi-ethnic, and multi-lingual fellowship of Jesus' followers. We believe people need Jesus, people need each other, people change the world, and people leave legacies. To Jesus' glory, we believe every church in America and the world can see God do the impossible. "Now to Him who is able to do far more abundantly beyond all that we ask or think, according to the power that works within us, to Him be the glory in the church and in Christ Jesus to all generations forever and ever. Amen" (Ephesians 3:20–21).

I pray that you and your church will experience the supernatural power of prayer and fasting. You will learn this supernatural reality: God can do more in a moment than you can ever do in a lifetime.

13

Pursuing God Together

In the summer of 2011, Julio Arriola joined our Cross Church staff team as the Global Worship Pastor. Julio's love for people, passionate heart for God, incredible musical talent, vision for evangelism, zeal for church planting, and commitment to the Great Commission set him apart in every way. We fell in love with Julio, Carla, and their family.

Julio assisted me in every way across this country. For example, when I served as the president of the Southern Baptist Convention, he led worship for us splendidly. Our Tuesday night sessions at the Southern Baptist Convention Annual Meeting in 2015 in Columbus, Ohio, and 2016 in St. Louis, Missouri, were incredible and unprecedented evenings. Thousands upon thousands of people joined us both years at these prayer gatherings. God also used Julio to lead worship for other multiple prayer gatherings called Praying Pastors.

When Julio Arriola joined our team, God led him to participate with us in many experiences of prayer and fasting. He began doing our 21 Days of Prayer for the first time and also fasted with us each year during those days. He informed me recently that he has observed the 21 Days of Prayer with fasting each year since his first year with us.

After our 21 Days of Prayer emphasis in January 2016, Julio Arriola informed me that God was calling him back to Guadalajara, Mexico, to plant a gospel church. It was obvious the Lord was calling him. So he stayed with us until the end of the Annual Meeting of the Southern Baptist Convention in St. Louis, Missouri, during which he led all worship sessions for us. Then our church sent Julio and his family to plant the church in Guadalajara and supported them financially. Our church loved Julio but sent him out, knowing God would use him extensively.

He spent the rest of 2016 preparing for the 2017 launch of the church. God supplied him with a core team, and this team spent twenty-one days fasting with him to kick off the church launch in 2017. God blessed the new church immediately. In the first two years, the church had over seven hundred members and an average attendance of five hundred people weekly. Prayer and fasting became a part of their church culture. The supernatural power of God was evident in their church as they were constantly reaching people for Jesus Christ.

Then, in late 2019, after my departure from Cross Church, Julio joined us in Nashville, Tennessee, to accept a role with us as the executive director of Hispanic Relations and Mobilization. Again, he provided exceptional national leadership to all the Hispanic leaders and churches across America. Once again, his commitment to prayer and fasting became a part of his leadership, and God gave him enormous favor and blessing.

Following my departure from my role in Nashville in late 2021, Julio accepted an incredibly influential position with the North American Mission Board as the director of the SEND Network in Texas, with the Southern Baptist of Texas state convention. Julio is now empowered to lead the church planting network in all of Texas for the Southern Baptist Texas Convention. In 2022, he led them to plant more churches in Texas than any year since 2005. Julio gives God the glory for these thirty-nine churches launched in Texas that year, knowing and testifying that God's supernatural power did this through prayer and fasting.[21]

In all the equipping he provides to these church planters, Julio instructs them about prayer and fasting and then calls upon them to practice prayer and fasting with him. As a result, he led all of them in January 2023 in 21 Days of Prayer and Fasting. Julio will tell you that his life has never been the same since his beginning days of fasting with us in 2011. So he has taken the baton of prayer and fasting and handed it to every church planting pastor as they launch their churches through-out Texas. To this day, God is using him powerfully and supernaturally across America and the world.

Pursue God through prayer and fasting as your church goes forward. Let the testimony of Julio be an extraordinary blessing to you to inspire you and your church to do great things for God. The supernatural power of prayer and fasting is real, and God will change your life by what he does in and through your church as you pursue God daily and seasonally, most especially when you are practicing prayer and fasting together.

The Bible Sets the Precedent

We read in Acts 8 that when the Jerusalem church was persecuted, many scattered to escape arrest. A band of Christians ended up three hundred miles away in the city called Antioch, which was the capital city of Syria. It was a pagan city but also very luxurious. At the time, Antioch was the third largest city in the world. In this city, God raised up a mighty church that began the missionary movement of taking the gospel to the ends of the earth. The book of Acts begins to shift its emphasis from Jerusalem to Antioch. From the city of Antioch, God did extraordinary things.

The power of Jesus Christ through the Holy Spirit was working supernaturally in and through the church at Antioch. The Spirit of Jesus made this a world-changing church. Scripture records the work of God in

Antioch beginning in Acts 11. It was in this city where the disciples were first called Christians. Then in Acts 13, we read more about what God was doing through the church. The Bible says:

> Now there were prophets and teachers at Antioch, in the church that was there: Barnabas, Simeon who was called Niger, Lucius of Cyrene, Manaen who had been brought up with Herod the tetrarch, and Saul. While they were serving the Lord and fasting, the Holy Spirit said, "Set Barnabas and Saul apart for Me for the work to which I have called them." Then, when they had fasted, prayed, and laid their hands on them, they sent them away. (Acts 13:1–3)

A diversity of spiritual gifts and Spirit-led leaders emerged in the church in Antioch. Although then, the presence of God became evident through this church as they worshiped the Lord and were ministering to him, they were also praying and fasting. The Lord instructed them to set Barnabas and Saul (Paul) apart for the work God was calling them to do. Therefore, as they fasted and prayed, they laid their hands on them and sent them away on their first missionary journey to advance the good news of Jesus Christ throughout the gentile world.

If the first-century church practiced prayer and fasting, why do churches today not do it? Likewise, if the church of Antioch in Acts 13 sent out their leaders and missionaries through prayer and fasting, why does the church today not do the same? While the early church's culture was permeated with prayer, fasting, and the fire of God's power, the church's culture today is not.

The church at Antioch was world-changing. If you want your church to be a church like Antioch, pray and fast! Their spiritual leaders walked with God intimately, passionately, and urgently. They were on a mission with God to take the gospel to the world. The church in Antioch was pursuing God together. Healthy churches send, and growing Christians go.

Consider this interesting observation I want to share with you about today's church versus what we read about happening in Acts 13 in and through the church at Antioch. We talk a lot about sending and going but little about fasting and praying. We cannot have the breadth and reach of the church at Antioch without the depth they practiced in prayer and fasting.

We must press into becoming the church Jesus wants us to be so Jesus can use us in the way he wants to. We need God's supernatural power, and prayer with fasting is critical to have it. It is time, past time, for the world to see what God can do. Pursuing God together will result in God working through his people and his church worldwide. Church by church, churches with churches must pursue God together through prayer and fasting.

Roaring Twenties Fast

Evangelist Matt Brown, founder of Think Eternity, and Pastor Malachi O'Brien, a national prayer leader, are committed intercessors and mobilizers for prayer and fasting. Since 2020, each January, they have extended the call for one million people who are in their "roaring twenties" to fast and pray for twenty-one days, asking God to move mightily among all people living right now in their "roaring twenties."[22]

They believe tens of thousands have responded to this vision each year since it began in 2020. So can you imagine this: tens of thousands of people of all ages, praying and fasting for twenty-one days each January for God to move mightily among the present younger generation that is right now living in their "roaring twenties." Matt texted these words to Malachi and me recently:

> Ronnie, the one thing I would add is that Malachi was a seminary student whose faith was dry and whose marriage was struggling. He was deeply impacted by hearing about the Cross Church revival and your fasting journey. The next day, he began his first 40-day fast, profoundly changing his life and bringing him close to the Lord. In a very real way, this "Roaring Twenties" fast would not have impacted millions of young people

over the past four years if you hadn't obeyed
God's call to fast and pray.

Matt was overly gracious with his words, and they
humbled me greatly before the Lord. To God be the
glory alone! Thank God for putting it on Matt's and
Malachi's hearts to do this fast annually. Then, Malachi
texted Matt and me these words:

> The roaring twenties fast is the passing of
> the baton of fasting from one generation
> to the next. That lane on a track where
> older and younger grasp the same baton
> momentarily. A decade-long initiative that
> will shift nations. The roaring twenties ended
> in depression, but we believe the new roaring
> twenties will end in revival.
>
> Thousands of millennials and GenZ have
> joined the fast, and more are joining every
> year. They desire the authentic presence of
> Jesus, and spiritual hunger through fasting
> is an escort to the deeper things of God. An
> accelerant to the Great Commission and a
> recalibration for all who deeply feel there has
> to be *more* of *God*.

I love both Matt and Malachi. They are great encour-
agers and prayer intercessors for Jeana and me. Together,
we believe and pray that this generation, all of us alive

today, will become known as the Revival Generation. Plan now to be a part of next year's "Roaring Twenties" by fasting and praying.

Can you imagine what the spiritual potential would be when church by church and churches with churches would pray and fast together? Pursuing God with this unity, focus, and purpose would transform our nation and world. It would also usher in what I believe God put in my heart in 1995 and have now prayed for each day for over twenty-five years: there is coming a day when God will bring forth a mighty spiritual revival to America that will transcend all denominational, generational, cultural, racial, and ethnic lines.

Friend, will you pray and fast with us? Will you mobilize your church to pray and fast? Will you mobilize pastors to pray and fast? Will you mobilize church leaders to pray and fast? Will you mobilize national leaders from all walks of life and living on various career paths to pray and fast?

God can do more in a moment than you can do in a lifetime. God can also do more in and through the church in a moment than programs, ministries, technical excellence, great worship, or mere machinery. No one can take the place of God! Nothing can take the place of God! Looking at the church today, we see what man can do. While we may have state-of-the-art technology, more expressive worship, or even more targeted ministries, do we have more of God? I am convinced today, more than ever, that it is time for the church to see what God can do.

This nation and world need Jesus desperately. They need to see Bible-based churches empowered by the Holy Spirit and preaching the gospel of Jesus Christ as the hope for the world. Everyone needs Jesus, and everyone needs Jesus now. Prayer and fasting move the focus away from what we can do and then adjust the focus to what God can do. I am overflowing and on fire with a God-given urgency for calling the church to relentlessly pursue God together.

The time is not tomorrow. The time is not later. The time is now! We live in critical times, and critical times call for radical, urgent actions. Urgent actions we can do personally and in our church *include* prayer and fasting—church by church and churches with churches pursuing God together.

Pursuing God Together

I want to share five ways your church can pursue God together through prayer and fasting. Each type of fast has a place individually, and a few can be done together. Consider which of these ways fits best for your season of life and the season of your church.

(1) One-Meal Corporate Fast

A one-meal fast with your church is an excellent place to begin. You may start even more simply by calling the church to fast over a specific meal, like lunch or dinner. For others to participate in this one-meal fast, they need to know that they should retreat for prayer when they usually eat. They also need to know what they are fasting for.

I recall at least one time when I called our people to pray and fast over a Sunday noon meal for a Solemn Assembly that we were having during our Sunday night worship service. The Solemn Assembly is the gathering of the church for repentance and crying out to God for revival. Therefore, I challenged the people to abstain from the Sunday noon meal and go to a private place, sit before God, talk with him, and let him deal with their life. All of this would be in preparation for the Solemn Assembly. I wanted them to understand that getting their hearts right before God personally would result in God doing something great during the Sunday evening Solemn Assembly.

How specific should you get? I quote directly from an article I wrote many years ago in our weekly church periodical:

> The Sunday noon meal on January 9 is also the time we set aside to fast. Then after the Solemn Assembly, the fast can be broken. The Solemn Assembly has been called for the purpose of crying out to the Lord for spiritual renewal personally, in our church, and in America. As we come together for the

purpose of renewing fellowship with God, we will experience repentance, cleansing, and renewal. Pray with me this week about this Solemn Assembly. This will be new ground for some of us, but the foundation is solid since it is based on the Bible. I believe God will meet with us mightily in the assembly.

I believe God's people will move toward this initial commitment to prayer and fasting when they understand it. Of course, biblical and practical teaching on fasting is essential, but specificity is also imperative for success.

Constantly challenge yourself to take the specified mealtime to draw aside privately, talk to God, and listen to what he is saying to you from the Word. Open the Bible, read it, and let God speak to you through the Scriptures. When the Bible speaks, God speaks. So again, a one-meal fast is an excellent place to begin. Therefore, begin!

(2) One-Day Corporate Fast

I have found, and still believe today, that the church will respond well when a pastor calls his people to a one-day fasting journey. I have done this numerous times, too many to count. But it is simple enough that most can get their arms around it and their hearts into it.

We have called people to one-day fasting journeys

for a specific need in our church to the needs of our nation and many needs in between. In addition, at times, we have encouraged people to fast for the National Day of Prayer, which is always the first Thursday in May. In our church specifically, I have led our people to observe a one-day fast to seek the Lord for specific matters like:

- A significant event that is coming up in our church,
- A time of prayer for our nation, like the National Day of Prayer,
- A time of crisis in our region, state, nation, or the world,
- A financial need or emphasis we are asking our people to participate in for a project ahead.

The critical questions are: What does God want to do among us? What does God want to do in me? When I lead our people into a one-day time of prayer and fasting, I encourage them not to eat from sundown on one day until sundown the next day. This is a proven and right model for everyone to consider.

(3) Seven-Day Corporate Fast

At least twice while serving Cross Church, I led our people to participate together in a corporate, church-wide fast over seven days. While our church had journeyed into several types of fasts during times of corporate fasting, I believed God wanted to take us into a new dimension spiritually, not only for our church but also personally for those who participated with us. Here is what we sensed God was calling us to do:

- I challenged people to pray and fast from food for seven days about the most significant burden in their life and to ask God to deliver them from it if he willed. If his will was to leave someone's burden in their life instead of removing it, they were to seek him for his power to learn, grow, and understand what he was doing in this season of their life. Additionally, I asked them to join me in praying and fasting for our church's most significant burden. Therefore, we prayed and fasted for seven days for their greatest personal burden and our church's most significant burden.

- I also realized some could only participate to a degree due to physical reasons or daily schedules. Additionally, if, due to these reasons or others, they could not do a food fast, then they could choose something they love to do and abstain from it, like watching television, scrolling social media, or something else.

- I wanted the people to be comfortable and prepared, so I preached the initial message four weeks before this seven-day fast so they could pray about it and pinpoint their personal burden. Also, I wrote a prayer guide for everyone to use if desired. Then we used commitment cards to help them, not to call them into accountability. It was their commitment to God and not to us. Just under one thousand people signed a commitment card, but participation was much greater. God did great things! We also had nightly prayer and sharing services to experience him and encourage the people wherever they were.

- A few years later, we did another seven-day fast that focused on asking God for a breakthrough. We asked them to pray and fast for seven days for personal and church breakthroughs. Whatever their wall or obstacle, it needed to come down, so I invited them to pray and fast that it would. We encouraged them to identify what was holding them back and fast for it. Identify it and then join me in prayer and fasting for it. As a church, we were asking God for a financial breakthrough. As I shared earlier, God was faithful, and the church remains blessed and flourishing financially. This time just under fifteen hundred people turned in commitment cards to God. Both were powerful and life-changing for many but also a huge blessing for the church as we pursued God together.

(4) 21 Days of Prayer

I have mentioned the twenty-one days of prayer in this chapter, along with fasting for those who desire to go a little deeper on the journey. These twenty-one days of prayer at Cross Church have occurred annually for over a decade, beginning on January 1. We have found this is the easiest way to communicate it and encourage people to make their own twenty-one days if this one does not fit their lives or schedule. Many participate in prayer and add fasting at some level.

We share devotions daily, and for at least one year, I did a Facebook live twenty-minute prayer time daily. This was received greatly, and the number of viewers grew significantly throughout each day. I would urge every pastor and every church to pray for twenty-one days consecutively in January. I have helped churches through these, speaking to their congregations on Sundays and encouraging their faithfulness.

Additionally, when serving as a pastor, I may speak about this occasionally in a specific sermon to prepare for this time or during another sermon in December. It is important to communicate well, given the people as many details as possible, and encourage them to participate, so plan accordingly. Sunday announcements via video during the Sunday services from Thanksgiving through the end of the year and during the twenty-one-day emphasis should be made weekly. The video can also be shared through social media.

You can always wait until the second week of January to begin, whatever is best for your church. Consistency is key. I have started every year like this for over a decade. I find it helpful, encouraging, and a blessing to me, and many have shared that this time of fasting blesses them physically, mentally, and emotionally following the Christmas season.

(5) Forty-Day Corporate Fast

Through the years, we have used a forty-day corporate fast to focus greatly on what God may want to do with us. We would encourage our people to pray and fast through one meal each day or even one day a week for prayer and fasting. Some may go on a seven-day fast to begin the forty days or conclude the forty-day journey. Here are some examples of the specific focus of some of these forty-day corporate fasts for our church:

- Evangelistic events: We did this for a major weeklong evangelistic event. We began the fast so the forty days would be completed on the event's final day. We were praying and fasting for one thousand people to come to Jesus Christ during this evangelistic event, which would take a God-sized movement. On the first night after the event began, we had a driving snowstorm that gave our region several inches of snow, resulting in all schools being closed for several days. On the surface, this was not good, but we believed God and decided during a staff meeting on Monday to add two more gatherings. All was in faith as we prayed and fasted. Miraculously and to the praise of God alone, after day seven was completed, we witnessed more than twenty-six hundred people come to saving faith in Jesus Christ in that one week. All for Jesus! God heard our cry through prayer and fasting and did what only he could do. It was incredible!

- The outpouring of the Holy Spirit for spiritual revival: God placed revival in America not only in my heart but also in the heart of the church. God opened mighty doors for our church through the years, including my leadership within our denomination and through the massive movement of Promise Keepers, where I preached to over 1.3 million men in the National Mall in Washington, DC, as well as serving as president of the National Day of Prayer for at least two years. All these and many other doors opened because of our church's commitment to pray and fast. To God alone be the glory!

- Major financial campaigns: One of these campaigns specifically we called Special Treasures. This campaign raised funds for the Pinnacle Hills Campus of Cross Church. At its completion, it was the largest financial campaign in our history. I felt God wanted me to lead this project, and I did not choose to use a consulting group in this experience. God did great things. I cast the vision of this campus ministry and facility in at least forty different settings for our adults, and God blessed us each time powerfully. We saw God's people commit more than twenty-five million dollars to Special Treasures.

A God-Sized Story

Get ready; this story is possible only through God's supernatural power. Early in this prayer and fasting journey for the Special Treasures Financial Campaign, an older woman came to me and gave me her only possession of worth, all she had. In our first of forty gatherings, she handed me her wedding ring. It was literally all she had to give. As she laid it in my hand, weeping, it was the most humbling experience in giving I had ever experienced. After continuing to cast the vision to our people, I felt led one night to tell the story about this woman and what she had given me for the campaign.

I deeply felt I needed to ask this question that night: "Will someone buy this ring, and when you do, will you give it back? It is God's ring." God kept one of our men up all night, and early that next morning, he offered to buy it for five thousand dollars. Then he gave it back to me. The next night I stood up to a different group, told the story, and asked them, "Is there anyone who wants to buy the ring for ten thousand dollars, and when you do, will you give it back? It is God's ring." Before I left that night, a couple bought the ring. Then they gave it back. I did the same the next night, and someone bought it for twenty thousand dollars. I kept doing it, and people purchased the ring for forty thousand dollars, then eighty thousand dollars, and yes, then one hundred sixty thousand dollars. Finally, a man called me and bought the ring for the final time for a huge amount. So when all the gifts for the ring were tallied together, the ring had brought a total of $1.3 million to the campaign. This is due to a simple, sacrificial gift by this woman of her wedding ring that, realistically, had little value by the world's standards but extraordinary, supernatural, life-changing eternal value from God's perspective.

Oh, how God used it! All these things occurred during the forty days of prayer and fasting. There is supernatural power when we pray and fast. I am convinced that the journey of prayer and fasting for forty days resulted in such radical giving. Only God, yes, only God, could have done all of that. When you pray and fast, God can do more in a moment than you could ever do in a lifetime.

In all these experiences I have shared with you, each journey went by a prayer plan for all forty days. As I wrote each of those plans, the Lord directed his people to honor him through prayer and fasting. God answers prayer.

My pastor friend, Shane Idleman, is the founder and lead pastor of the Westside Christian Fellowship in Leona Valley, California. He has a big heart for God and is a passionate prayer warrior who practices the power of prayer and fasting. In his book, *Feasting & Fasting,* he writes, "Have a prayer list available. It's a battle—a hunger strike against hell. It's challenging and difficult, but the pain of discipline far outweighs the pain of regret."[23]

Shane lives this out personally. I preached for Shane before and will go back again in his weeklong series of services seeking God for revival called "Rend the Heavens." His church is pursuing God together! Will your church pursue God together?

The Value of a Prayer and Fasting Guide

People must have a prayer guide for any corporate fast. Keep it simple but clear. These are the components for one of these guides:

- Spiritual Goal: What is your specific desire or goal you want to see God do? Fasting is abstinence from food with a spiritual goal in mind.
- Unity: A prayer guide unites the church in prayer together. It promotes oneness in spirit and heart as you pray and fast.
- Specifics: When we pray specifically in unison,

something powerful occurs because God answers prayer! Build these specifics for prayer upon Scriptures, which give the people the Word of God to stand upon as they call out to the Lord.

- Consistency: A prayer and fasting guide will provide a clearer path for each person to be more consistent.

Prayer and Fasting Inspires Others

My friend and fellow pastor, Kie Bowman, served the Hyde Park Baptist Church in Austin, Texas, for over twenty-six years. In 2023, Kie retired from his church so he could give himself entirely to the prayer movement in America. It was Kie, along with Trey Kent, whom God used to begin the Unceasing Prayer Movement in Austin, Texas. As Kie was cleaning out the office he had inhabited for twenty-six years and moving everything out of it, he came across something he wanted me to share with you. Here is what occurred.

In 1996, I was asked to give the convention sermon to the Southern Baptist Convention in the New Orleans Superdome. Thousands and thousands were present at that time in Southern Baptist life. I shared with them a message about prayer and fasting from the book of Joel. I offered a public invitation that saw hundreds and hundreds of pastors and wives coming forward, pleading with God, seeking God for repentance and spiritual revival, and even committing to prayer and fasting.

Kie Bowman discovered what he had written in his prayer journal about this experience in New Orleans and beyond. I preached that message in early June of 1996. Kie had written in his prayer journal: "July 13, Day 30: What a victory to have fasted for one month. Prior to Ronnie's fast, I would have thought that this length of a fast would be impossible. Praise the Lord. Ten days to go to emulate the fast that Jesus did. I want to be like my Lord."

Kie would tell you that his forty days of prayer and fasting changed his life and future. Glory to God that he can use anyone to inspire others. Kie has been used in mighty ways to inspire many, including me.

There is nothing like inspiring others and being inspired by others through prayer and fasting. Pursuing God together is what every church should do. Whom will you inspire, and whom will your church inspire to pray and fast? This story that I told in that message in the New Orleans Superdome is what God used to encourage Kie Bowman to press on that June morning in 1996 and consider going on a long-term fast. I closed my message in New Orleans that day with the following passionate plea.

What Will Our King Jesus Say?

There was once a page in the king's court. He did not have many important responsibilities until the king called him into the throne room one day. The king handed the boy a scroll, and the following words were written on that parchment: "In the prison across town, there is a man who is going to be hanged today. I have decided to pardon him."

"Quickly," said the king, "take this message to the head jailer."

The little boy was excited about what the king wanted him to do. He ran through the town, thinking over and over about how grateful that prisoner would be, knowing he was now pardoned and would not be hanged. As the boy passed a store, he saw some clothes and thought, *You know, the prisoner will surely need some new clothes for his new life.* So he went into the store and bought a splendid outfit for the one who would soon be free.

He ran a little bit longer, and then, suddenly, he saw a place to eat, so he ran in and got some food for the convicted man because he knew the prisoner would be hungry. So then he started running with all his strength toward the prison. When he arrived, the young boy entered the jailer's office. With a smile on his face, the youngster handed the head jailer the scroll of pardon from the king. The boy said, "This is from the king himself. The man who would be hanged today is to be pardoned."

The jailer shook his head and began to cry. He said, "Oh, son, we executed that prisoner five minutes ago. He is dead. He is dead."

Tears welled in the little boy's eyes as he walked out of the prison and returned to the palace. As he shuffled toward the throne room, the guards could hear him mutter repeatedly, "What is the king going to say? What is the king going to say? What is the king going to say?"

Our King, the Lord of lords, Creator, and Sustainer of all, King Jesus, is coming again. But before he appears, he wants to see a mighty awakening stirring in your life, my life, and churches throughout this nation. If we don't choose to fulfill the spiritual challenges God has issued to us, we may one day walk away in grief, even as that little boy did. In this *kairos* moment—our last, fleeting, opportune moment before the judgment—you and I will know in our hearts that God wanted us to do something great through his power but that we, somehow, were too preoccupied with other distractions to meet the challenge.

Then, on our way to stand before our God, it will dawn on us just exactly what we missed. The breakthroughs were ours for the receiving, but we settled with where we were. As we approach the judgment seat of our Lord Jesus Christ and come face-to-face with the King of kings, the fear of God will overcome us as we realize it is now too late in the day to humble ourselves before the Lord, too late to fast and pray, too late to help others see God's gateway to spiritual breakthroughs.

As these thoughts slam into our hearts, we will find ourselves whispering those same words, *What is our King going to say? What is our King going to say? What is our King going to say?*

Section III

Experiencing the Supernatural Power of Prayer and Fasting Devotions

DAY 1

It Is Time to Fast

I proclaimed a fast there at the river of Ahava.
Ezra 8:21

Knowing God is calling you to pray and fast is very compelling. When you believe it is time to fast, the Holy Spirit has convinced you that now is the time to do it. Whatever the length of the fast, you are making the spiritual decision that God is up to something in your life; therefore, you are pursuing him with all you are and all you have. God's irresistible invitation is for you to elevate your walk with him through prayer and fasting. Knowing God is interested in deepening your relationship with him moves you to enter this moment and season.

Fasting is abstinence from food with a spiritual goal in mind. Fasting is when you choose to give up one of the most natural things your body desires, which is food, to pursue the God of heaven to do something supernatural in your life. Ezra 8:21–23 speaks of Ezra proclaiming a fast for everyone. He was calling the people to submit their lives totally to God. Ezra made a spiritual decision: it is time to fast. This is the same decision you have made today; it is time to fast.

Why did you make this decision? What is driving you and compelling you to fast today? Whatever is moving you to pray and fast, write it down in one statement. This will keep you focused on why you are doing this today and what you are trusting God to do about it. For Ezra, he had a specific and spiritual goal in mind: a safe journey. To get to Jerusalem, they had to go through enemy territory; therefore, he asked the people to pray and fast with him that God would give them safety throughout this journey.

Write down in one clear sentence *why* you are praying and fasting today. Keep it before you all day. If God has given you a Scripture verse or passage to stand upon, write it underneath your request. If you do not have a Scripture verse, ask the Holy Spirit to provide one. It will energize your prayer dynamically and supernaturally when you stand on the Word of God.

God, you have called me to pray and fast today. Please answer my request. Amen.

DAY 2

Humble Yourself before God

I proclaimed a fast there at the river of Ahava,
to humble ourselves before our God.
EZRA 8:21

Whether you are on your first fasting journey or have been on a few already, you learn quickly that a call to fast is also the call to humble yourself before God. The word "humble" means to make yourself low before God and place yourself underneath him. When you respond to God's call to fast, you are simultaneously taking the initiative to humble yourself before God.

I believe there is a link between walking humbly before God and praying with fasting. You are far more likely to walk before God humbly when practicing prayer and fasting. The story of Ezra leading the people to fast is a simple, specific, and clear illustration of the basics of fasting. Ezra proclaimed the fast so that everyone would humble themselves before God. Before God does great things through you, God wants to do great things in you.

When you humble yourself before God through prayer and fasting, he will do great things *in* you, resulting in him doing significant things *through* you. This is precisely what God did with Ezra and the people of God. As they submitted themselves before God, the

Lord provided for them his protection on their journey to Jerusalem. Genuine fasting is never about us. Biblical fasting is about each of us humbling ourselves before God. Whether it was Moses, Isaiah, Ezra, David, Daniel, Jesus, or the early church, fasting always involved humbling oneself before God. We need God and his supernatural power.

Your body may feel weak when you fast, but this can remind you that God is in the process of humbling you. God is strong, and the weaker you become, the more you discover his strength and power. So even as you pray and humble yourself before God, consider kneeling before God at times or lying prostrate on the floor before God, or even sitting before the Lord in a chair just listening, meditating, and waiting before him. Each of these is a way to humble yourself before God.

Lord, I am taking the initiative to humble myself before you. I need your supernatural power in my life. Amen.

Nothing but Prayer and Fasting

*He said to them, "This kind can come out
by nothing by prayer and fasting."*
MARK 9:29 NKJV

As Jesus came down from the Mount of Transfiguration, someone informed him that they had brought their son to his disciples to heal and deliver him from an evil spirit. Yet his disciples were unable to do it. This man also told Jesus that the spirit had possessed the boy since childhood, had made the boy mute, and would throw him down to the ground as he foamed at the mouth. The man asked Jesus if he could do anything about it. Jesus made sure the man understood that Jesus *could* do something about it because all things are possible to those who believe. Jesus then healed the boy, rebuking the unclean spirit, which immediately came out of him. Then he took the boy by his hand and lifted him up.

Jesus' disciples were stirred to ask him why they could not cast out the evil spirit. Jesus told them, "This kind can come out by nothing but prayer and fasting." He pointed out that this miracle over the demonic spirit was an act of faith in God, who can do anything. While some translations of this verse say prayer and fasting, others have only prayer.

The ultimate point here in this passage is that faith

becomes much more significant with prayer and fasting. This kind of faith will move mountains, expel demons from people, and result in mighty miracles to the glory of God. Jesus was very straightforward; this movement of faith comes through prayer and fasting. I call this the supernatural power of prayer and fasting. Right now, you are praying and fasting about some specific matters. Please know that you may be on the verge of seeing God do a miracle. God answers prayer, and he does great things.

Now I realize that you may be on the third day of your fasting journey. This is usually a physically challenging day. If you will continue this fast, on day four, you may physically feel a significant improvement. While this is the usual pattern, each person is different, and their bodies respond uniquely to a fast. God can see you through as you trust him in this prayer and fasting journey.

Jesus, since you can do all things, please answer the prayers I am praying as I fast before you. Amen.

Examining Yourself Honestly before God

If we confess our sins, He is faithful and just to forgive us our sins and to cleanse us from all unrighteousness.
1 JOHN 1:9 NKJV

In these first few days of your fast, it is essential that you examine yourself honestly before God. Refuse to be deceived by yourself. Ask the Holy Spirit to show you any public or private areas of your life that are not pleasing to God. When you try to hide, ignore, or downplay any sin, especially secret sin, remember that God already knows all about them.

Therefore, I want to encourage you to find thirty minutes today with just you and God. Take your Bible with you and open to 1 John 1:9. This text tells us that we are to confess our sins to God. Confession means saying the same thing God says about your sin. What does God say about your sins? Your sin, my sin, and all the sins in the world deserve death, judgment, the grave, and hell. But God also says that he gave his one and only Son, Jesus Christ, to die in our place for our sins. First John 1 also says God "is faithful and just to forgive us our sins and to cleanse us from all unrighteousness." Yes, our sins are washed away by the blood of Jesus.

One of the significant verses in the life of all Jesus'

followers is 1 John 1:9. Therefore, stand upon this Word from God and dive into the challenging waters of evaluating yourself honestly before God.

Now that fasting is quickening your spirit, you will become much more aware of and alert to sinful practices in your life. The Holy Spirit will arrest, convict, and move you to repentance and forgiveness. You will deal with God honestly and perhaps become aware of the need to make things right with other people.

One of the helpful tools in this book can be found toward the end of chapter four but also in the Appendices section of the book. Look to the section called "Examine Yourself" at the end of chapter four. As God reveals your sin, confess it, turn from it, and receive God's forgiveness. Then rejoice; you are forgiven!

Lord Jesus, wash me and cleanse me from all my sin. I want you to cleanse me of all sin and unrighteousness. I receive it now. Amen.

Seeking God Specifically

*I proclaimed a fast there at the river of Ahava, to humble
ourselves before our God, to seek from Him a safe
journey for us, our little ones, and all our possessions.*

EZRA 8:21

For many of you going through these forty days of
prayer and fasting devotions, you are now fasting on
your fifth day. In most of my extended prayer and fasting journeys, day five is when I feel so much stronger
physically and even more empowered spiritually. So to
God's praise and glory alone, I hope you will become
stronger throughout this entire day as you pursue God
on this prayer and fasting journey.

I believe that some of your strength spiritually
comes on this day because you are beginning to have
a greater understanding and clarity about your concerns and various matters you are addressing with God
through the fast. As the Holy Spirit awakens and ignites
your spirit, he will bring much greater clarity when you
approach God in prayer.

Now I would like to be clear about all of this. God
is not the problem. We are the problem. Due to running so fast through life and, at times, living all over the
map of our schedules and places we are supposed to be,
we become disoriented spiritually. We lose our spiritual

equilibrium. But when we practice prayer and fasting, we hear God calling us into order again.

Seeking God specifically about your concerns is essential. When you look further into Ezra 8:21, you will see that not only did Ezra proclaim a fast and call the people to humble themselves before God, but he did so with a specific goal that God had put in his heart: a safe journey for everyone! This includes even the little ones and the possessions God had given everyone. In your present prayer and fasting journey, seek God specifically. As you become more alert to the Spirit of God, you will receive a growing clarity about *what* you are praying for and *how* you should pray for it. I have discovered through the years that this is the purifying process of God adjusting your mind, emotions, and will to his sovereign and providential will. Therefore, seek God about your requests specifically.

Father, please purify my mind, emotions, and will to your sovereign and providential will throughout this journey. I trust you. Amen.

God Is Remaking You

*"Behold, like the clay in the potter's hand,
so are you in My hand."*
JEREMIAH 18:6

Throughout my life, I have repeatedly had to come to this reality: God is making a man. As difficult as some situations and circumstances are that may alter my entire life and trajectory, I still must come to the biblical reality that my life and future are in God's hands. Therefore, the only way to go forward purposefully is to know God is still making a man, and I am this man.

In Jeremiah 18:1–6, we learn how the potter takes the spoiled clay and remakes it into another vessel. He does this in a way that pleases him. The application of this story is powerful. God is the Potter. We are like the clay in his hand. He takes us as we are, broken, sinful, and spoiled. Then, he remakes us into another vessel. By God's grace and for his glory, God fashions us and forms us into something different and new, always doing with us whatever he deems is best.

Even as I share this with you, I am overcome with God's personal involvement in our lives. When walking through personal problems and difficult circumstances that may be entirely out of our control, we may question where God is and what God is up to in our lives.

However, we must do all we can to see things from God's perspective. He is our Potter. We are like the spoiled clay in his hand. Our Sovereign Father takes each of us in his hands and remakes us into another vessel. We become newly created vessels God has prepared for his purpose in these times. As David declared, so we must join him in declaring with confidence and faith, "My times are in Your hand" (Psalm 31:15).

When you pray and fast, truths like this will become ever more prevalent in your life and future. Through this journey that you are on presently, God is remaking you into another vessel, whatever he deems as best. He creates a new you, constantly reshaping you to become more like Jesus. God *is* at work in your life.

Father, I am in your hands. Remake me to be the person you deem best for today and the future. Amen.

Trusting God through Prayer and Fasting

We fasted and sought our God over this matter.
EZRA 8:23

After decades of studying the Scriptures about prayer and fasting, as well as teaching, preaching, and writing about it through the years, and practicing prayer and fasting personally, I have recently come to believe that Ezra 8:21–23, along with verse 31, is the simplest, clearest, and most concise passage of Scripture to teach about fasting. It summarizes the biblical principles you need to know and will take you on any experience you will have through prayer and fasting. So whenever you pray about and prepare to enter either a one-day fast or an extended season of fasting, remember Ezra 8:21–23 and verse 31.

Ezra and the Israelites made the spiritual decision to fast and decided to humble themselves before God through fasting, seeking God for a specific need and trusting God to hear and answer their prayers. Reread this, "So we fasted and sought our God concerning this matter" (v. 23). This verse demonstrates the importance of trusting God through prayer and fasting.

Some of you who are reading this are on your seventh consecutive day of praying and fasting. Whether you conclude your fast at the end of today or continue to fast through ten days, twenty-one days, or even forty days, you may have discovered already, and will even more so in the immediate future, that you are trusting God continually. Moment by moment, day by day, and night by night, you are trusting him to see you through physically but also to see you through spiritually as you constantly share with him your concerns and the matters on your heart in this fast. By the way, congratulations on praying and fasting for seven days. Now, praise the Lord for seeing you through. If God leads you, continue the journey with trust and humility.

Whether you are walking on this prayer journey or have joined it with fasting, keep your eyes and heart on trusting God. Continually seek him about what he is leading you to pray through. Call it out to him constantly.

Dear Lord Jesus, I trust you with all the concerns and burdens I am presenting to you constantly. Amen.

DAY 8

Resetting Your Life

"Behold, I am going to do something new."
ISAIAH 43:19

While we trust God through prayer and fasting, we also trust God through the days when we are not fasting. One of the plentiful treasures we have in the Bible is that God reminds us of how he has worked in the past to prepare us for the uncertain days ahead of us.

In Isaiah 43, God reminds us that no god was formed before him, and there will be none after him (v. 10). No one can formulate future history, and no one can revise the history of the past. Nevertheless, God is alive and active everywhere. As God was faithful to lead his people out of Egypt, through the wilderness, and into the promised land, so he will do the same for his people in the future. Therefore, you can trust him. His character is pure and holy. Consequently, he does everything he says he will do.

Based upon all these things, God declares remarkably that his people do not need to call to mind the former things he has done or to live in the past. Why is this? God resounds triumphantly: "Behold, I am going to do something new." God called his people to reset their thinking and their lives in Isaiah 43, and I believe this is one of the greatest needs today. Resetting your

287

life means that you are changing to a new direction. Sometimes this may require you to delete the past to readjust your life to a new future.

The powerful hope in Isaiah 43:19 is that God promises you that he is going to do something new. Remember, he always does what he says he will do. I believe God is calling upon us to reset our lives. So expect God to do something new in you![24]

Praying and fasting are spiritual instruments that God uses to reset you for the future God has ready for you. When you pray and fast, whatever God does in resetting your life will transform you, guide you, protect you, and provide for you. So by faith, expect God to do something new.

God, I am counting on you to do something new in and through me. So please reset my life and future to your will. Amen.

God Resets Your Life Continually

"Behold, I am going to do something new, now it will spring up; will you not be aware of it? I will make a roadway in the wilderness, rivers in the desert."
ISAIAH 43:19

God resets your life continually. This should be no surprise to us because nothing ever stays the same. This includes you and me. God cherishes his relationship with each of us. He created each of us uniquely and has a plan for our lives. Therefore, be assured and be encouraged to know that God resets your life continually. He does it for your good and his glory.

This does not minimize or diminish a prayer and fasting journey because these are spiritual instruments that God uses supernaturally. Furthermore, when we initiate prayer and fasting in our lives, God uses them to forward our walk and relationship with Christ Jesus our Lord. As today's Scripture verse tells us, his work will spring up suddenly. Just as grass springs up and leaves and flowers will come forth seemingly overnight, so God works in our lives. He resets us continually. His providence becomes evident in life. There are times when God's providence makes roadways in the wilderness, and other times when he creates rivers in the desert. God's providence is always with us, and he is the one who always resets our lives.

Recently, I was studying the life of Joseph. Do you realize that when Jesus was born, God reset Joseph's life for the future? First, God sent Joseph, Mary, and Jesus from Bethlehem to Egypt, and then after Herod's death, sent them to Israel to live in the Galilean region in Nazareth. Reset upon reset occurred in Joseph's life, and God used adversity to bring about some of them. When you walk through adversity, God is resetting your life. Even the delays you face, the detours that may frustrate you, and the failures that you will experience—none of these are fatal, but God uses each to reset your life in ways you may not understand.

Therefore, Jesus' followers, please understand that one of the blessings of grace is that Jesus never gives up on you and will reset your life continually.

Jesus, thank you for your grace. Thank you for resetting my life continually. Amen

God Answers Your Prayer and Fasting

He listened to our pleading…He rescued us from the
hand of the enemy and the ambushes by the road.
EZRA 8:23, 31

I have some great news to share with you on this, your
tenth day of prayer and fasting. Before I share this good
news from the Scriptures, I praise God with you for his
empowerment upon you for these ten days. His miraculous and supernatural hand is helping you in this
journey. If anyone has cast suspicion upon you or even
criticized you for doing this, let it go. Unless someone
has been here, they will never understand that for Jesus'
followers, fasting for ten days is only possible through
God alone.

In these first ten days, what has God said to you?
What sin has he revealed in your life that you have
repented of already? Is there anything he has already
spoken to you about the future? Did you make sure you
wrote it down? Every time God speaks to you specifically, always write it down. This documents your walk
with Christ, which will create even greater faith in years
to come. Therefore, I have saved these words for this
important day because I want you to know that God
answers your prayer and fasting.

It was a powerful decision when Ezra declared the fast. It was a powerful decision when the people affirmed it and followed his lead. With prayer and fasting, they humbled themselves before God and sought God specifically for a safe journey. As they trusted God, look at what God did. Their testimony was powerful as they declared that God had listened to their pleading and that God rescued them "from the hand of the enemy and the ambushes along the way." So the great news is that God answers your prayer and fasting!

In the future, pray and fast as God leads you, but above all, you must have the hand of God upon you as Ezra and the people had God's hand upon them. This demonstrated the supernatural power of prayer and fasting before the world. God can do more in a moment than you can ever do in a lifetime. God can do anything he desires anytime, with anyone, anywhere. This includes you.

Oh God, put your hand on me. Please be sure to keep your hand on me. Amen.

DAY 11

Reconnecting with the Manifested Presence of God

"Yet even now," declares the LORD, *"Return to Me with all your heart, and with fasting, weeping, and mourning."*
JOEL 2:12

One of the most significant realities that occur when we pray and fast is that we reconnect with the manifested presence of God. In Joel 2, God tells the people how to reconnect with him and his manifested presence. God expressed his urgent appeal to return to him with the words, "Even now." How did God instruct his people to return to the Lord? God wanted them and he wants you to return with your whole heart today by fasting, weeping, and mourning.

Indeed, God's desire is for you not to have dual allegiance but a singular allegiance to God alone. In other words, God wants you to have a 100 percent commitment to him. This leads to how God wants you to return—with all your heart, fasting, weeping, and mourning over your personal sin. So if you want to reconnect with God's manifested presence, now is the time to do it with all your heart through fasting, weeping, and mourning.

We should be broken over our sins, the church's sins, and the nation's sins. We demonstrate our brokenness over these matters through weeping and mourning. God is calling his people to repent and turn back to him. If we do this, we will reconnect with God and his manifested presence. Revival is the manifested presence of God. Brokenness leads to repentance. Repentance leads to revival. Revival leads to awakening.

For those fasting right now, be encouraged because you are on the pathway to experiencing the manifested presence of God. It is possible that through eleven days of fasting, you are much more aware of Jesus' manifested presence now than when you started fasting. The world is noisy and very distracting. It distracts you from God working in your life. However, I have found that when I pray and fast, the noise disappears, and God's voice, the Lion of Judah, becomes a roar. So now is a great time to reconnect with God's presence through your prayers and fasting.

Holy Spirit, I want to experience your presence mightily. Revive me! Amen.

What Burden Is Moving You to Pray and Fast?

When I heard these words, I sat down and wept and mourned for days; and I was fasting and praying before the God of heaven.
NEHEMIAH 1:4

God often places upon us a burden that moves us to think about praying. When he does this, it serves as an invitation from him to pray and fast. While some burdens we obtain bring us concern, there are other burdens that move us so much that we feel this burden personally, deeply, and significantly. It should also move us to consider addressing this burden through prayer and fasting.

What burden has moved you to pray and fast for the past eleven days? If a burden is driving you, then identify it. Write it down and keep it before you. Then, when a desire for food comes, refer to what you have written down and call it out to God immediately. Stand upon Scripture and ask the Father in Jesus' name to do what you desire him to do about the burden you are carrying.

Nehemiah was a great example of someone who had a heavy burden. While in exile from Jerusalem, Nehemiah became extremely burdened when he heard the news that the walls around Jerusalem were down, that the gates had been burned with fire, and that God's people were in great distress. He was moved to prayer and fasting. He asked the king to send him back there to rebuild the walls. King Artaxerxes permitted him to return and rebuild the wall. God moved Nehemiah and the people of God to finish the wall in fifty-two days. It was a mighty miracle of God. The Lord did a mighty miracle in the face of threats, false accusations, and multiple rumors. This happened because it began with a burden, a genuine prayer and fasting burden.

God controls the outcome, but we get the privilege of carrying our burdens to God through prayer and fasting.

I have discovered these realities about burdens and prayer and fasting:

- The greater the burden, the more you will be compelled to carry it with fasting and prayer.
- The greater the burden, the more it may impact the length of your fast.

Is God speaking to you right now? If so, what is he saying? Do what God says.

Lord, help me to discern when you want me to pray and fast about a burden. Amen.

Personal Desperation Moves You to Pray and Fast

As the deer pants for the water brooks,
so my soul pants for you, God.
PSALM 42:1

I have been told that in the desert regions of the Middle East, one can see herds of deer gathering near the water brooks. The heat is so high that the water brooks are a major relief for them. Conversely, the Scripture says that the deer pants for the water brooks. The panting demonstrates the intensity and desperation for water. This specific word chosen here in the Hebrew text was used only one other time in Scripture, in Joel 1:20, which describes the animals' intense desire for water during the drought. "Even the animals of the field pant for You; for the stream beds of water are dried up, and fire has devoured the pastures of the wilderness." The drought described by Joel was the result of God's judgment.[25]

The deer had an intense desire to be able to drink from the water brooks. They were desperate for water. The Scriptures say we need to have this same intense desire to go after and come to God. Do you have that same kind of intense desire to walk with God closely, follow him, chase after him, spend time with him, or have him work powerfully in and throughout your life?

When we do, we will practice prayer and fasting. When we do not have that intensity, we should consider prayer and fasting as a way to regain the intensity for God we may have once had in our lives.

I believe parents, pastors, politicians, and even powerful CEOs are becoming more desperate by the day for something positive to occur in their lives, families, businesses, communities, and across our nation. As desperation increases across America and the world, we must act in these unprecedented times. Praying and fasting are proper responses for Jesus' followers to take when we yearn for, desire greatly, and intensely need a move of God in our life, family, business, or community. Desperation may indicate that God wants to do something about your concern; therefore, intensely pursue him through prayer and fasting. Then overflow with hope. Help is on the way!

God, I desire you intensely, so please work in my life. Please lead me. Amen.

Your Personal Need May Move You to Pray and Fast

Do not be anxious about anything, but in everything by prayer and pleading with thanksgiving let your requests be made known to God.

PHILIPPIANS 4:6

I believe that God creates or allows a need, a problem, or a challenge, to call us to seek him through prayer and fasting. Have you found this to be true? Everyone has needs. Everyone has problems. Everyone faces challenges. Not one of us is exempt from any of these. So when we have them, what is one godly response? One response is entering a day, several days, or a season of prayer and fasting.

Prayer and fasting can lessen or even eliminate your anxiety and worry about any personal need, problem, or challenge. The Scripture verse above says to take these things to the Lord in prayer and plead with him to intervene. He will not shun you because he says to make your requests known to God. While prayer and fasting are not mentioned in this text, does this mean they do not apply? Absolutely not! When these needs, problems, and challenges occur, we must take whatever action possible, including even prayer and fasting.

While we may think up ten reasons why we should

not do it, God is calling us to him. Whatever the need, whatever the challenge, whatever the problem, most often, seeds of prayer, faith, and at times fasting precede God's mighty and miraculous intervention. This intervention may give you greater wisdom, perspective, or even the miracle of eliminating the problem, challenge, or need. Our God is certainly able! He can do anything! So you can talk to him about it. Make your requests known to God.

Your personal need may move you to enter a season of prayer and fasting. I can tell you this through personal testimony that each time I take a need to God in prayer with fasting, God moves powerfully in my life or situation. As I have said, prayer and fasting prepare your heart and shape your perspective on life and situations.

What problem are you facing? What is your challenge? What is your need? Whatever it may be, pray and fast for God to intervene and help you.

God, please intervene in my life. I need your favor, wisdom, and miracle. Amen.

Decision-Making Moves You to Pray and Fast

"Truly, truly, I say to you, the Son can do nothing of Himself, unless it is something He sees the Father doing; for whatever the Father does, these things the Son also does in the same way."

JOHN 5:19

Jesus gave profound insight into decision-making in John 5:19. Notice what Jesus said. Jesus told the people that the Son could do nothing of himself unless he saw the Father doing it. Then Jesus said the Son could do these things if he saw the Father doing them. Whatever the Father is doing is God's will. Therefore, the question is, *What is the Father doing?*

Decision-making is a huge part of life. Each of us is a product of the decisions we make. We usually do not delegate others to make our personal decisions, nor should we. Once we are adults, each of us is responsible for our own decision-making. If we make good decisions, we will likely continue to make more good decisions. Conversely, we will most likely continue on an unfortunate path if we do not make good decisions.

As Christ-followers, we need to consider prayer and fasting before we make major decisions. Fasting awakens your spirit and calls your body, mind, will, and emotions to attention. The more your spirit is aligned with God's Spirit, the more you will see things more accurately and clearly. Anyone who has ever fasted has experienced this; you know what I am talking about. If decision-making has moved you to pray and fast, as you do, I want to share these steps with you:

- Identify the decision you are making. Write it down.

- Ask God to show you his will as you pray and fast.

- Focus on what God says about this decision by reading his Word because it is our most reliable source of decision-making, and it can guide you to the will of the Father.

- As you pray and fast, you will also learn God's will by evaluating the circumstances, listening to people around you, and meditating on what he is putting in your heart.

If we want to do God's will, we must continually ask what the Father is doing. What is God doing right now around the world? The critical question is: What does God want you to do? Whatever you believe he is doing, join him in it.

Lord, many decisions are before me each day. Lead me, Holy Spirit. Amen.

Prayer and Fasting Prepare You

For forty days, [Jesus was] tempted by the devil.
And He ate nothing during those days,
and when they had ended, He was hungry.
Luke 4:2

Jesus spent forty days praying and fasting before his public ministry began. Following Jesus' water baptism in the Jordan River by John the Baptist, the Holy Spirit led Jesus into the wilderness to go on a forty-day journey with God. The Bible says that during this time, Jesus fasted from food entirely. Throughout those days, he encountered ongoing attacks and temptations from the devil, but Jesus prevailed victoriously.

Jesus prayed and fasted forty days before his public ministry began. This preparation time was well spent because he communed with God only, withdrawing from everyone and everything else. Jesus knew this one-on-one time with his Father was exactly what he needed for the days ahead. These days were days of preparation.

One of the most significant values of prayer and fasting is preparation. God uses prayer and fasting to prepare us for whatever may be ahead of us. God uses prayer and fasting to clean us up internally and spiritually, and he uses prayer and fasting to purify and prepare us physically. This spiritual and supernatural experience also calls into order the mind, the will, and the emotions. Yes, God prepares us through prayer and fasting.

God uses every journey in prayer and fasting to prepare us for whatever may be ahead. Through this spiritual experience, he creates within you a new perspective about the prayer requests you wanted to talk to him about on this fasting journey. Prayer and fasting do not guarantee that he will answer your prayers as you desire them to be answered. Nonetheless, he will supernaturally prepare your heart for however he responds to your requests, burdens, and challenges.

God also uses prayer and fasting to prepare you for any specific task, calling, or vision he has asked you to do. For example, when significant opportunities have come to me for preaching, leadership, or vision, God used days of prayer and fasting to prepare me for what he asked me to do. Prayer and fasting prepare you for whatever is before you.

Lord, please prepare me for whatever lies ahead of me. I surrender to you. Amen.

DAY 17

Prayer and Fasting Empower You Supernaturally

Jesus returned to Galilee in the power of the Spirit, and news about Him spread through all the surrounding region.
LUKE 4:14

The Bible tells us that when Jesus was baptized with water by John the Baptist, heaven opened, and the Holy Spirit came upon Jesus in bodily form like a dove. From heaven, God said to Jesus, "You are My beloved Son, in You I am well-pleased" (Luke 3:22). Then we read in Luke 4, "Now Jesus, full of the Holy Spirit, returned from the Jordan and was led around by the Spirit in the wilderness" (v. 1). The Holy Spirit came upon Jesus.

After John baptized him, Jesus was full of the Holy Spirit, and then the Spirit led him around in the wilderness for forty days as he prayed and fasted. The Bible says that when his days of prayer and fasting were over, Jesus returned to Galilee in the power of the Spirit. It is significant for us to note this progression. After the Holy Spirit came upon Jesus, he was full of the Spirit, was led around by the Spirit, and following his time of prayer and fasting for forty days, he returned to Galilee in the power of the Holy Spirit.

Jesus experienced fresh power and anointing through prayer and fasting. He even publicly proclaimed this when he said, "The Spirit of the LORD is upon Me, because He anointed Me to bring good news to the poor" (v. 18). Jesus was given this special anointing of the Holy Spirit to do his ministry on this earth. Jesus was the living manifestation of the presence and power of God on this earth.

Praying and fasting can empower you supernaturally. We cannot ignore that there is something powerful about simply obeying what God says to do. Do you want fresh spiritual power in your life? Do you desire a new and powerful anointing in your life? Since Jesus, the Son of God, felt the personal need to practice prayer and fasting, you should also feel the need. Whatever your vocation, desire to live with the Holy Spirit upon you, filling you, leading you, and empowering you supernaturally.

Holy Spirit, come upon me, filling, leading, and empowering me supernaturally. I need Holy Spirit power and anointing daily. Amen.

Restlessness Moves You
to Pray and Fast

The peace of God, which surpasses all comprehension,
will guard your hearts and minds in Christ Jesus.
PHILIPPIANS 4:7

If you are still participating at some level of prayer and fasting during this forty-day journey, I know the personal challenge in this period of the fast. On day eighteen, you are probably feeling the challenge mentally and spiritually. You may even wonder, *Can I continue going forward?* At the same time, I know well from my extended fasting journeys that I usually feel very well physically during this time. So the challenge to continue to completion, whether twenty-one days or forty days, is more mental and spiritual at this point. Additionally, you may begin to feel emotional because you are missing the special times of fellowshipping over mealtimes. I have found that participating at some mealtimes while I am fasting does not bother me or tempt me when I am fasting. On the contrary, I find it refreshing to do this.

So how do you work through this restlessness? First, let me remind you that many times, an ongoing feeling of restlessness moves us into a journey to pray and fast. You are feeling that same restlessness again but differently at this point of the journey. Anytime a spirit of restlessness comes upon us, we can be sure that God wants us to come to him and experience his peace.

We can find God's peace only in his presence. God can give us supernatural peace during our most complex and challenging times. This peace, described in Philippians 4:7, can be so obvious and powerful that it rises above our ability to understand how it occurs, and simultaneously, God's peace serves as a guard over our lives when we present our requests to him.

God's peace overcomes the spirit of restlessness, worry, and other anxieties. He is calling us to come to him. After all, he is the Prince of Peace. God wants to give you a spirit of peace about who you are, what you are doing, and where you live while doing it. So when you have that restless feeling, go to God in prayer and fasting. You will always find peace in the presence of God.

Prince of Peace, Jesus Christ, give me peace today on my spiritual journey with you through prayer and fasting. Amen.

Praying with Others
While Praying and Fasting

*All these were continually devoting themselves
with one mind to prayer.*

ACTS 1:14

Extraordinary prayer precedes every great movement of God. After Jesus was crucified, buried, and then rose from the dead, he walked on this earth for forty days, speaking of things regarding the kingdom of God. After his ascension into heaven, there was a ten-day period before the coming of the Holy Spirit on the day of Pentecost. What happened during those ten days?

In the first chapter of Acts, we learn that about one hundred twenty believers had a prayer meeting together. "They were continually devoting themselves with one mind to prayer." It is evident from the language used in this verse that there was an ongoing experience of prayer happening over those ten days. I am assuming there was a constant movement of prayer occurring. During those days, they may have had personal moments to refresh themselves with rest and food. But what we do know is that they prayed together. They were praying in agreement and with unity. They obeyed Jesus because he told them to wait and that power would come upon them. On the day of Pentecost, this occurred.

This prayer journey was extraordinary because of its length, which was over ten days. It was extraordinary because of its content because we know it was a prayer meeting. It was extraordinary in power because they were unceasingly praying with one mind and in one accord. Therefore, the church was born in and through a prayer meeting. While their extraordinary prayer was occurring, the Holy Spirit came upon the people on the day of Pentecost, three thousand were baptized, and the world has never been the same.

We do not know if any or all of the apostles were fasting as they prayed over these ten days, but we do know they were together and praying. I encourage you to pray with other people even while you are on this journey of prayer and fasting. Many churches that practice church-wide fasts also try to have prayer gatherings when they are doing it. Prayer meetings change the world.

God, bring to my mind some people I can reach out to today so we can pray together. Amen.

Write Down Whatever God Is Saying

*The word that came to Jeremiah from the L*ORD*, saying,
"This is what the L*ORD*, the God of Israel says: 'Write all
the words which I have spoken to you in a book.'"*
JEREMIAH 30:1–2

Do you realize we have the Bible to read and study because someone wrote it down for us? Someone wrote down every book of the Bible. We know that each of these books, chapters, and verses is inspired by God. Yes, God breathed these words into people's minds and hearts. Then someone wrote it down as a matter of record, a record of what God said to write down. The Scripture tells us these words, "Men moved by the Holy Spirit spoke from God" (2 Peter 1:21).

In the book of Jeremiah, the Lord spoke to the prophet and told him to "write all the words which I have spoken to you in a book." God wanted Jeremiah to document and record what God was saying to him so he could share it with others. We benefit from the Bible because someone wrote down whatever God inspired them to write.

Are you writing down what God is speaking to you? Since January 1, 1990, I have done this daily. This becomes even more intentional when I go on a prayer and fasting journey. What do I do? Let me tell you:

- I write down the Scripture text, truth, principle, or even strong impression I am getting from God on this journey.
- Throughout the fast, I try to review it regularly.
- On the final day of the fast or the morning after I complete the fast, I take a highlight pen and go through my journal, asking the Holy Spirit to speak to me about those things that are the most impactful.
- Then I go back through it, reading only the highlighted sections, and ask God to speak about any of these he wants me to pray about daily. If God so directs, those intentions go into my prayer journal so that I will pray for them daily.
- Writing down what God speaks to you is a beneficial exercise.

Lord, as you speak to me, I will write it down so I can put it into my life daily. Amen.

Ask God to Set
Your Heart on Fire

They said to one another, "Were our hearts not burning within us when He was speaking to us on the road, while He was explaining the Scriptures to us?"
LUKE 24:32

This is a very significant day for each of you on an extended fast. If you are fasting for twenty-one days, your fast will conclude today. I rejoice with you and praise God for sustaining you this entire time. If you are on your way to accomplishing a forty-day fast, your fast is more than halfway completed. This is a huge blessing and a testimony of God's sustaining power in your life. As you go forward, you will need God's power more than ever before.

So whether you are completing the twenty-one-day fast or on your way to the forty-day fast, ask God to set your heart on fire with the Holy Spirit's power and fire. We must have the fire of the Holy Spirit!

After Jesus had been resurrected from the dead, he walked on the road to Emmaus. As he walked, he began talking to two sad-looking men who were also traveling on this road. The men, who did not recognize Jesus, told him they had hoped that Jesus, who had just been crucified, would be the Messiah to redeem Israel. But now, even his body was missing. As Jesus talked to them, he explained what the Scriptures said about him. When evening came, Jesus came into their house to stay with them. But when Jesus took the bread, blessed it, and handed it out to them, they suddenly realized who they had been talking to. It was Jesus! Yes, the resurrected Jesus! As they ran back to Jerusalem to tell the other disciples, they made the powerful statement that their hearts were burning when Jesus spoke to them from the Scriptures.

When you pray and fast, Jesus is the only one who can set your heart on fire. Likewise, Jesus' Word, the Bible, sets us on fire as we learn it and grow to hear what God is saying to us. Therefore, from this day forward in your life, ask God to set your heart on fire with the Holy Spirit and the Word of God.

Lord, please set my heart on fire with your Holy Spirit and the Word of God. Amen.

DAY 22

The Power of One Hour with God

In the morning, L<small>ORD</small>, You will hear my voice;
in the morning I will present my prayer to You
and be on the watch.
P<small>SALM</small> 5:3

One of the most defining moments in my life happened in the spring semester of my first year in college. After spending some time with a great man of God who was mentoring a friend and me, I asked him this question: "If you could tell me one thing I could do as a minister that would really make a difference, what would it be?" Without hesitancy, he looked at me with piercing eyes from under his bushy eyebrows and said: "Ronnie, if you could begin to spend one hour a day with God, there is no telling what God will do with you." I was young but hungry and thirsty for God. Therefore, the next day I implemented this one hour with God.

Throughout all these years, I have spent at least the first hour of the day with God. My time alone with God now goes for almost two hours daily. This is my most important appointment each day, and I never compromise it. It is the first thing I do very early each morning.

As you are on day twenty-two of your fast, stretch your spiritual life each day by spending the first hour with God. You may be doing this on the fast already but consider continuing to reserve the first hour for God each day once your fast is complete. If you can pray and fast for twenty-two days consecutively, then you can start each day by spending at least one hour with him. David spent the early mornings with God. With urgency in the mornings, he would pray daily and ask God for protection, and he expected God to move in to help him. David was a mighty prayer warrior and a man after God's own heart.

I want to urge you to do everything you can each morning to rise and spend at least the first hour of your day with God. The power of one hour with him will become a significant and defining decision in your life.

Lord, I will call upon you in prayer in the morning. I will prioritize this time and pray that you will make it a defining decision in my life. Amen.

Praying Early in the Morning

In the early morning, while it was still dark, Jesus got up, left the house, and went away to a secluded place, and prayed there for a time.

MARK 1:35

There is great value in praying in the early morning. Jesus did this, and we should consider doing it also. The Scripture tells us what Jesus did. Jesus disciplined himself to rise early before the day dawned, leaving his house and going to a secluded place to pray for a time. These principles are priceless.

We learn that before the day's dawning, we should rise from sleep, go into a private place, and pray for a time. If you cannot get the privacy you need to pray in your home, consider leaving your house to find a place to pray. The most important thing you need to do is pray, so set a time and place daily for prayer.

I do want to ask you this question, and I challenge you to wrestle with it until you settle it: If Jesus, the Son of God, needed to rise early in the morning, even before the dawning of the day, to pray for a time, don't you think you will find some value in doing the same? Your prayer life each day is between you and God. I want to challenge you to consider what Jesus did. I am convinced that the first hour of your day, every day, will help you keep the lens clear in your life and give you a greater perspective for each day.

As you develop your prayer life with this incredible commitment to fasting for these twenty-three days consecutively, you will desire to elevate your prayer life once this fast is over. What we discussed in the devotions for yesterday and today will help you immensely. I close with these important realities:

- Your prayer life in your walk with God determines everything about your life.
- The power of one hour of early morning prayer and devotion will transcend into every segment of your entire life.
- As you deepen your prayer life while walking with God, he will broaden your influence.

Praying in the early morning will add great value to your life.

Oh God, I desire to spend time with you daily in the early morning. Empower me to rise and meet with you. Amen.

Praying in the Holy Spirit

You, beloved, building yourselves up on your most holy faith, praying in the Holy Spirit.
JUDE 1:20

Jude was a man for his time as he had significant concerns about the culture and its godless influence invading the church. Therefore, he wrote a letter to Christians about the basics of the faith and living the Christian life. Jude contended earnestly for the faith.

Jude understood the importance of truth and the significance of prayer in the life of Jesus' followers. Prayer and the Holy Spirit are connected. Jude presents a healthy balance of having the most holy faith built upon God's truth and understanding the importance of praying in the Holy Spirit. Jude was a Christian leader committed to the Word and the Spirit. We should also be. The Scriptures teach us to pray in the Holy Spirit. What does it mean to pray in the Holy Spirit? It means to pray

- As the Holy Spirit leads you. Be willing to sit before the Lord and let the Holy Spirit lead you in what to pray for and how to pray for it. As the Spirit leads you, you will pray by the Word of God and with the Word of God.

- As the Holy Spirit assists you. There are times when you do not know how to pray; therefore, be still, open the Bible, and ask the Holy Spirit to help you.
- As the Holy Spirit empowers you. The power of God in prayer precedes the demonstrations of the power of God through his people publicly. Everything goes to a new level when the Spirit's power comes.

Praying and fasting elevates praying in the Holy Spirit, and praying in the Holy Spirit elevates prayer and fasting. The key to a powerful prayer life is praying in the Holy Spirit. In your private prayer life and in your church's prayer time, consider sitting before the Lord quietly, letting the Holy Spirit speak to you, and asking him to lead you to pray as the Spirit wills, which will always be built upon the Word. Then pray as he leads you. Pray in the Holy Spirit.

Father, I want to pray in the Holy Spirit. Please teach me how to do this built upon the Word of God and with the power of the Holy Spirit. Amen.

Praying and Fasting
in Jesus' Name

*"Truly, truly I say to you, if you ask the Father for
anything in My name, He will give it to you."*
JOHN 16:23

When you pray and fast, God teaches you many things
about prayer. The Bible is full of incredible insights, such
as praying early in the morning in a private place and
praying in the Holy Spirit as you stand upon the Word
of God. There is another one I want to share with you
today that you may practice now.

In John 16, Jesus taught us one of the critical principles of prayer that also influences fasting. When we
pray to the Father and ask him for anything, we know
he is our King of kings and Lord of lords. He is superior
to us in every way and everything. But we have access
to God always and can talk to him about anything, anywhere, at any time. This is possible when we come into
his holy presence and make our requests known to God
in Jesus' name. Doing this is so powerful that Jesus said
that when we ask anything in Jesus' name, God will give
it to us.

As we pray and fast, we do so in Jesus' name. Why is
praying and fasting in Jesus' name so important?

- Jesus' name is the entry point into the presence of God. Remember, Jesus is the only way for you, the only truth for you, and the only life for you eternally. So the next time you are given an entry code or key into a room or any door, remember that this is what Jesus' name is to you so that you can come into the presence of God.

- Jesus' name is your authority in all your requests to God. Since Jesus is the most powerful name in all of heaven and earth, tie your request in prayer and fasting to Jesus' name because Jesus is Lord and has all authority. When you offer your requests to God in Jesus' name, you submit everything to God's will, and the Father knows this.

Connect your prayer and fasting with Jesus' name. There is really something powerful about that name.

Father, in Jesus' name, I am praying and fasting. So God's will be done. Amen.

Total Surrender to God's Will

*"Father, if You are willing, remove this cup from Me;
yet not My will, but Yours be done."*
LUKE 22:42

One of my favorite places in Israel is the Garden of Gethsemane. This area is sacred ground to Christians because it is where Jesus poured his heart out to the Father in prayer in such a way that his sweat became like drops of blood dripping onto the ground. Even knowing crucifixion was ahead, Jesus totally surrendered himself to the Father's will: "Not My will, but Yours be done."

Total surrender to God's will when you pray and fast should emulate the heart and prayer of Jesus that night in Gethsemane. While this is not easy, it is important that you do it. At all times, we must totally surrender everything to God.

It is good for us to remember that our role is to pray and fast; then God alone determines when and how he will answer those prayers. God alone determines the timing and the results; we do not. Prayer leads us to experience the power of God, most especially when we pray in Jesus' name and do so according to his will as recorded in the Bible. We must never forget that we can discover God's will in God's Word. Prayer and fasting move our hearts toward God's will more than our prayers ever move God. Therefore, total surrender to God's will when you pray and fast is more likely to occur when you do these things:

- Pray according to the Scriptures and stand upon the Scriptures when you pray. In the Bible, God reveals to you his will.

- Present your request to God, trusting in him alone to determine when and how he will answer. When we do not know God's will regarding a decision we must make, we need to present it to God and trust him alone to determine what happens.

- Prayer is faith, and your dependence upon God builds faith.

Therefore, you should learn to surrender totally to God's will when you pray and fast. Always remember Jesus' words: "Not My will, but Yours be done."

Father, in Jesus' name, I am standing upon your Word, praying now: Not my will, but your will be done. Amen.

Prayer and Fasting Strengthens Warfare Prayers

*Be of sober spirit, be on the alert. Your adversary,
the devil, prowls around like a roaring lion,
seeking someone to devour.*
1 PETER 5:8

The closer you get to God, the more you will face spiritual attacks. The devil is dangerous. He slanders, accuses, destroys, and devours. Just as an animal swallows its prey, so Satan can eat you up and drink you down. You must always know who your real enemy is, as Peter writes in 1 Peter 5:8. Satan is your fiercest enemy and your most threatening opponent in everything. So take him seriously and always be alert and awake, ready for his attacks.

When we pray and fast, we are more prepared to encounter the Enemy with greater spiritual strength and to do warfare praying. Therefore, as we humble ourselves through prayer and fasting, we should be more on the alert for the Enemy's attacks and have God's perspective about them.

So what is warfare praying, and how can you apply it to your life? Warfare praying is praying against Satan. We are told in Ephesians 6 to stand firm against the schemes of the devil by putting on the armor of

God and praying in the Spirit. As Jesus' followers, the name of Jesus is our banner, the blood of Jesus is our covering, and the Word of God is our sword. We can fight the Enemy knowing that Jesus is victorious over Satan, and Jesus wins. Warfare praying is also praying against strongholds. Strongholds include bad habits, evil thoughts, vain imaginations, or lustful desires. We must pray these down and away in Jesus' name, standing upon the Word of God.

When you are praying and fasting and confronting the devil and any strongholds in your life, always pray in and through Jesus' name, the blood of Jesus, standing upon the Word of God, and the word of your testimony, and then you are more than equipped to stand in the Lord's strength victoriously through all warfare praying.

Holy Spirit, empower me today to pray like this and experience victory. Amen.

Prayer and Fasting Increases Your Persistence in Prayer

"I say to you, ask, and it will be given to you; seek, and you will find; knock, and it will be opened to you."
LUKE 11:9

Prayer and fasting usually elevate your spiritual life and your entire prayer life. While every prayer and fasting journey is unique, God will use each one to elevate your walk with him and to deepen your prayer life. Therefore, prayer and fasting increase your persistence in prayer.

What is persistence in prayer? Persistence is when you pray about something specific in your life and cannot let it go, so you continue to pray about it, persevere through it, and believe tenaciously for God to answer your prayer, even if that means praying for years or even decades. This is praying with persistence.

Jesus talked about this as recorded in Luke 11. After Jesus told the disciples a story about a man who persistently asks his neighbor for bread, he amplified the principle in the story by going straight to the point in Luke 11:9: "Ask and it will be given to you." In so many words, Jesus taught his followers to never give up in prayer. We refer to this at times as "praying it through." Prayer and fasting can help you increase your tenacity and persistence regarding prayer requests you call out to the Father in heaven. I have found this to be true personally.

Jesus was telling us to ask and keep on asking, to seek and keep on seeking, and to knock and keep on knocking until the door is opened. When you ask, you receive; when you seek, you will find; and when you knock, the door will be opened. All of this can happen due to your generous heavenly Father.

So how long should you pray about something even when there is no visible response? I want to encourage you to persistently call out your request to God in prayer until you know it is not God's will or until you see God answer it or until you receive a spiritual release from praying about it any longer. When you are persistent in prayer, it means you have great faith in God. I have walked with God for many years, and I can tell you that prayer and fasting have increased my persistence in prayer.

Father, I desire greatly to have great faith and to never give up in prayer. Amen.

Call Out to God
through Prayer and Fasting

People began to call upon the name of the LORD.
GENESIS 4:26

In Genesis 4, the Bible mentions that people began to call upon the name of the Lord. Earlier in this chapter, Adam and Eve had two sons, Cain and Abel. Sadly, this chapter shows that Cain came against Abel and killed him. Then later, the chapter records that Adam and Eve had another son named Seth. Seth had a son named Enosh, and at some point in Enosh's life, people began to call upon the name of the Lord.

Calling upon the Lord, or calling out to the Lord, has its origin in Genesis. People began to appeal to the Lord, summon the Lord, and even invite the Lord into their lives. When we call out to the Lord, we summon God's assistance. Sometimes, we may even cry or shout aloud our need and beg assistance from God.

When you pray and fast, you are more cognizant of the need to call upon the Lord and should develop the practice of calling out to him. The more I pray and fast, the more I know I need to summon God's assistance. I need Jesus every day, all throughout the day and the night. The good news is that we can call out to God every day, each day and night. This is the most significant action you can take when you encounter a crisis: summon the Lord's assistance immediately. When you call out to the Lord, you depend upon the Lord and no one else, including yourself.

As you encounter real-time daily needs in your life, call out to God. As a parent, you love it when your children call out to you for assistance in some way. God is a greater heavenly Father than any of us can ever be. Therefore, he genuinely wants to help you.

Whether you are worshiping the Lord, concerned for your future, or even in your daily time of prayer with God, call out to the Lord. Pour out your heart to God and summon his assistance in your life. Call out to God through prayer and fasting.

God, I call out to you today, asking you for your assistance in my life in every way and everything. In Jesus' name. Amen.

Interceding for Others When You Pray and Fast

For this reason we also, since the day we heard about it, have not ceased praying for you and asking that you may be filled with the knowledge of his will in all spiritual wisdom and understanding.

COLOSSIANS 1:9

Interceding in prayer for others is one of the most outstanding gifts you can give. When you intercede for someone in prayer, you are pleading with God because you know of a special need or challenging time someone else may be going through. The Lord is pleased as you offer prayers to him on their behalf. Praying for others is one of your highest callings in the Christian life.

Just think of all the people who have prayed for you. One of the greatest joys of pastoring a church is knowing people are praying for you. We need God's help and power to live like Jesus wants us to. Therefore, everyone needs to pray for others and receive prayers from others.

Many years ago, I learned the importance of praying for others regarding their specific needs. Since then, I have an ongoing and ever-changing prayer list of people for whom I call out to God in prayer. I have already talked about the importance of praying biblically for others, standing upon the Word of God as you pray for them. When you stand upon God's Word as you pray, it elevates and empowers your prayers.

In Colossians 1, the apostle Paul prayed for people unceasingly. When he heard how some of the people were being influenced by the anti-Christ philosophy that man could attain a higher knowledge than God, which was their salvation, Paul began to intercede unceasingly for the believers. He pleaded with God for them to live with spiritual wisdom and to be strengthened by God's power so they could bear fruit. His prayer was for them to be filled with God's will.

There are so many ways you can intercede for other people. One of the significant biblical sections about how to pray for others is Colossians 1:9–12. Call out specific names of people as you pray through this passage. Lift the points from this text to become your prayer points for others. When you are praying and fasting, always intercede for others in prayer.

God, I want to be an intercessor and pray for others, specifically and biblically. Please teach me how to do this. Amen.

Looking into the Depths of Your Heart

If I regard wickedness in my heart,
the Lord will not hear.
PSALM 66:18

As you have now prayed and fasted for thirty days consecutively, you may be more sensitive before the Lord than ever. While you are at this unique point in your life, finish these last ten days strong. Look deep into your heart to ensure all is well and pure.

One of the Bible's most stirring and convicting verses is our Scripture verse for today. The word "regard" in this verse is also translated as "cherish." Therefore, we could read it, "If I cherish wickedness in my heart." This is a strong biblical word we cannot ignore. This Hebrew word is *rasah*, which means "to approve of, enjoy, or even show respect for something."[26] Consequently, it could be written, "If I approve of wickedness," "If I enjoy wickedness," or "If I show respect for wickedness." That really creates a much more robust understanding of the verse. Sadly, all wickedness and evil offend God. Furthermore, why should we expect God to pay attention to our prayers when we honor the wickedness in our hearts more than we honor God?

While repentance forsakes all sin, we often have

secret and private sins settled in our human hearts. So let the Holy Spirit place God's holy searchlight into the depths of your heart, and if some secret sins are there, remove them through repentance immediately. This is when spiritual freedom in your life goes to a higher level.

Almost every house has a junk room, and the door to that room is always shut. So if a guest comes into the house and they open the door mistakenly, you say to them, "No, shut the door now!" The human heart can also have a junk room filled with our private sins and attachments. Yet God knows it is there. While you may have tamed those secret sins like pets, if you do not deal with them one day, they will strike you like a rattlesnake. It is time to clean out the junk room of your heart.

Lord, please reveal any secret sins lodged deep in my heart and give me the courage to turn from them now. Amen.

DAY 32

Cleaning Out the Junk Room in Your Heart

You ask and do not receive, because you ask with the wrong motives, so that you spend what you request on your pleasures.
JAMES 4:3

I want us to continue to give God ample opportunity to clean out the junk room in our hearts. God is ready to do this in each of us. But it starts with us by letting God reveal the hidden sins that may be lodged right now deep in our hearts. Yesterday's verse was: "If I regard wickedness in my heart, the Lord will not hear" (Psalm 66:18). So now, where do we go from here?

Sometimes when we ask, even when we are fasting, we do not receive from God what we have asked from him. Sometimes it is because we have poor motives or even evil motives if there is a compromise in our hearts. The one thing about God is that we cannot hide anything from him. He already knows everything about us. He waits for us to get our hearts right and do the Lord's will.

We must stop sinning those same secret sins. We must stop ignoring the Holy Spirit's conviction. We must stop hardening our hearts to God. Many with secret sins think they have control or are not really hurting anyone, but they are mistaken. God does not want us to manage our sin more effectively but to turn from it and walk in his victory over it.

I encourage you to review yesterday's devotion illustration about the junk room. Open that room in your heart and ask the Holy Spirit to shine his searchlight into every corner and reveal anything that is evil, wrong, or, as you think, hidden from everyone. Are you willing to turn from those secret sins, receive God's forgiveness, and release them from your heart so you can be free again?

When we cherish, approve, enjoy, and respect sin more than we do God, our spiritual life will soon suffer the consequences. If we want our prayers and times of fasting to go up to the Father in heaven, then the wall of our unrepentant hearts must come down. You are in a defining moment. Take a significant step toward purity, holiness, and freedom. Ask God for courage now.

God, help me now to take steps toward you in purity, holiness, and freedom. Amen.

DAY 33

Relationships

*Being diligent to keep the unity of the Spirit
in the bond of peace.*
EPHESIANS 4:3

Every relationship in your life matters—your relationship with God and your relationship with other people. Your relationship with others is either healthy and flourishing or unhealthy and strained. When you assess your marriage, family, friendships, workplace, community, and church, how would you evaluate your relationships in these areas? Is each one healthy and flourishing, or are any of them unhealthy and strained?

Your vertical relationship with God will affect your horizontal relationships with people. Your horizontal relationships with people will affect your vertical relationship with God. There is no relationship in your life that is insignificant. Every person matters to God; therefore, every person should matter to us.

Because of this, Ephesians 4:3 is relevant to everyone. God calls upon us to make every effort and take the personal initiative to keep the unity of the Spirit in the bond of peace. We must do all we can and make every effort to see that each of our relationships is healthy and flourishing. Yes, we want unity, and unity takes work. But God also factors in human relationships, and in this passage, we learn that the Holy Spirit is the one who brings unity. So then peace serves as an adhesive wrap around each relationship or community of relationships so we can walk in unity with one another.

What about your relationships? Are you walking in unity like this? Do you think you are taking the initiative to walk in unity with everyone? Our prayers will be hindered when any of our relationships are unhealthy or strained. This is true for a husband and wife, a parent with their children, a church, a workplace, or a community.

As followers of Jesus, we are told to love one another. This means that we must be committed to loving others unconditionally, willfully, and sacrificially. How we treat others will determine how God responds to our prayer. In these days of praying and fasting, I appeal to you in Jesus' name to recognize that each relationship in your life matters. Therefore, make every effort to keep the unity of the Spirit in the bond of peace.

Lord, I want to walk in unity with every person. Please help me to do so. Amen.

Bridges or Barriers

*He Himself is our peace, who made both groups into one
and broke down the barrier of the dividing wall.*
E<small>PHESIANS</small> 2:14

The book of Ephesians teaches us how to live the
Christian life. We know from Scripture that Jews and
gentiles had been at odds for years. They had a huge
wall up between them. When Jesus came and died on
the cross, he shed his precious blood for the sins of
the entire world. Since that moment, anyone far away
from God can now have a relationship with God and
have direct access through Jesus Christ. This is not only
true of someone's relationship with God, but it is even
possible with human relationships. Since Jesus died, if
you are struggling with any person or group, there is no
longer a need for a spiritual wall to exist between you.
In fact, there should be no walls between any human
relationships.

Jesus' shed blood and death on the cross are so
powerful that he can make all people one. Even the wall
of separation between Jews and gentiles came down
when Jesus died on the cross. Therefore, through Jesus'
death, every barrier, every wall, and every dividing
force between the two parties should now come down.
Furthermore, Jesus' resurrection from the dead has the

power for us to experience unity with each other rather than division and disunity.

Unity is possible through the power of Jesus Christ. Jesus takes relational barriers and transforms them into bridges. Consequently, as you evaluate each relationship you have in your life, you will either see barriers you have built up that have led to division or bridges you have built that resulted in unity.

I do want to remind you from the Ephesians 4:3 passage that, as Christians, we always need to make the first move to make things right with others and to bring unity. We must stop saying, "If only they did," and start saying, "I will make the first move." We must get into the business of building relationships and stop being a part of the business of demolishing relationships. Build bridges and stop building barriers. With Jesus, there is always a way. Let these words rest on you: "If possible, so far as it depends on you, be at peace with all people" (Romans 12:18).

Holy Spirit, empower me supernaturally to build bridges with people and stop building barriers. With Jesus, there is always a way. Amen.

Forgiving Others

It keeps no record of wrongs.
1 CORINTHIANS 13:5 NIV

On the thirty-fifth day of your fast, I want to praise God with you that you are nearing the conclusion of your forty-day experience with God. Day by day and night by night, you have pursued God diligently. Therefore, I want to share some truth, a significant subject that, when you embrace it, will elevate your spiritual life and this entire forty-day fasting experience.

If you are like most people, you have had a time in your life when someone has taken advantage of you, abused you in some way, mistreated you, lied about you, dismissed you from your job, or hurt you deeply. Whatever may have happened to you, it left you with a deep hurt and wound in your heart. If you are honest with yourself, you are still angry, resentful, and bitter. Sometimes it still consumes you, and sometimes it is all you can think about.

The Scriptures say that love "keeps no record of wrongs." There is no benefit to keeping a record of wrongs. Whether it is in your marriage, with your children, parents, pastor, supervisor, friend, or anyone else, God is serious about this and these powerful words: "Keep no record of wrongs." This includes those who have hurt us deeply. God has not appointed you to be the judge of all the world. God's Word says, "Keep no record of wrongs."

In R. T. Kendall's phenomenal book, *Total Forgiveness*, he writes: "Total forgiveness is a choice. It is not a feeling—at least at first—but is rather an act of the will."[27] Therefore, it is not your role to punish someone or hurt someone back or retaliate against someone. Come to God, be honest with yourself, forgive, release the offense, and live out what R. T. calls total forgiveness. Release your hurt, anger, and bitterness to God. Let God clear the record in your heart. When you let go of the negative emotions and sins like unforgiveness, bitterness, and anger you have carried throughout your life, the Holy Spirit will come and anoint you again with a greater anointing. Just keep the record clear.

Lord, please help me to refuse to keep a record of wrongs done against me. Forgive me. Amen.

Your Words Matter

*The tongue also is a fire, a world of evil among the parts
of the body. It corrupts the whole body, sets the whole
course of one's life on fire, and is itself set on fire by hell.*
JAMES 3:6 NIV

The third chapter of the book of James is very direct
about the destructive nature of the tongue. Look at the
basics of what verse six says about the tongue: "It is a
fire, a world of evil…corrupts the whole body, sets the
whole course of one's life on fire, and is itself set on fire
by hell." Therefore, the tongue can be the most destructive part of the human body. By the nature of the words
that it speaks, the tongue can set the whole body on fire.
A tongue out of control demonstrates that it is on fire,
and this fire is from hell. Consequently, for the person
who speaks evil, who boasts, or who curses others, their
entire life becomes like an uncontrolled fire.

Jesus said, "By your words you will be justified,
and by your words you will be condemned" (Matthew
12:37). The Lord Jesus Christ said these words well
before James wrote his epistle, but James was so closely
connected with Christ that he built upon Jesus' words
with enormous strength. Your words will set you free,
or your words will condemn you. Do your words set
people and situations free, or do your words condemn

others and imprison others? Take careful note of this: negative words are set on fire from hell. Choosing words like this in your communication will result in quenching and grieving the Holy Spirit of God. This is *not* the Lord's will. Negative and harmful words separate and divide. Choose the better way of honoring, blessing, and encouraging other people.

I know you have probably been in meetings or gatherings where someone's words are so out of control that your meeting shuts down abruptly. Everyone in the group feels so awkward even though the person who spoke those words appears desensitized to other people's feelings. Conversely, when someone is blessing others within a gathering like this and leading with grace and wisdom with their words, people flourish into high-level productivity. So honor the Lord and other people with your words.

Oh Lord, I want my words to be helpful and kind. Please speak through me. Amen.

Prayer Makes the Difference

When they had prayed, the place where they had gathered together was shaken, and they were all filled with the Holy Spirit and began to speak the Word of God with boldness.

ACTS 4:31

There are times in the New Testament when it is undeniable that prayer makes the difference. One of these times is recorded in the fourth chapter of Acts. In the previous chapter, Peter and John had just healed a lame man. As a result, when they preached the gospel to the crowds, two thousand people began following Jesus. Now in chapter 4, five thousand people were following Jesus. Peter's message to everyone was courageous as he told people there was only one way to be saved: through Jesus Christ. This resulted in the religious authorities warning the apostles to shut up and stop teaching in the name of Jesus. However, Peter and John responded that they could not stop speaking about what they had seen and heard. After the religious leaders took them into custody, they continued their threats, but eventually, they released Peter and John.

Jesus' followers began to pray together in unity, appealing to God as if they were one voice and heart. The result of their prayer was God-sized and supernatural. A great Jesus movement occurred.

- The church's message strengthened as they declared that Jesus Christ was the only way to heaven. We read, "There is salvation in no one else; for there is no other name under heaven that has been given among mankind by which we must be saved" (4:12). This created an urgency in the church to reach all people for Jesus Christ.

- The ministry of prayer preceded the power of God shaking the place where they had gathered. Their extraordinary prayer ushered in a great move of God. When God's people pray, great things happen.

- The people were filled with the Holy Spirit, and the power of God was released. God was supernaturally using ordinary people.

- The people proclaimed the Word of God with holy boldness. They preached and witnessed to everyone everywhere about Jesus Christ. Will you?

The Scriptures profoundly explain why all this occurred: "When they had prayed." Prayer precedes every great movement of God. Therefore, we must pray. Prayer makes the difference.

God, when your people prayed, great things occurred. So please, do it again. Amen.

DAY 38

Watching for the Lord

As for me, I will be on the watch for the LORD;
I will wait for the God of my salvation.
My God will hear me.
MICAH 7:7

You are three days away from completing your forty-day fast before the Lord. As you are nearing the conclusion, what do you do between now and then? I want to urge you to do as Micah did in his life: "I will be on the watch for the LORD." Stay alert and aware of what the Lord has been doing in your life and what he may still do before day forty is complete.

Micah was a part of the remnant in Jerusalem, yet he also said that looking for the godly and faithful was like looking for the fruit after the harvest. The energies and skills of the godless never stopped. As the nation of Israel was decaying and hope was passing away, God raised this lamenting prophet Micah to declare that he would still watch for the Lord, expecting and believing God for the future. As he declared his hope in the Lord and his commitment to wait on God to act, Micah put his faith only in his God and Savior. Facing difficult and dire circumstances, Micah still believed God would make known all his work and power. With firm, holy conviction, he knew that God would hear him. What faith! What trust! Therefore, I strongly urge you to take these practical steps as you wait for the Lord:

- Determine how God has been working in the first thirty-eight days of this season of fasting. One way to do this is to read through any journals you recorded or reflect on experiences you remember. Collect them in one list of how you believe God may have spoken to you. This is like Micah saying he would watch for the Lord. Start discovering, reading, and collecting these now.

- Resolve to wait for the Lord about the requests you have presented to him that you feel he has not yet spoken to you about. There is still time!

- Know that God has heard and will hear your prayers and see your fasting. When and how he answers you is up to him.

God, in these evil days, give us the vision and persistence to watch for the Lord in faith and with expectation. Amen.

Pouring Out Your Heart to God

The effective, fervent prayer of a righteous man avails much.
JAMES 5:16 NKJV

As your prayer life goes, so goes the rest of your life. Prayer is central and influential in our lives. I am unsure why people often downplay or dismiss the power of prayer or relegate prayer as a last resort, but praying is the greatest action a person and a church can take. For many years, I have repeatedly stated that we must do all we can to bring fervent prayer back into the church. Prayer is more than a one-minute transition in a worship service. Jesus wants his church to be "a house of prayer for all the nations" (Mark 11:17). The spiritual investment of prayer can bear fruit for generations to come.

Fervency in prayer is pouring your heart out to God. Fervency in prayer is praying with such commitment that you are stretching and straining like an athlete running a race. It is also intense and intentional praying, travailing and prevailing praying, passionate and persuasive praying. Fervent prayer is so strong that it calls you to be convicted by the Spirit. The terms describing fervent prayer are unusual, and you might hear someone say, "We should be prayed up and always praying." The intensity and intentionality of pouring out your heart to

God are strong. This kind of prayer involves discipline, conviction, energy, and faith.

Pouring out your heart to God in prayer moves your heart toward God and his will. This kind of prayer also changes situations and circumstances. I love this translation of James 5:16 because it exudes with confidence how powerful fervent prayer is: "When a believing person prays, great things happen" (NCV).

So be encouraged because you have joined fasting with your fervency in prayer for thirty-nine days consecutively, knowing you have been praying, straining, stretching, believing, prevailing, travailing, and pouring out your heart to God. Do the same all day today and on your final day tomorrow. You are experiencing and will continue to experience the supernatural power of prayer and fasting. There is no telling what God will do in you, through you, and around you today, tomorrow, and in your future. Great things are going to happen!

Lord, with fervency in prayer, I pour out my heart. Speak to me, work in me, and use me supernaturally. Amen.

DAY 40

After This,
I Will Pour Out My Spirit

*After this I will pour out my Spirit on all humanity; then
your sons and your daughters will prophesy, your old men
will have dreams, and your young men will see visions.*
JOEL 2:28 CSB

Welcome to your fortieth consecutive day of praying
and fasting. While God has been active and powerfully
working in and through you these days, tomorrow will be
the beginning of a new God-sized future based on your
faithfulness and commitment to be all in on seeking God
humbly with all your heart. The best is yet to come!

The term "After this" in the above Scripture text
is very significant because everything Joel is about
to describe in verse 28 and in the verses that follow
occurred because of all that happened in Joel 1:1–2:27.
Let me explain briefly. First, God's people were under
the judgment of God. In 1:1–14, God took away their
provision, protection, and joy. In 2:12–17, God's people
responded to him by returning to him in prayer, fasting,
and repentance. Then in 2:18–27, God answered their
prayer and saw the change in their heart and lifestyle.
When he saw it, God lifted the judgment against his
people. God supernaturally responded to their praying,
fasting, repenting, weeping, and mourning. Once again,

God provided for them, protected them, and granted them joy.

The initial fulfillment of God pouring out his Spirit happened on the day of Pentecost. However, the complete fulfillment of it will come in the season just before the return of Christ. It will usher in evangelism as we have never seen and a gospel explosion in our generation in a supernatural way.

We are on the brink of the mightiest outpouring of the Holy Spirit that has ever happened in the world. I believe God calling you to this prayer and fasting journey is all part of preparing his people for his supernatural outpouring of the Spirit that will come in the last days. You are experiencing the supernatural power of prayer and fasting now and for the future. After this, including your forty-day fast, God will pour out his Spirit on all humanity. Even so, Lord Jesus, come!

Lord, please pour out your Spirit on me today and in my future. I want to experience your supernatural power. Amen.

Appendices

Appendix 1

Daily Prayer Guide
and Church Evaluation

During any season of prayer and fasting, take an inventory of your heart. For example, use the following inventory daily during your prayer time while on a one-day or three-day fast. You could also use this in the first three days of a ten-day or twenty-one-day fast. Then, during a forty-day fast, use this in the first three days and again on day twenty-one of your fast. Using it this way will help you go deeper into a spiritual inventory in your heart.

Whether you use this inventory personally, in a prayer group, or in a church or region, always personalize it. Be honest with yourself and God as you reflect on the questions. This is an important spiritual exercise because when we desire to experience God's supernatural power and presence, we must recognize that every "yes" to these questions suggests we have a sin to confess. So we must immediately confess it, ask God to forgive us, and then walk in this forgiveness.

Stand upon these promises as you walk through this daily:

> If we walk in the Light as He Himself is in the Light, we have fellowship with one another, and the blood of Jesus His Son cleanses us from all sin. If we say that we have no sin, we are deceiving ourselves and the truth is not in us. If we confess our sins, He is faithful and righteous, so that He will forgive us our sins and cleanse us from all unrighteousness. If we say that we have not sinned, we make Him a liar and His word is not in us. (1 John 1:7–10)

May the searchlight of God's holiness reveal every reality to you as you do. Pray now: *Holy Spirit, speak to me and bend me, oh Lord.*

- "In everything, give thanks; for this is the will of God in Christ Jesus for you." (1 Thessalonians 5:18 NKJV)

Do I worry about anything? Have I forgotten to thank God for all things, the seemingly bad and the good? Do I neglect to thank him for my breath, health, and life?

- "Now to Him who is able to do exceedingly abundantly above all that we ask or think, according to the power that works in us." (Ephesians 3:20 NKJV)

Do I avoid attempting things in our heavenly Father's name because I fear I am not talented, smart, or skilled enough? Do feelings of inferiority keep me from fulfilling my desire to serve God? When I accomplish something of merit, do I choose to give myself the glory rather than God?

- "You shall receive power when the Holy Spirit has come upon you; and you shall be witnesses to Me in Jerusalem, and in all Judea and Samaria, and to the end of the earth." (Acts 1:8 NKJV)

Have I hesitated to thank God for the miracles he has performed? Have I believed that living my Christianity casually is good enough and that sharing the good news of my deliverance with others is not all that important? Am I hesitant to share the gospel? Am I intentionally missing opportunities to advance the message of Christ in my region, in America, and worldwide?

- "I say...to everyone who is among you, not to think of himself more highly than he ought to think." (Romans 12:3 NKJV)

Am I overly proud of my accomplishments, talents,

and family? Do I need help putting the concerns of others first? Do I have a rebellious spirit at the thought that God may want to change me and rearrange my thinking? Do I brag or boast to others about what I have? Do I swell up with pride when I receive compliments?

- "Let all bitterness, wrath, anger, clamor, and evil speaking be put away from you, with all malice." (Ephesians 4:31 NKJV)

Do I complain, find fault, or argue? Do I nurse and delight in a critical spirit? Do I carry a grudge against believers of another group, denomination, or theological persuasion because they don't see the truth as I see it? Do I speak unkindly about people when they are not present? Do I find that I'm often angry with myself? With others? With God?

Is there disharmony in any of my relationships? Am I unwilling to let it go and start over again? Is there anyone with whom my relationship is not right? Do I grieve the Holy Spirit with my unforgiveness toward others? Am I unwilling to make everything right with everyone, resulting in a greater anointing from God?

- "Do you not know that your body is the temple of the Holy Spirit who is in you, whom you have from God, and you are not your own?" (1 Corinthians 6:19 NKJV)

Am I careless with my body? Do I defile my body with unholy sexual acts? Do I overeat? Do I neglect to take care of my body? Do I ignore the need to be physically fit?

- "Let no corrupt word proceed out of your mouth." (Ephesians 4:29 NKJV)

Do I use language that fails to edify others? Do I tell off-color jokes or stories that demean another person's race, habits, or culture? Do I condone these comments from guests in my home or when my colleagues share them with me at work? Do I curse?

- "Do not…give place to the devil."
  (Ephesians 4:26–27 NKJV)

Do I ignore the possibility that I may be a landing strip for Satan when I open my mind to him through ungodly practices, psychic predictions, occult literature, and violent, sex-driven, sexually perverted movies and online videos? Do I seek counsel for daily living from horoscopes in the paper, on television, or the internet rather than God, our faithful and ultimate source of living? Do I let Satan use me to set up barriers that inhibit the cause of Christ in my church and home through criticism and gossip?

- "Not slothful in business." (Romans 12:11 KJV)

Am I chronically late in paying my debts, sometimes choosing not to pay them? Do I charge more on my credit cards than I can afford? Do I believe I don't need to keep honest income tax records? Do I engage in shady business deals? Do I inflate my financial worth? Do I get into business partnerships with unbelievers?

- "Beloved,…abstain from fleshly lusts which war against the soul." (1 Peter 2:11 NKJV)

Am I guilty of a lustful eye toward the opposite sex? Do I fill my mind with sexually explicit internet sites, suggestive television programs, lewd movies, or unsavory books? Do I commit the sin of lust by willfully looking at lascivious magazine covers or centerfolds, especially when I sense no one is watching? Do I indulge in lustful activities God's Word condemns, such as fornication, adultery, or perversion? Do I have inappropriate online relationships? Do I belong to dating sites I should not be in? Am I engaged in pornography in any way? Do I gamble, place bets, or play the lottery in any way, searching for instant gratification or the desire to get rich quick?

- "Bearing with one another, and forgiving one another, if anyone has a complaint against another; even as Christ forgave you, so you also must do." (Colossians 3:13 NKJV)

Have I failed to forgive those who may have said or done something to hurt me? Have I written off certain people as not worthy of my friendship?

- "Even so you also outwardly appear righteous to men but inside you are full of hypocrisy and lawlessness." (Matthew 23:28 NKJV)

Do I portray an image to others that is not who I truly am? Am I using my active involvement in my church as a cover for my sinful activities when I'm away from the body of Christ? Am I mimicking the Christian faith for social status and acceptance in my church or community? Am I living hypocritically?

- "Finally, brethren, whatever things are true, whatever things are noble, whatever things are just, whatever things are pure, whatever things are lovely, whatever things are of good report, if there is any virtue and if there is anything praiseworthy—meditate on these things." (Philippians 4:8 NKJV)

Do I enjoy listening to conversations that hurt others? Do I pass on what I hear? Do I believe rumors or partial truths, especially about an enemy or a competitor? Do I spend little or no time each day allowing God to speak to me through his Word?

The Spiritual Condition of Our Church

Sometimes, we need a tool to help us get more honest about the spiritual condition of our personal life and the local church. In desiring to break through spiritually into all God had for us personally and as a church, we created this assessment tool to help us evaluate our church. I am trying to remember how many times I have used it but probably at least twice through the years, with various prayer and fasting emphases corporately. I have updated this tool for you in case you desire to use it in the future.

Standing on the Word of God, our church worked through these matters spiritually and collectively. "Call to Me and I will answer you, and I will tell you great and mighty things, which you do not know" (Jeremiah 33:3). As a church, when we call out to God together and pray in agreement, we realize that God alone can show us and do through us great and mighty things that we do not know. We pray this for us today and the future generations of our church until the Lord comes. Therefore, join together in lifting our church up to God in prayer concerning the following areas.

Confessing the Sins of Our Church

Ask God to forgive us and give us the power to repent from our sins. The following could be a sin in our personal lives and our church. We must confess each and turn away from them, individually and as a church body.

What Is Limited or Missing in Our Church?

- Excitement about Jesus Christ and what he is doing in our lives and church?
- Enthusiasm for God and the things of God?
- Focus on God and his work through our church?
- Service to God through our church?
- Love for people and concern for the needs they have?
- Involvement in ministry to others?
- Attendance at worship services?
- Involvement in small groups?
- Response privately or publicly when God's Word is preached or taught?
- Desire for people to come to Christ?
- Desire for our church to grow?
- Passionate love for God?
- Time or priority given to the things of God?
- Love expressed for other Christ followers, replaced by a critical or judgmental spirit?
- Prayer for spiritual leaders in our church?
- Sensitivity to God's Word and his movement?
- Honor and respect for God regarding the

giving of the first-tenth (tithe) of all one's resources to and through the local church, such as one's entire salary, bonuses, stocks, inheritances, and including the church in one's will or trust?

- Burden to see our region reached for Jesus Christ, taking the gospel to every person in the region?

- Desire to share our faith with family, friends, associates, or neighbors who desperately need Christ?

- Desire, passion, and strategy to advance Jesus' good news to our region, America, and the world?

- Desire to participate personally in God's work?

- Desire for broken relationships to be restored?

- Desire to engage and participate in the private and public worship of God?

Prayer for Spiritual Breakthrough in Our Church

Ask God to grant each of the following requests as we seek his will and trust him for our future.

Spiritually

- We need deliverance from the sins of our church.
- We need a spiritual downpour that will rain on us mightily.

- We need a drenching and anointing of God's Spirit.
- We need passion, enthusiasm, and fire for God, his activity, and our church.
- We need deeply spiritual men and women in our church body.
- We need God to call people into ministry and missions.
- We need God to do in us whatever we need and do around us whatever will allow us to be recipients of God's special anointing, blessing, and calling as a church.
- We need a spiritual revival to occur in our church, our worship services, our small groups, and every ministry in and through our church.
- We need God to break our hearts for friends, coworkers, neighbors, and family members who don't have a personal relationship with Jesus.

Strategically

- We need a defined direction for our future.
- We must dream without parameters about what God can and wants to do in our church.
- We need a defined strategy about how to reach a changing world.
- We need a defined and robust strategy to reach

the next generation from their birth through being children, teenagers, college students, and all young adults under thirty years of age.

- We need a defined strategy for how to reach the ethnic groups of our region.
- We need a defined strategy that is God-sized.
- We need a defined strategy about what our church can do to reach our region, America, and the world.
- We need a defined strategy for each age group in our church.
- We need a defined strategy for mobilizing people for Christ in our region, America, and worldwide.
- We need a defined strategy for equipping the ministers and missionaries God wants to connect us with in the future.
- We need God to give each of us a spirit of willingness to give up our preferences and to walk away from things that hinder our ability to minister to as many people as possible in our region.
- We need the Lord to give us a clear vision for our future that we can articulate, run to, and lead our people to follow.

Financially

- We need the walls of financial strongholds to be broken in our people.
- We need the national and local economy to move positively.
- We need God to abundantly bless our people.
- We need our people to prosper financially with integrity in every way.
- We need God to clear major financial hurdles in our church so we can seize the future wholeheartedly.
- We need our people to obey God by giving generously at least one-tenth of all God has entrusted to them, including remembering the church in their wills and trusts.
- We need God to bring and develop new givers in our church.
- We need God miraculously and generously to meet our ministry budget for the coming year.
- We need God to show our people how to create businesses that will generate funds for the cause of Christ.
- We need God's people to believe in the power and blessing of giving and to give generously and enthusiastically to the causes of Christ.
- We need God to provide our church with

major financial miracles now that will impact our future dramatically.

Pray for This Week

Pray for God's power to be evident this week in the following areas:

- Pray for our pastor and ministry staff team as they lead us this week.
- Pray for the following Sunday to be a powerful spiritual breakthrough Sunday for many individuals and our entire church.
- Pray that God will change our church forever spiritually, strategically, and financially.
- Pray that God will bring a mighty spiritual revival that will transcend all denominational, generational, cultural, racial, and ethnic lines.
- Pray that God will place the burden of extraordinary prayer upon our church in everything we do.

Thank God for answering our prayers and for the great miracles God will do for you, others, and our church.

Here is my personal testimony about what you just read. When I updated this evaluation for you, I was overflowing with gratitude for how God has answered so many of these prayers for our church. It is amazing, and I give glory only to Jesus our Lord. Therefore, proceed with faith through this evaluation.

Appendix 2

Fasting and Prayer
as Spiritual Worship

The disciplines of prayer and fasting are not reduced to a formula or a hoop that we are to jump through as if we are in a kind of spiritual circus. Nor are they physical tests or exercises in mental discipline. True prayer and fasting are attitudes of the heart and cries of the soul. God's Word has a strong rebuke for those who fast for the wrong reasons or in an improper manner. I have never seen God respond favorably to prayer and fasting based on pretenses or impure motives.

Improper Reasons and Motives

Prayer and fasting are improper when a person seeks

- to fulfill selfish desires and ambitions.
- to attempt to manipulate God.
- to elevate one's status or personal agenda.
- to promote false piety, legalism, or religious duty.

Improper Manner

Prayer and fasting are improper when we

- draw attention to our personal glorification.
- attempt them without sufficient seriousness and respect.
- conduct them while intentionally continuing in sin.
- conduct them while continuing to pursue selfish desires in pleasure and business.
- conduct them while harboring improper, ungodly attitudes.
- conduct them while promoting or continuing acts of injustice, oppression, or impropriety.
- conduct them without drawing aside daily and dedicating ample time for sincere seeking, quiet communion and devoted prayer with God.

A God-Honoring Fast

The Bible is filled with references to the prayers and fasting of his people. In Matthew 6, Jesus placed fasting on the same level as praying and giving. He said, "When you fast" (v. 17), "when you pray" (v. 5), and "when you give" (v. 2). I wonder why Christians today and churches in our generation don't place fasting on the same level as praying and giving. Jesus, by his example and his teaching, demonstrated that prayer and fasting are critical and integral ingredients in the lives of his followers. One purpose of prayer and fasting is to bring our hearts to a place filled with a sacrificial love that results in godly attitudes. True fasting will draw us closer to God and his purposes.

I cannot explain why God has chosen prayer and fasting to be what I believe is the gateway to supernatural power. One thing I do know: studying Scripture, praying, and fasting are how believers humble themselves in the sight of the Lord. When we humble ourselves, he promises to exalt and lift us at his appointed time (1 Peter 5:6; James 4:10). God also indicates that he will resist the proud but will give grace to the humble (James 4:6). God calls his people to humble themselves, pray, seek his face, and turn from their sins (2 Chronicles 7:14).

Fasting focuses on the dramatic difference between our physical and spiritual natures. Eating is one of the most fundamental things we do as physical beings. One of the most natural desires we have is for food. Without proper nourishment, we die. By exercising our wills and depriving ourselves of food for spiritual purposes, we acknowledge our spiritual natures and honor our Creator-Father.

When we are willing to deny ourselves and call out to the Lord in prayer and fasting, God may choose to move upon us supernaturally. When we fast, we confirm the words uttered by Jesus in the face of temptation during his forty-day fast, "Man shall not live on bread alone, but on every word that comes from the mouth of God" (Matthew 4:4 NIV).

Through prayer and fasting, we forsake our physical needs and the human comforts of this world and call upon God as the originator, giver, source, and sustainer of all life, especially our own. We exalt Jesus as our hope and salvation. True spiritual fasting will result in our submission and devotion to God.

God Blesses Us When Our Fasts...

- Focus on God and honor God. (Although you will receive spiritual blessings, these are not proper motives for fasting.)
- Have spiritual purposes. (Although you may realize certain physical benefits, these are not proper motives for spiritual fasting, e.g., fasting to lose weight.)
- Cause us to humble ourselves and submit to the authority of God and his Word.
- Cause us to acknowledge and repent of sin.
- Deprive our natural desires and lusts to focus on the spiritual.

A Practical Guide

Even when we honor God by praying and fasting, this does not mean that our heavenly Father will grant everything on our wish-and-whim list. God will only work and bless in ways that are consistent and in harmony with his will and purpose. One of the primary functions of prayer and fasting is to help us discover his ordained purposes and will for our lives.

Below are some practical help and hints rooted in my experience—guidelines I follow as I fast and pray.

Spiritual Suggestions

- If God does not call you to fast, don't fast! Unfortunately, most people don't have a call to fast, possibly because they are not open to God's leadership, have not been taught the biblical foundation for fasting, or are caught up in other types of sin that interfere.
- Determine the length of the fast God is calling you to undertake.
- If God calls you to a fast, he has specific reasons and purposes. Before you fast, determine the purposes of your fast and write them down. For example, *Lord, I am fasting for the spiritual purposes of (1) spiritual revival and awakening in the church of America, (2) spiritual revival and awakening in my local church, and (3) spiritual revival and awakening in my own life.* Under each major heading, several subpoints could detail what you trust God for in each area.
- Identify, confess, and repent of all revealed sins

before and during your fast. Continue to ask the Holy Spirit to search your heart and show any concealed areas where you may feel separated from God. Unconfessed sin and disobedience will hinder your prayer and fasting.

- Be sensitive to the Holy Spirit's prompting in all areas of your life since God often requires you to seek reconciliation or restoration in broken relationships.

- Pray fervently and continually.

- Absorb large quantities of Scripture through hearing, reading, studying, memorizing, and meditating on God's Word. Ask God to reveal what he wants you to read and study in his Word.

- Always reserve time to be still and quiet before the Lord.

- Keep a journal of your purposes for the fast. This should contain specific prayer requests, written prayers, devotional thoughts, and spiritual insights you gain during your fast. For example, I handwrite many of my prayers to God. I also document whatever I feel God is teaching me even though they may seem insignificant at the time. I include the specific day and time in the journal entry. These daily writings have been a consistent source of encouragement, strength, and insight long after the fast has ended, reminding me, often months later, of God's direction and calling for my life.

- Skipping meals alone will not result in a meaningful fast. You must *set aside time* to pray and seek spiritual insight. Dedicate at least as much time for prayer and the study of God's Word as you would typically spend in food preparation and eating.

- At times, consider praying audibly in a kneeling position. At times try getting on your face before God. This may help foster an attitude of humility in prayer and keep you focused on your purposes. Then, at other times, just sit before the Lord in silence, meditate on him and his Word, and pay attention to see, hear, or sense what God has put in your heart.

- Praise God verbally and in song for who he is and what he has done. Worship him.

- Use scriptural prayers during some of your prayer time.

- Ask God with whom, when, and how you may want to share your fasting experience when it has ended. If God so allows it, your testimony can challenge, inspire, and help increase the faith of others. Always give God the glory for what he has done in your life.

Physical Suggestions

- As a precaution, check with your doctor before beginning your first fast.

- If you (a) undertake a water-only fast (which is rare), (b) plan an extended fast, (c) have a medical condition, or (d) are taking medication, you should consult a medical doctor familiar with fasting before you begin your fast.

- Drink plenty of water for a few meals before you begin your fast.

- Decrease the size and frequency of meals before your fast, especially before a prolonged fast.

- Determine what kind of fast you will undertake, like total abstinence, water only, or water and juice. I recommend water-and-juice fasts. They help you accomplish the spiritual and physical purposes of the fast while, at the same time, they help you maintain your energy level and your health.

- Avoid chewing gum during the fast. Chewing activates the digestive processes.

- Days two through four of the fast are often the most physically challenging. Just realize going into the fast that these may be more challenging days in your spiritual journey.

- When drinking juice on the fast, unsweetened and nonacidic juices seem best. Tomato and orange juice are hard on the stomach unless considerably diluted.

- I prepared most of my juice at home during my initial fasting years. However, today, you can easily purchase 100 percent pure juice. Since I knew I would be entering a prolonged fast, one of the purchases I made was a high-quality juicer, which we still use in addition to juices we purchase. However, this is not as necessary today as it was years ago.

- Consult other resources on fasting.

- You may need to restrict some of your physical activity during the fast, and incredibly rigorous exercise is not recommended. However, most of the time through the years, I have been able to exercise normally and regularly most days during my fast. But, as you know, this is personal. Be wise.

- Sudden movements, especially standing up quickly, may cause temporary dizziness or light-headedness while you are fasting.

- Expect some physical, mental, and perhaps even some emotional discomfort. Headaches, sleeplessness, and irritability often accompany a fast, but don't allow the fast to become an excuse for improper actions and attitudes. Remain prayerful, and hopefully these times will be brief.

- You will likely experience some weight loss during a fast, but the weight usually returns quickly once you break the fast.

- It's essential always to consider the feelings of others, particularly family members, when planning a fast. For example, planning a fast during a holiday or a family reunion could unnecessarily offend others or draw attention to yourself. Ask God for the right time to conduct your fast. Use your calendar to plan this and be wise. Furthermore, realize that there is no perfect time to fast.

- Some people, even those with good intentions, may try to keep you from fasting. Others may encourage you to end your fast before the appointed time. You should anticipate this and be prepared with a kind yet resolved response.

- End the fast, especially an extended one, gradually. After my prolonged fasts, I eat only soft foods for at least a few days (baked potato, soup, yogurt, etc.). I begin with small portions and gradually increase my intake. I then move to other foods that are more easily digestible. I often wait five or more days before returning to a full meal without restraint. Returning to standard eating patterns too quickly after a fast can cause serious medical problems and may also minimize some of the physical benefits of the fast. Please remember, each person's body is different, so be wise.

Appendix 3

Answers to Commonly Asked Questions

How do I know if I am called to a fast?

The calling from God for me to fast has always been as clear and specific as anything he has ever asked me to do. In all cases, the deep burden and sincere conviction I experience are unmistakably from God. Usually, if confusion prevails regarding the fast, I know that it is not God's timing to draw aside. The Lord will make it clear if he wants you to fast, especially for a prolonged period. The first chapter in this book will help answer this question.

During your extended fasts, what type and quantities of liquid do you consume?

I consume only water for the first couple of days during my extended fasts. After the second day or the beginning of the third day, I begin drinking various kinds of juices prepared at home in a high-quality juicer or purchased juices that are 100 percent pure. My wife prepares these juices from fresh fruit and vegetables. I mostly enjoy watermelon, cantaloupe, grape, pineapple, and grapefruit juices. Watermelon juice is particularly effective for reducing an occasional headache that sometimes results from fasting. Grapefruit juice helps with the cleansing effect of the fast. Typically, I drink eight to twelve ounces of juice four times a day. I also consume water throughout the day. On some days, I drink some electrolyte sports drink because it is refreshing, offers variety, and helps ease an occasional headache.

What are some of the biggest challenges you have faced during your fasts?

Physically, my most significant challenges have come between the second and fourth days. On the first day, because my body is accustomed to caffeine and generous food portions, the sudden withdrawal causes some major headaches. Later in the fast, my body begins to feel great. I typically do not experience any physical hunger. I have adequate energy and feel better than usual, especially after the tenth or fourteenth day. In recent years, I have had caffeine as desired, like coffee or tea.

Although I am not physically hungry after day four or five, I often face mental challenges. Focusing on how many days remain in your designated fast can be intimidating and discouraging, especially early in the fast. Instead, take one day at a time. You have heard the old question, "How do you eat an elephant? One bite at a time." Similarly, "How can you fast for forty days? By fasting one day at a time." It can be a problematic mental battle to count and anticipate that you have twenty or thirty more days to go in your fast. So instead, I remain focused on today's fast only.

How does a fast affect your bodily functions?

Fasting cleanses your body. You may visit the bathroom more than usual. You may experience bad breath or some unusual body odor as the body starts to release toxins that have built up in your system. Again, each person's body is unique; therefore, it is difficult to say, "This is what you will experience." But at the least, these are some possible symptoms you should be aware of.

Have you ever failed in a fast? What should someone do if he or she fails in the fast?

No, I've not failed if failure means not completing the number of days I had initially committed. I felt deeply that God had called me to the fast, and I remained confident that he would enable me to accomplish what he had asked me to do. If God has called you to a fast and you fail to start or finish, confess this inaction, repent of it, ask God to give you another opportunity, and then wait for him to call you to another fast.

What do you write in your spiritual journal?

In prolonged fasts, I have recorded many pages of handwritten notes to myself and God. I will often begin by simply writing, "Dear God," and then continue to write whatever is on my heart. The prayers are usually related to the specific purposes of my fast, but I don't intentionally restrict what or whom I pray for.

I also record, *God, you have spoken to me through this Scripture passage*, then I write down the scriptural reference and the principles he has revealed to me. I always record the date and time I write my journal entry. This helps me document my spiritual journey. I also develop a list of things to pray for before the fast and add to this list during the fast. The point is not how many pages you write but that you record God's work.

What Scripture passages do you recommend for study during a fast?

Each person should seek God's direction in this matter. Often, when God calls you to fast, he has already given you the passage on which to focus. Isaiah 58 and Luke 4 are good foundations on which to build your fast. I freely mark in my study Bible, identifying key quotes, phrases, or words. I also make notes on its pages. If you choose to read other books to supplement your

Bible reading and study, I recommend books on fasting, such as this one, and books that will inspire you to faith and vision. Additionally, whatever the number of days in your fast, please read the devotions in this book. They will help you on your journey, whether it be a one day fast or a forty day fast.

How do you handle mealtimes with your family or business associates during a fast?

During the first few days, I draw aside to be alone during mealtime. After a few days, I return to sitting with the family at the table. The time for sharing is essential. At that point, I am comfortable being around food. The hunger pangs are gone. The food smells good, but I'm not drawn to it. Additionally, each family member is aware of the fast and my reasons for it; therefore, they help make the experience pleasant for all of us. However, I typically limit my lunch appointments, and when meeting with associates at lunchtime, I simply state, "I'm not eating today, thank you."

How do you know when to plan or schedule a fast (including length and type)?

There is no simple answer to this question. I am confident that when God calls you to a fast, he will help you designate the length and type of your fast. Once convinced that God has called me to a forty-day fast, I prayerfully consider my calendar and look for the best opportunity to draw aside. The magnitude of the need may determine the length of the fast. There have been times when I knew I would go at least three days but felt I would navigate it day by day. While writing this book, I felt God was leading me to lengthen the fast.

Have you ever been frustrated because God did not answer or lead you during a fast?

One of the results of a fast is always increased faith and trust in God and his sovereign will. Of course, I often have unanswered questions, but I am increasingly less anxious about specific answers to my concerns. Instead, I trust God to supply wisdom, guidance, and direction for each need. True prayer and fasting result in less worry about having God confirm or bless my plans while it increases my awareness of his plans and purposes.

Do you believe women can and should fast in the same manner as men?

Absolutely. Although there are physiological differences between men and women, prayer and fasting are not gender specific. Women can and should pray and fast. Several women in our church have gone on prolonged fasts, some for as long as forty days.

How did your family relate to you during the fast?

The number one thing my family did was to pray for me. I was encouraged by their prayers, especially during our family prayer time. When I would fast in an extended way when our two boys were at home, Josh and Nick were great sources of inspiration to me. In addition, my wife, Jeana, saw her role as keeping me supplied with fresh juice and water. She faithfully, continually ministered to me and walked with me in the fast. In the recent global pandemic, in the summer of 2020, I went on a forty-day fast, and Jeana joined me in the first fourteen days of fasting.

Did you suffer any adverse effects because of fasting? How do you keep from allowing irritability and fatigue to affect family relations?

Although I suffered a few headaches, I don't believe I have had any adverse results from fasting. I didn't have any increased irritability. I would draw aside and briefly nap if I felt tired, but this only happened three or four times. My family and I approached the prolonged fasts as something of a journey. They did their best to understand the spiritual significance of the task and were tolerant, even encouraging, of my extra time alone with God and his Word. Although sometimes things around the house were slightly different because Dad was so preoccupied, they all knew this experience would be temporary.

Whom do you tell about your fast, and when do you talk about it? Should I tell anyone about the short fast, or is that drawing attention to myself?

People who go on a prolonged fast should notify those around them who will be most affected, which may be only four or five people. Beyond your family, you may even wait a few days until needing to inform others. My purpose is to help them understand my heart and the reasons for my fast and to encourage them to pray for me. I am reluctant to share my fast with unbelievers.

The teaching of Matthew 6:16–18 on "whenever you fast" is clear about how we should conduct ourselves. Once the fast is over, I don't believe that telling people about the experience is inappropriate, especially if I have maintained pure motives. Think about it this way: Moses received the Ten Commandments while fasting and praying for forty days. Imagine if he had not shared his experience with us. God gave Moses something meaningful in his fast, and he communicated it to the people, including us, many generations later. None of the instances of prayer and fasting would appear in the Bible if fasting and its results were meant to be concealed. Maintaining the right spirit, attitude, and motives is critical. Much of what God reveals is a private matter; at the same time, you may help expand the faith of others by sharing with them your experience and insights if God permits. During the fast, do your best not to talk about it unless someone asks you and you cannot avoid it. Share about it only following the fast and only if God permits you.

Do you violate the principles of a God-chosen fast by publicly speaking about it?

No, I do not believe so. Indeed, we need to hear and heed the warnings of Jesus issued in the Sermon on the Mount. His instruction does not prohibit all preaching, teaching, and discussion of prayer and fasting, but it does demand that all such communication bring glory and honor to God. So do it if God leads you to humbly talk about your fast with others. Fasting is something God teaches us. Just like praying or any other principle or discipline, we can share it as we learn it. As we do, it builds our faith and helps increase the faith of others.

How should I determine what to pray for?

Before I go on a prolonged fast, I ask God what purposes he wants me to pray and fast for. For example, at times in my prolonged fasts, God directed me to pray for revival in America, our church, and my life. Under each theme, God gave me more than ten related specific concerns or topics, like the kind of awakening we need in America and how I would be involved in this revival. I prayed for each of these daily, asking the Spirit of God to teach me what to pray for and trust God for during this special time in his presence. These main points were built upon unique Bible promises I stood upon as I prayed.

During my fasts, I begin my prayer time by confessing the sin in my life and then enter a prayer time over each topic. I typically end with some other specific concerns. I then begin my reading and study of God's Word. Usually, during a prolonged fast, I spend up to two hours each morning in prayer, reading the Word of God, and journaling. I am convinced that a person who wants a God-honoring fast will have a similar emphasis on drawing aside to pray and study God's Word.

Practically speaking, what is important to remember when you fast?

Avoid getting caught up in the details, like whether you should drink caffeine or minor matters like this. Here is what you need to remember: God looks upon your heart. You are abstaining from food with a spiritual goal in mind. Keep this on your mind constantly. Juice and water fasts are the best methods unless you are doing a Daniel Fast, as written about in the book of Daniel. Our spiritual motives must be pure. Leave some of the unknowns with God. Again, God examines your heart. While we need to be wise and attempt to honor God's intention for us, we do not become legalistic and judgmental because this shows we do not have the right heart.

Appendix 4

Results to Expect from Your Fast

Expect results. A properly motivated and executed fast will enormously impact your life. Invariably the primary place where God will work is in you. As I respond to his lordship and leadership, I must change my thoughts, attitudes, activities, and motives. As I begin to make these changes, everything about my ministry and relationships changes. Some of these changes are uncomfortable, challenging, and difficult.

For example, because of one fast, I had to confront my pride and arrogance, after which I asked forgiveness from those I had offended. I needed to change how I thought, acted, and reacted. Although my tendency for self-worship may resist some of the spiritual principles God teaches, obedience to God and his Word is non-negotiable. I am convinced that obedience honors and glorifies God and will conform me to the image of Christ.

God promises to reward and bless true prayer and fasting. I have not found a single promise that God has failed to fulfill. On the contrary, he honors each promise he has ever made.

Promises from God's Chosen Fast in Isaiah 58:6–14

- He will set you free from self and your sinful nature. He will loosen the bonds of wickedness and undo the bands of the yoke.
- He will bring freedom from oppression.
- He will transform you into a giver.
- He will give you the desire and ability to meet and minister to people's needs.
- He will allow you to see yourself as you are.
- God will give you spiritual insight and influence.
- No matter how dark and dismal the situation is, your light will break forth like the dawn. You will help dispel the darkness and its power.
- You may experience recovery and healing of various kinds.
- Righteousness will precede you.
- The glory of God will be your protection and rear guard.
- God will answer your prayers. You will call, and he will answer.
- God will manifest his presence with you. You will cry out, and he will reply, "Here I am."

- He will adjust your attitude. Your gloom will become like midday.
- He will continually guide you.
- He will fulfill your desires in the midst of harsh and adverse circumstances.
- He will give you strength and energy.
- He will make you fruitful like a watered garden.
- He will make you like living water that never runs dry.
- You will become a rebuilder of right traditions and a godly heritage.
- You will become a restorer.
- You will become a repairer of breaches and gaps.
- God will lift you and exalt you.
- He will give you more faith.

When fasting, I pray through these promises each day and ask God to let them occur in me and through me.

Corporate Fasting

Even as I have written about the biblical mandate of personal fasting, I must address more fully one other important issue I touched on in an earlier chapter—corporate fasting, the fasting and praying of an entire church or congregation.

The forty-day prayer and fasting devotions I have written for this book can become a pathway to take your church day by day at whatever level of fasting each person may choose to do. Even if the church's fast is seven or twenty-one days, the devotions are written for anyone or any church to use regardless of the length of their own fast.

Pastors and church leaders need to understand the value of emphasizing fasting in their churches for seven days, twenty-one days, or even forty days. They must be aware of what a fasting focus can do for the church. The purpose of these forty days is to involve individual Christians in fasting and prayer for the purpose of fulfilling the spiritual goals that they believe God wants their church to achieve. This all-church ministry can take any congregation to a higher level with God.

So why do we need this ministry? Because individual Christians will seldom go any further than they are led to go in their walk with Christ. I pray pastors and church leaders will be persuaded to seriously consider a ministry such as this.

Concluding Remarks

I challenge you to boldly and confidently enter the fullness of God's will and purpose for your life. True spiritual champions know that when Jesus Christ is not preeminent in their lives, they are open to failure and defeat. True spiritual champions give total allegiance to their Lord. Spiritual champions demonstrate absolute dependence on their Savior and reckless abandonment to the authority and leadership of their Sovereign God. Spiritual champions understand the privilege and responsibility of being children of the King.

Human efforts will fail. Natural attempts will not satisfy. Ordinary tactics are ultimately reduced to mediocrity. There is no lasting contentment apart from God's will and purpose for our lives. Unless we surrender completely to God's plan, we will drift into a sea of disappointment, disillusionment, and depression. We are in constant need of supernatural power. Our only hope is in the life and love of our wonderful Lord, Jesus Christ.

Revival *will* come. Christians *will* be awakened. The world will be shaken from its catatonic complacency. You can take part and make a difference. "The difference you make with your life is totally contingent on the difference God makes in you. The difference you make in others will never be any greater than the difference which has been made in you by Jesus Christ. The dent we can make in our world will be insignificant without the power of Jesus Christ flowing through our lives."[28]

I encourage you to join me and many others as we pray and fast for revival and renewal in our lives, families, churches, and nation. Believe that God will soon bring a spiritual revival that will transcend all denominational, generational, cultural, racial, and ethnic lines. The church needs revival, and America needs the next Great Awakening.

Appendix 5

Fasting in Scripture

The Bible references the words "fast" or "fasting" in fifty-seven verses and uses the words sixty-nine different times. These are only the references regarding abstaining from food. When I requested assistance regarding this information, Davin Benavides, Vice President of Student Development and Mentoring in the Cross Theological Seminary in Northwest Arkansas, provided this so I could share it with you.[29]

The following is a list of these references and their usages in the Bible. As you study and practice fasting, I pray this list will be helpful to you.

Scripture Verses That Mention Fasting

Old Testament

Fast (tsum)

Judges 20:26 – Then all the sons of Israel and all the people went up and came to Bethel, and they wept and remained there before the LORD, and fasted that day until evening. And they offered burnt offerings and peace offerings before the LORD.

1 Samuel 7:6 – They gathered to Mizpah, and drew water and poured it out before the LORD, and fasted on that day and said there, "We have sinned against the LORD." And Samuel judged the sons of Israel at Mizpah.

1 Samuel 31:13 – They took their bones and buried them under the tamarisk tree in Jabesh, and fasted for seven days.

2 Samuel 1:12 – They mourned and wept and fasted until evening for Saul and his son Jonathan, and for the people of the LORD and the house of Israel, because they had fallen by the sword.

2 Samuel 12:21 – His servants said to him, "What is this thing that you have done? You fasted and wept for the child while he was alive; but when the child died, you got up and ate food."

2 Samuel 12:22 – He said, "While the child was still

alive, I fasted and wept; for I said, 'Who knows, the LORD may be gracious to me, and the child may live.'"

2 Samuel 12:23 – "But now he has died; why should I fast? Can I bring him back again? I am going to him, but he will not return to me."

1 Kings 21:27 – It came about, when Ahab heard these words, that he tore his clothes and put on sackcloth and fasted, and he lay in sackcloth and went about despondently.

1 Chronicles 10:12 – All the valiant men got up and took away the body of Saul and the bodies of his sons, and brought them to Jabesh; and they buried their bones under the oak in Jabesh, and fasted for seven days.

Ezra 8:23 – So we fasted and sought our God concerning this matter, and He listened to our pleading.

Nehemiah 1:4 – When I heard these words, I sat down and wept and mourned for days; and I was fasting and praying before the God of heaven.

Esther 4:16 – "Go, gather all the Jews who are found in Susa, and fast for me; do not eat or drink for three days, night or day. I and my attendants also will fast in the same way. And then I will go in to the king, which is not in accordance with the law; and if I perish, I perish."

Isaiah 58:4 – "Behold, you fast for contention and strife, and to strike with a wicked fist. You do not fast like you have done today to make your voice heard on high!"

Jeremiah 14:12 – "When they fast, I am not going to listen to their cry; and when they offer burnt offering and grain offering, I am not going to accept them. Rather, I am going to put an end to them by the sword, famine, and plague."

Zechariah 7:5 – "Say to all the people of the land and to the priests, 'When you fasted and mourned in the fifth and seventh months these seventy years, was it actually for Me that you fasted?'"

Fasting (tsom)

1 Kings 21:9 – She had written in the letters, saying, "Proclaim a fast and seat Naboth at the head of the people."

1 Kings 21:12 – They proclaimed a fast, and seated Naboth at the head of the people.

2 Chronicles 20:3 – Jehoshaphat was afraid and turned his attention to seek the LORD; and he proclaimed a period of fasting throughout Judah.

Ezra 8:21 – Then I proclaimed a fast there at the river of Ahava, to humble ourselves before our God, to seek from Him a safe journey for us, our little ones, and all our possessions.

Nehemiah 9:1 – On the twenty-fourth day of this month the sons of Israel assembled with fasting, in sackcloth and with dirt upon them.

Esther 4:3 – In each and every province where the command and decree of the king came, there was great mourning among the Jews, with fasting, weeping, and mourning rites; and many had sackcloth and ashes spread out as a bed.

Esther 9:31 – To establish these days of Purim at their appointed times, just as Mordecai the Jew and Queen Esther had established for them, and just as they had established for themselves and for their descendants, with instructions for their times of fasting and their mourning.

Psalm 35:13 – As for me, when they were sick, my clothing was sackcloth; I humbled my soul with fasting, but my prayer kept returning to me.

Psalm 69:10 – When I wept in my soul with fasting, it became my disgrace.

Psalm 109:24 – My knees are weak from fasting, and my flesh has grown lean, without fatness.

Isaiah 58:3 – "Why have we fasted and You do not see? Why have we humbled ourselves and You do not notice?" Behold, on the day of your fast you find your desire, and oppress all your workers.

Isaiah 58:5 – "Is it a fast like this that I choose, a day for a person to humble himself? Is it for bowing one's head like a reed and for spreading out sackcloth and ashes as a bed? Will you call this a fast, even an acceptable day to the Lord?"

Isaiah 58:6 – "Is this not the fast that I choose: To release the bonds of wickedness, to undo the ropes of the yoke, and to let the oppressed go free, and break every yoke?"

Jeremiah 36:6 – "You go and read from the scroll, which you have written at my dictation, the words of the Lord to the people at the Lord's house on a day of fasting. And you shall also read them to all the people of Judah who come from their cities."

Jeremiah 36:9 – In the fifth year of Jehoiakim the son of Josiah, king of Judah, in the ninth month, all the people in Jerusalem and all the people who came from the cities of Judah to Jerusalem proclaimed a fast before the Lord.

Daniel 6:18 – Then the king went to his palace and spent the night fasting, and no entertainment was brought before him; and his sleep fled from him.

Daniel 9:3 – I gave my attention to the Lord God, to seek Him by prayer and pleading, with fasting, sackcloth, and ashes.

Joel 1:14 – Consecrate a fast, proclaim a solemn assembly; gather the elders and all the inhabitants of the land to the house of the Lord your God, and cry out to the Lord.

Joel 2:12 – "Yet even now," declares the Lord, "Return

to Me with all your heart, and with fasting, weeping, and mourning."

Joel 2:15 – "Blow a trumpet in Zion, consecrate a fast, proclaim a solemn assembly."

Jonah 3:5 – Then the people of Nineveh believed in God; and they called a fast and put on sackcloth, from the greatest to the least of them.

Zechariah 8:19 – "The LORD of armies says this: 'The fast of the fourth, the fast of the fifth, the fast of the seventh, and the fast of the tenth months will become joy, jubilation, and cheerful festivals for the house of Judah; so love truth and peace.'"

Hungrily; in fasting (tevath)
Daniel 6:18 – The king went to his palace and spent the night fasting, and no entertainment was brought before him; and his sleep fled from him.

New Testament

Fast (nhsteuw)
Matthew 4:2 – After He had fasted for forty days and forty nights, He then became hungry.

Matthew 6:16 – "Whenever you fast, do not make a gloomy face as the hypocrites do, for they distort their faces so that they will be noticed by people when they are fasting. Truly I say to you, they have their reward in full."

Matthew 6:17 – "As for you, when you fast, anoint your head and wash your face."

Matthew 6:18 – "So that your fasting will not be noticed by people but by your Father who is in secret; and your Father who sees what is done in secret will reward you."

Matthew 9:14 – The disciples of John came to Him, asking, "Why do we and the Pharisees fast, but Your disciples do not fast?"

Matthew 9:15 – Jesus said to them, "The attendants of the groom cannot mourn as long as the groom is with them, can they? But the days will come when the groom is taken away from them, and then they will fast."

Mark 2:18 – John's disciples and the Pharisees were fasting; and they came and said to Him, "Why do John's disciples and the disciples of the Pharisees fast, but Your disciples do not fast?"

Mark 2:19 – Jesus said to them, "While the groom is with them, the attendants of the groom cannot fast, can they? As long as they have the groom with them, they cannot fast."

Mark 2:20 – "The days will come when the groom is taken away from them, and then they will fast, on that day."

Luke 5:33 – They said to Him, "The disciples of John often fast and offer prayers, the disciples of the Pharisees also do the same, but Yours eat and drink."

Luke 5:34 – Jesus said to them, "You cannot make the

attendants of the groom fast while the groom is with them, can you?"

Luke 5:35 – "The days will come; and when the groom is taken away from them, then they will fast in those days."

Luke 18:12 – "I fast twice a week; I pay tithes of all that I get."

Acts 13:2 – While they were serving the Lord and fasting, the Holy Spirit said, "Set Barnabas and Saul apart for Me for the work to which I have called them."

Acts 13:3 – When they had fasted, prayed, and laid their hands on them, they sent them away.

Fasting (nhsteia)

Matthew 17:21 – "This kind does not go out except by prayer and fasting" (NKJV).

Luke 2:37 – She did not leave the temple grounds, serving night and day with fasts and prayers.

Acts 14:23 – When they had appointed elders for them in every church, having prayed with fasting, they entrusted them to the Lord in whom they had believed.

Acts 27:9 – When considerable time had passed and the voyage was now dangerous, since even the fast was already over, Paul started admonishing them.

Synopsis

- *Fast* or *fasting* occurs in fifty-seven passages of the Bible.
- *Fast* or *fasting* occurs sixty-nine times in these fifty-seven passages of the Bible.
- These are only the passages regarding abstaining from food.

Acknowledgments

I want to thank my Lord and Savior, Jesus Christ, who began in my life the ministry of prayer and fasting during my collegiate years. Then I did not know how God would use prayer and fasting in such a powerful way throughout my life and ministry. I am thankful to him for each of these times and seasons when he has used, and still uses, prayer and fasting to change me from the inside out.

I must also thank God for my wife, Jeana, who has helped me through these journeys in prayer and fasting. In some of these seasons, it has not been easy for her, but she has continually served and prayed for me. Even at times, she has joined me in praying and fasting. To God's glory, he has always been faithful to us.

I am also very thankful to Carlton Garborg and BroadStreet Publishing for encouraging me to write a new book on this subject. Carlton's gifted team of Nina Rose, Tim Payne, Bill Watkins, Caroline Rock, and many others have assisted me throughout this project. Thank you for this partnership.

As God has developed this message of prayer and fasting in my life, I pray he will continue to open doors of opportunity for me to share the message of this book with everyone everywhere. I believe deeply that *The Supernatural Power of Prayer and Fasting* will equip and inspire churches and ministries, pastors, church leaders, and all Christ-followers, to encounter God in ways like never before and to experience his presence mightily.

God can do more in a moment than we can ever do in a lifetime.

Endnotes

1   Larry Gormley, "The Greatest Inventions in the Past 1000 Years," Department of History, The Ohio State University, accessed December 21, 2023, https://ehistory.osu.edu.

2   "The 1904 Welsh Revival," The Bible College of Wales website, accessed April 25, 2023, https://www.bcwales.org.

3   James A. Stewart, *Invasion of Wales by the Spirit through Evan Roberts* (Fort Washington, PA: Christian Literature Crusade, 1963), 9.

4   Stewart, *Invasion of Wales by the Spirit,* 10.

5   Stewart, *Invasion of Wales by the Spirit*, 61.

6   "Welcome," Moriah Chapel, Birthplace of the Welsh Revival, accessed December 23, 2023, http://www.moriahchapel.org.uk.

7   James A. Stewart, *When the Spirit Came* (Philadelphia, PA: Revival Literature, 1963), 30.

8   Stewart, *Invasion of Wales by the Spirit*, 28–34.

9   Stewart, *Invasion of Wales by the Spirit*, 35.

10 To learn more about Liberty Live Church and the Twenty-One Days of Prayer, visit their website at https://libertylive.church/pray21.

11 Joseph Halliday, "Transforming Lives since 1865: The Story of The Salvation Army So Far," The Salvation Army International, accessed December 26, 2023, https://story.salvationarmy.org.

12 Charles Bateman, *Life of General Booth* (New York, NY: Association Press, 1912), 94.

13 Richard Collier, *The General Next to God: The Story of William Booth and the Salvation Army* (New York: HarperCollins, 1965), 210.

14 Jim Cymbala, *Fresh Wind, Fresh Fire: What Happens When God's Spirit Invades the Hearts of His People* (Grand Rapids, MI: Zondervan, 2018), 19.

15 Fritz Rienecker and Cleon Rogers, *Linguistic Key to the Greek New Testament* (Grand Rapids, MI: Zondervan, 1976, 1980), 534.

16 John MacArthur, *The MacArthur Study Bible* (Nashville, TN: Word Publishing, 1997), 1,811.

17 Jeff Henderson, *What to Do Next: Taking Your Best Step When Life Is Uncertain* (Grand Rapids, MI: Zondervan Books, 2022), 6.

18 Henderson, *What to Do Next*, 7.

19 Ronnie Floyd, *How to Pray: Developing an Intimate Relationship with God* (Nashville, TN: W Publishing Group, 2019), 142–45.

20 Trey Kent and Kie Bowman, *City of Prayer: Transform Your Community through Praying Churches* (Terra Haute, IN: PrayerShop Publishing, 2019), 105–107. See also Brett Walton, "Central Texas Drought Is Worst on Record," Circle of Blue, February 25, 2015, https://www.circleofblue.org; and Billy Hallowell, "Here's What Happened after Christians Begged God to Bring Rain to Water-Starved Texas," Blaze Media, May 29, 2014, https://www.theblaze.com.

21 To read more about Julio Arriola and SEND Network SBTC, visit https://sbtexas.com.

22 To read more about Matt Brown, Malachi O'Brian, and the Roaring Twenties Fast, visit https://thinke.org/roaring-twenties-fast.

23 Shane Idleman, *Feasting & Fasting: What Works,
What Doesn't, and Why* (Leona Valley, CA: El Paseo
Publications: Shane Idleman, 2022), 12.

24 Gary V. Smith, *New American Commentary, Isaiah 40–66,
Vol. 15B* (Nashville, TN: B&H Publishing Group, 2009),
210–11.

25 Albert Barnes, *Notes on the Old Testament, Psalms Volume
II* (Grand Rapids, MI: Baker Book House, 1977), 3–4.

26 Floyd, *How to Pray*, 199–211.

27 R. T. Kendall, *Total Forgiveness* (Lake Mary, FL: Charisma
House, 2007), 32.

28 Ronnie W. Floyd, *The Meaning of a Man* (Nashville, TN:
B&H Publishing Group, 1996), 11.

29 The Cross Theological Seminary is a church-based,
church-centered seminary that trains students to fulfill
the Great Commission. You can visit their website at
https://crossseminary.com.

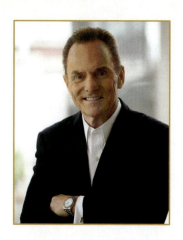

About the Author

As a proven high-capacity leader of multiple large and influential ministry organizations, Ronnie Floyd is known for being a leader of leaders. He is the founder of the Northwest Arkansas Business Persons' Summit, which has had an attendance of over one hundred thirty thousand business leaders since its inception in the fall of 2001. He has a passionate commitment to investing in, inspiring, and influencing leaders.

For over thirty-two years, he served as the senior pastor of Cross Church in Northwest Arkansas. During his tenure, the church exploded in growth and became a large multi-campus church with over twenty thousand members. With three major campuses in the region, the church is still impacting major corporations that have their global headquarters in the region: Walmart, JB Hunt, Tyson Foods, and the University of Arkansas.

Dr. Floyd's personal and communication skills help create unity around a common purpose and strategic vision that influences and invests in leaders who will change the world. His commitment to developing leaders for over three decades resulted in establishing a successful succession plan, which was implemented in 2019. Today, the church is flourishing and advancing into the future with a strategic vision and dynamic hope through the leadership of Dr. Floyd's son, Nick, who is now the senior pastor of Cross Church.

As a speaker, author, and former president of the National Day of Prayer Task Force, Dr. Floyd has led across denominations and ministries. He was elected in 2014 to 2016 to serve as the President of the Southern Baptist Convention. Then, in the spring of 2019 through 2021, Floyd served as the President and CEO of the Southern Baptist Convention Executive Committee. Today, he speaks, writes, consults for organizations, and coaches leaders.

He received his bachelor's degree from Howard Payne University and his master's and doctoral degrees from Southwestern Baptist Theological Seminary. He